States-Within-States

States-Within-States

Incipient Political Entities in the Post–Cold War Era

Edited by

Paul Kingston and Ian S. Spears

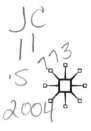

STATES-WITHIN-STATES
© Paul Kingston and Ian Spears, 2004

First published 2004 by
PALGRAVE MACMILLAN™
175 Fifth Avenue, New York, N.Y. 10010 and
Houndmills, Basingstoke, Hampshire, England RG21 6XS
Companies and representatives throughout the world

PALGRAVE MACMILLAN is the global academic imprint of the Palgrave Macmillan division of St. Martin's Press, LLC and of Palgrave Macmillan Ltd. Macmillan® is a registered trademark in the United States, United Kingdom and other countries. Palgrave is a registered trademark in the European Union and other countries.

ISBN 1–4039–6385–1 hardback

Library of Congress Cataloging-in-Publication Data
    States-within-states : incipient political entities in the post Cold War era / edited by Paul Kingston and Ian Spears.
        p. cm.
    Includes bibliographical references.
    ISBN 1–4039–6385–1
        1. National state. 2. Dismemberment of nations. 3. Legitimacy of governments. 4. Developing countries—Politics and government. I. Title : States within states. II. Kingston, Paul W. T. III. Spears, Ian.

JC11.S773 2004
320.1—dc22   2003064806

A catalogue record for this book is available from the British Library.

Design by Newgen Imaging Systems (P) Ltd., Chennai, India.

First edition: April 2004
10 9 8 7 6 5 4 3 2 1

Printed in the United States of America.

To My Family—P.K.
To Sarah, Jordan, Jack, and Nicholas—I.S.S.

Contents

Acknowledgments

There are many we would like to thank. This endeavor has been generously funded by a number of institutions. Our first thanks go to the Canadian Council of Area Studies Learned Societies (CCASLS) for helping us get this project off the ground as well as to its administrator, Linda Thériault, and Roxanne Welters for their more than generous time and efforts on our behalf in organizing the initial "states-within-states" workshop. We also received generous support from the John Holmes Fund of the Canadian Centre for Foreign Policy Development of the Canadian Department of Foreign Affairs and International Trade as well as from the Social Science Division of the University of Toronto at Scarborough, the Political Science Department of the University of Windsor, and the Centre for International Studies at University of Toronto in conjunction with the Munk Centre for International Studies. We would especially like to thank its Director, Lou Pauly, and Tina Lagopoulos who provided us with much needed moral and logistical support in hosting the initial workshop. Thanks also to our editor David Pervin and Palgrave Macmillan for their support of our project and to Mary Pardi for the preparation of the index.

We would also like to thank all those who participated in our workshop, not all of whom have chapters in this volume. We would like to mention especially Robert Jackson, Jeffrey Herbst, Bob Matthews, Catherine Legrand, and Ken Bush—all of whom provided stimulating commentary as discussants. We would also like to make particular mention of Hussein Adam, Jonathan Barker, Andrew Grant, Don Hubert, and Susan Henders for their keen interest and penetrating insights into the topic at hand during the workshop and beyond.

On the personal front, there are many people who proved to be invaluable sources of support. Ian would like to thank Sarah Atkinson, Martha Spears, and Ellen Spears for their considerable time and energy in the workshop's preparation. Paul would like to thank Nancy Kokaz and Rebecca Kingston for their generous gift of time in reading and discussing some of the initial drafts of his chapters as well as Sue Horton and Audrey Glasbergen of the Division of Social Sciences and Catherine Moffatt of the International Development Studies Programme at the University of Toronto at Scarborough, all of whom stepped in for him more often than he would care to know while he labored with the preparations for both the workshop and the edited volume.

Introduction

States-Within-States: Historical and Theoretical Perspectives

Paul Kingston

The end of the Cold War, the rise of globalization, and failed governance have all contributed to a weakening of political authority in much of the developing world. Already described as being "weak"[1] and, in some cases, "quasi,"[2] many Third World states have experienced dramatic declines in their administrative capacity and societal legitimacy. J. Forrest has described this process as one of "state inversion" whereby "the state grows increasingly irrelevant for society . . . culminating at its most severe levels in the disintegration of the central government."[3] But, what happens when a state is unable to maintain any semblance of a regime of compliance or, more seriously, collapses? Much of the literature tends to write about such processes in cataclysmic terms as if, without a functioning state, societies descend into some kind of chaos. This interpretation is, perhaps, best exemplified by Robert Kaplan's phrase "the coming anarchy" in which he plots the explosion of societal anger throughout much of the developing world brought about by deteriorating social and environmental conditions.[4] At its worst, Allen writes of the emergence of a "new violence" characterized by quantitative increases in civilian victims, a ubiquity of social violence, and a dramatic rise in interpersonal violence—in short, the emergence of a polity and society characterized by extreme insecurity where violence has become the norm.[5]

In this volume, we are interested in challenging this notion of an emerging anarchy in much of the developing world, one which, as Michael Ignatieff has effectively pointed out, often leads to the misplaced but disengaging sentiment of "moral disgust" on the part of policy-makers in the West.[6] Rather than chaos and anarchy, this volume works from the premise that the crumbling of one form of political order can reveal or give rise to the emergence of new or incipient kinds of political order. Indeed, in some cases, one sees the emergence of political entities that are in sharp and favorable contrast to the juridical states that rule above them—especially in their capacity to control defined pieces of territory, collect taxes, and conduct business with international and transnational actors. It is for the purpose of investigating the nature and significance of these emerging incipient political entities—ones that we are calling states-within-states—that this volume has been compiled.

There are three principle questions that we are seeking to examine. First, what is the context out of which states-within-states have emerged? This question requires that we delve into debates about the relative significance of the end of the Cold War and of the emergence of powerful transnational economic forces, often pushed forward politically, in weakening existing states in the developing world and in creating conditions conducive for the emergence of social and political movements from below. In other words, what are the forces that have spearheaded a significant relocation and "diffusion of power" in the political economy of developing countries?[7] Second, what is the significance of these non-state political entities that are emerging to challenge weakening state structures in a variety of developing countries? Are these substate units the real and organic political units in waiting whose emergence has only been delayed and frozen in embryo form due to the distorting effects of international norms of sovereignty that have artificially supported the existence of numerous "quasi-states"?[8] Born in conflict, are they simply delayed versions of Tilly-like states in the making[9] and, if so, what institutional features do they share in common with the juridical states above them? Finally, what significance do these political entities have for practitioners and theorists of international relations? Are they a significant addition to the increasing pluralism found within the international arena? What are the challenges, and effects, of using them as channels for humanitarian and development assistance and what implications might this have for the future practice surrounding the norm of sovereignty?

The Emergence of States-Within-States

The dominant context in which the issue of states-within-states must be discussed is state–society relations in the developing world. With the exception of the "developmental states" in South East Asia, many states in the developing world are now defined as being "weak," possessing both limited capacities and legitimacy in their efforts to mold the social order within the territories under their jurisdiction.[10] However, this has not always been the prevailing understanding nor, indeed, the reality in the early years of independence. The Cold War, for example, seemed to tip the balance dramatically in favor of the state in the newly emerging postcolonial world. Through the delivery of financial and military assistance, it provided leaders with a tangible safety net and this was reinforced by the prevailing postcolonial norm of sovereignty that provided numerous Third World regimes with immediate international legitimacy—despite their inability to fulfill some of the basic requirements associated with notions of "positive sovereignty."[11] Moreover, this aggrandizement, or "overdevelopment,"[12] of the postcolonial state was further reinforced by the prevailing étatist economic orthodoxies of the postcolonial era that provided these states with the justification to pursue development strategies that James Scott has called "authoritarian high modernism"—policies aimed at centralizing power and destroying the autonomy of local customs and practices.[13] Hence, from a short-term perspective, it is clear that the Cold War provided means by which states in the developing world could enhance their Weberian status.

However, with the end of the Cold War, it is less clear that these means were really taken advantage of, at least not by all. Perhaps this failure is due to the relatively short duration of the Cold War. Or perhaps, as Jeffrey Herbst argues with respect to Africa, it was precisely because of the availability of a variety of Cold War safety nets that African leaders felt a reduced sense of the urgency to "broadcast" state power into the periphery of their countries.[14] Whatever the case, it is clear that with the end of the Cold War, many societies reverted back to the era of more enduring and contested patterns of state–society relations—ones that seemed to transcend the beginning and the end of the

Cold War.[15] Indeed, in the case of the historically deep-rooted and recurring patterns of conflict in two of the case studies in this volume, Colombia and Lebanon, one can in fact argue that the Cold War period had the reverse effect of exacerbating rather than muting these enduring patterns of state–society contestation. All of this adds weight to Debrix's point that the Cold War regime of sovereignty established a series of "fictions" around the world that acted as a veil covering over the more "ambiguous, artificial, fragile, and inconsistent" reality of political authority.[16]

Yet, while the effect on the Cold War on enduring patterns of state–society relations can be debated, it still seems to be the case that there is something different about the global environment in which "weak" states of the developing world now operate and in which the phenomenon of states-within-states has now arisen. No doubt, the reduction in Cold War aid plays a role here. However, perhaps the more profound changes revolve around the emergence of a new economic orthodoxy of neoliberalism supported by an array of forces promoting its extension throughout the world. In short, it is the emergence of a globalizing dynamic that is the real agent of change here. Clapham, for example, writes of a "two-pronged assault" on weak developing world states in the global era. Structural adjustment policies, for example, that call for a more open economy and a smaller state represent a "severe attack on post-colonial political structures based on patronage and clientelism" and will have "profound implications for the structure of political as well as economic life."[17] At the same time that it has further debilitated already "weak" states, however, globalizing influences may also be serving to empower social networks underneath the state—facilitating their participation in trans-border trading systems unmediated by the state in addition to providing them with access to resources from transnational networks. As such, whereas states seem to have had a fleeting advantage during the era of developmentalism and Cold War politics, the present neoliberal era of globalization may serve to tip the balance in more profound ways in favor of contesting social and political forces. All of this points to the likelihood of an intensification of conflicts between "weak" states and their challengers and/or contenders.

All the case studies in this volume are located in what we would describe as "weak" states. Within that general category, however, we find a wide variety of political contexts out of which have arisen significant substate actors. Some states are of recent creation such as those in Africa; others have deeper historical roots such as those of Colombia and, arguably, Lebanon. Some are in the midst of protracted civil war as is the case in the Sudan and Colombia; others have embarked on a process of reconstruction after a period of state collapse as is the case with Lebanon and, more recently, Somalia and Sierre Leone. Perhaps the most unique case in this volume is that of Kurdistan, a state-within-a-state born with the support of the international community after the defeat of the authoritarian and coercively powerful "fierce" Iraqi state in war.[18] By bringing together this wide and rich diversity of case studies and contexts across the developing world, we hope to provide useful comparative insights into the conditions that have given rise to their emergence.

Defining States-Within-States

One of the principal challenges facing the contributors to this volume is how to define the concept of states-within-states itself. Indeed, there is a twofold problem here, revolving around not only the criteria for identifying states-within-states but also determining the significance of these incipient political entities for both comparative politics in the developing world and for international relations. In this section, we shall examine some of the definitional dilemmas for those in comparative politics, leaving a discussion of its implications for the field of international relations, to the final section.

The basic dilemmas revolve around the criteria for "statehood" or "stateness." Is there a template around which debates about the state revolve? On the one hand, most of the literature within comparative politics adheres to the Weberian notion of the state—defined in minimal terms as a compulsory association with a territorial base claiming a monopoly over the legitimate use of force.[19] In its ideal-type form, such a state is regarded "as legitimate by its members and is run by an impersonal bureaucratic staff, in the context of a legal-administrative order regulated and limited by legislation and representative government."[20] Developed from observations of the process of state formation in the European context, the Weberian tradition of state theorizing, especially in its ideal-type form, has been widely applied as a benchmark for studies of state formation in the developing world.

It is increasingly recognized, however, that most states fall short of these criteria, even those in the West. Joel Migdal, for example, has been an articulate and insightful critic of exaggerated emphases on the power and effectiveness of the state, highlighting instead the existence of a disjuncture in our understanding of the state between "the image of a coherent, controlling organization in a territory" and "the actual practices of its multiple parts."[21] Rather than assuming the existence of a unified state "firing on all cylinders,"[22] Migdal offers a new definition of the state, characterized by contradictions and paradoxes. The state must be thought of in two ways, writes Migdal: "(1) as a powerful image of a clearly bounded, unified organization . . . performing in an integrated manner to rule a clearly defined territory; and (2) as the practices of a heap of loosely connected parts and fragments, frequently with ill-defined boundaries between them and other groupings inside and outside the official state borders and often promoting conflicting sets of rules with one another and with 'official' law." Indeed, as Migdal remarks, the state is often "a contradictory entity that acts against itself."[23]

This volume will continue the tradition in the social sciences of using Weberian criteria as an essential template for judging degrees of "stateness." However, it will also recognize, as stressed by Migdal, that these criteria set a standard in much of the developing world that is rarely reached by many states, let alone by states-within-states. Hence, while some earlier studies of de facto states tended to adopt strict definitional criteria—excluding entities characterized by informal, predatory, and/or de-territorialized activities[24]—our list of criteria in this volume is much more open-ended in recognition of the diverse manifestations of political authority and of its possible transformation over time. In short, our interest is more with "incipient" rather than full-blown political entities.

This leads us into a similarly inconclusive debate over the question of trajectory—where are these states-within-states going and how does this path connect to broader processes of state formation? The answers to these questions will depend upon how one views processes of state formation in the developing world more generally. On the one hand, stand the arguments of those like Charles Tilly who draw connections between war-making and state-making. Although Tilly advised caution in transposing his European and historically based arguments to the contemporary Third World, many developing-area scholars, including Spears in his contribution to this volume, have found his arguments attractive. According to Tilly, conflict can force those involved in making war to devise increasingly centralized, routinized, and extensive systems of revenue generation and collection. The more war-makers penetrate society, the more they are forced to strike bargains or contracts with their subjects, transforming what had originally resembled extortion racquets into more accountable and institutionalized political entities.[25] At this stage, as Robert Bates has more recently argued, one can see the emergence of a modern state that uses its monopoly over the use of force, not for the purposes of predation, but in order to enhance the productive basis of society.[26]

On the other hand are those scholars that challenge the universality and teleology of European models of state formation. There have been a series of fascinating studies on state formation in the developing world in recent years that highlight alternative, less intrusive, and less conflict-oriented routes to state centralized control. Karen Barkey's book *Bandits and Bureaucrats* (1994), for example, examines state formation in the Ottoman Empire. While dealing with the seventeenth century, Barkey's work is not irrelevant to our discussion in that, of all the various states and/or entities in the modern Middle Eastern region, it is Lebanon and the enduring social structures of Kurdish society that find their deepest roots in the Ottoman era. Barkey argues that processes of state centralization in the Ottoman lands were contrary to those in Europe. Rather than being characterized by a zero-sum conflict between state-makers and local forces, the Ottoman experience was characterized more by incorporation and accommodation. Hence, while local power was more often than not "crushed" in Europe, in the Ottoman Empire, it was "managed" allowing for a coexistence with the political center of variably developed political entities on the periphery. She concludes by arguing more generally that processes of state formation worldwide are "neither unidirectional nor without variation."[27]

A similar argument emerges from a recent work on state formation in Latin America in the nineteenth century by Fernando Lopez-Alves (2000) in which he argues that Tilly's state formation models only "partially apply" to the Latin American experience.[28] Indeed, Lopez-Alves argues that paths to state formation vary considerably within Latin America—combining the use of both conflict and incorporation. In determining the nature of the state formation process, therefore, he argues that one must examine it in a more open-ended and differentiated way than any one model can provide. He highlights, for example, the importance of examining the diversity of social and political alliances that underlie state formation processes—much as did Barrington Moore in his classic *Dictatorship and Democracy* (1966)—and, in an interesting point that is central to his argument, he emphasizes the importance of distinguishing between "types of conflict" and their effect on state formation processes. This latter point has been echoed by Mary Kaldor in her recent book *New and Old Wars: Organized Violence in a Global Era* (2001) when she argues that new "globalized" wars, given their dependence on predation and external support, their low levels of participation, and their targeting of civilians, tend to lead to the fragmentation rather than consolidation of political authority.[29]

Finally, Jeffrey Herbst, in his exceedingly stimulating book called *State and Power in Africa* (2000), outlines an altogether unique state formation trajectory—characterized neither by war nor by incorporation. Faced by what Herbst calls "the daunting nature of Africa's geography" that militated against the establishment of "profound links between cities and the surrounding territories," Africa's outlying regions remained relatively unincorporated by its political systems.[30] Indeed, he argues that this limited pattern of state centralization has been a continuous feature of state formation in Africa—be it in the precolonial, colonial, or postcolonial periods. He, therefore, concludes, like Barkey and Lopez-Alves, "the European experience does not provide a template for state-making in other regions of the world."[31]

The implications of these debates over the nature of the state and of state formation processes in the periphery raise profound questions about the underlying processes at work guiding the relationship between states and their substate challengers—questions that revolve around the degree to which there is a zero-sum game at play here. The Tillyan paradigm suggests that the stakes are high; that conflict will not only generate the emergence of political entities with state-like features but that it will create a teleological dynamic pushing these units toward statehood itself. On the other hand, the perspective from the periphery suggest more accommodative possibilities characterized by mutual—if uneasy—coexistence between state and the institutionally separate substate. Jeffrey Herbst, for example, has described many of these incipient political entities as "survival strategies." They emerge out of broader structural weaknesses of states but are themselves fragile and vulnerable; they are not what a universal social planner would have designed. Moreover, given the entrenchment of the state system in the twentieth century, it is now extremely difficult for such political entities to make the transition to statehood—even if they wanted to. As a result, he argues that most are destined to remain as "indeterminate and intermediate forms" whose political influence will ebb and flow depending on the strength of the state above.[32]

What do our case studies in this volume reveal with respect to these definitional questions about "stateness" and "trajectory"? Certainly, war and conflict between state and "substate" features prominently in all of our case studies in this volume. Moreover, out of these conflicts have emerged "substates" that have acquired a number of state-like Weberian features. These start with the nascent and more predatory-like institutions of revenue collection and extraction, as in the case of many of the "sub-state" actors described by William Reno in chapter three on Sierre Leone or the Sudan People's Liberation Army (SPLA) as discussed by Kenn Crossley in chapter eight in this volume. But, they also extend to such subpolitical entities as the *Fuerzas Armadas Revolucionarias de Colombia* (FARC) in Colombia, as described by Bejarano and Pizarro (chapter six), or the various Lebanese cantons during the Lebanese civil war, as described by Kingston and Zahar (chapter five), that claimed to be more public- and service-oriented. Chapter nine by Romano on Kurdistan suggests a further way to measure the degree to which a viable political entity has emerged linked to development of a vibrant civil society underpinned by a strong sense of national identity. Perhaps the arch typical example of state formation is found in Matt Bryden's (chapter ten) and David Romano's (chapter nine) description of the emergence of representative political institutions complete with elections in the case of Northern Somaliland and Kurdistan. In all cases, war and conflict has played a catalytic role in the emergence of more institutionalized micropolitical entities.

Yet, as most of the chapters make clear, the political units that emerged were also highly imbalanced in their institutional makeup. One of the important contributions of this volume is the wealth of empirical date uncovering the institutional nature of these subpolitical entities, data that shows the difficulty that most of these entities have had in fulfilling Weberian standards of statehood in a comprehensive way as outlined by Spears.[33] Chapter six by Bejarano and Pizarro on Colombia, for example, argues that Colombia's non-state actors lack many of the most basic criteria of "stateness." Despite controlling defined pieces of territory, they do not hold sway over large densities of population and their coercive and fiscal capacities are small relative to the larger state. In short, Bejarano and Pizarro argue that these non-state entities cannot challenge the existential legitimacy of the Colombian state. Moreover, even fulfilling the most basic of

Weberian functions—defined territoriality—can be problematic as shown by both Young's chapter on the politics of contestation over the status of the frontier South Blue Nile region in Sudan as well as Kingston and Zahar's chapter that highlights the gap between the identity and territorial contiguity of Lebanese wartime cantons. Neither, as Romano makes clear, can the Kurdish autonomous entity safeguard its own territorial integrity without a security guarantee from the international community. Finally, as the chapters by Reno on Sierre Leone as well as that by Romano on Kurdistan show, these entities are not immune from the debilitating emergence of internal "shadow states" themselves—indeed, their criminalization[34]—that weakens and divides the loyalties of the populations within these subpolitical entities and saps them of their institutional coherence. As a result, most of the states-within-states examined in this volume exhibit severe imbalances in their institutional development. With the exception of Eritrea and possibly Somaliland, there are no clear capacities or processes pushing these political entities in an unequivocal way toward statehood. Indeed, as is also made clear from all the case studies in this volume, despite the "weak" nature of juridical states, we are not witnessing their demise in the post–Cold War globalizing era. Rather, the result is more ambiguous leading to an uneasy coexistence and symbiosis between state and "substate."

Hence, while recognizing the historical connection between conflict and state forma-tion processes, we also recognize the need to be careful about adopting teleological and Eurocentric assumptions in our discussion of these micro-entities that we are calling states-within-states. There is no "end of history" here—no one road to statehood that these entities will ultimately find themselves on. Rather, using the same insights that have emanated from discussions about new theoretical directions in development stud-ies,[35] there is a need to recognize in our deliberations, the diversity of contexts and the ambiguity and contingency of processes and outcomes. It is for that reason that we have brought together a series of "area studies" experts on the countries that are being exam-ined, ones who can provide the rich historical detail that is needed if one is to transcend teleological models and assumptions.

Implications of the Rise of States-Within-States

This leads to the discussion of one final but related point: if substate actors including the diverse array of states-within-states take advantage of the empowering opportunities provided by the newly emerging and more open global arena, what challenges does this pose for both the theory and practice of global politics? Ann Mason, for example, has argued that international relations theory has a "blind spot" when it comes to the consideration of non-state actors in world politics, stressing that it must "go beyond its state-centered vision . . . and . . . develop conceptual tools better equipped with global realities."[36] It is certainly clear in the real world of international relations, for example, that sovereignty is no longer the sole and uncontested principle around which global politics revolves. To use a phrase of Robert Jackson, there is an emerging set of actors and networks that he describes as "escaping from sovereignty"[37]—be they unregulated global financial markets and/or a variety of transnational and subnational networks of which *al-Qaïda* would be a prime if clandestine example. This has serious implications for our entire notion of states-within-states in that it may shift potential trajectories away from statehood altogether. James Mittelman, for example, has written of a process of "de-territorialization" whereby substate actors no longer need to rely on control of a defined and local piece of territory in challenging state authority.[38] Duffield has gone further, discussing the phrase "durable disorder" to warn against the increased possibility—and utility—of protracted conflicts in this new unregulated age. Rather than conflict setting would-be states on the road to statehood, conflict becomes merely a method of economic accumulation[39]—leading to the emergence of an ambiguous no-man's land between sovereignty and subordination within the existing state. Whatever the case, the result is the emergence of a wider array of non-state actors in global politics—what some have called the beginnings of a "new medievalism" characterized by overlapping and constantly shifting lines of political authority.[40]

One of the most important questions to be answered by this volume, therefore, is how should policy-makers respond to the emergence of these additional non-state actors—some of which we are calling states-within-states? Up until now, the response of the international community has been a conservative one. As Jackson has commented, maps with borders remain paramount and it is states that continue to fill these spaces on the maps. Despite recent tinkering with the norm of sovereignty—symbolized by international efforts to create and support the Kurdish "safe haven" in northern Iraq as described by Romano—the international community continues to effectively shut the door to alternatives to statehood, resisting the establishment of any kind of precedent that might lead to the opening up of pandora's box.[41] On the other hand, however, the association of states-within-states with situations of conflict and humanitarian crisis in the developing world dictates that these entities cannot be ignored. Whether they are about "killing, stealing, or serving,"[42] many of these states-within-states have important impacts on attempts by the international community both to deliver humanitarian assistance to those caught in the middle of conflict (see chapter seven by Lauchlan Munro) as well as to bring to an end the conflicts themselves and so set in motion postwar processes of reconstruction and reconciliation.

Consistent with the varied agendas of the states-within-states described later, the chapters in this volume present a diverse set of policy implications. Some, indeed most, point to the need to reassert the power and authority of juridical states themselves, arguing that emerging non-state actors are unrepresentative and predatory in nature and often have the effect of prolonging conflict and humanitarian crises. This is certainly the case put forward by Bejarano and Pizarro who argue that it is only the Colombian state that has the national scope, legitimacy, and resources to effectively serve its citizenry. On the other end of the spectrum are those chapters that call for greater international support for fledgling states-within-states, calling, in effect, for their recognition as sovereign entities and arguing that they have become viable and legitimate political entities. Romano, for example, in the case of Kurdistan, argues that the internationally supported safe haven offers the best mechanism for the protection of Kurdish rights and opportunities.

However, the challenge facing policy-makers in the international arena does not lie so much with the two polar ends of the spectrum: recognition or rejection. Rather, the key challenge is to decide how to respond and interact with those more ambiguous cases where state and state-within-state coexist together in an uneasy symbiosis and where neither the state nor the substate possess significant legitimacy or capacity. The various specialized agencies of the United Nations, for example, have already set the precedent of establishing a working—though not political—relationship with non-state actors, especially in cases of humanitarian disaster. Yet, as the chapters by Munro and Crossley clearly show, keeping such working relationships apolitical is easier said than done. Not only must they resist attempts by these entities to deflect UN assistance away from their humanitarian purposes, they may also, as revealed by Munro's fascinating chapter on UNICEF's operations in the Eastern Congo between 1996–1998, face immense challenges in establishing a working relationship in the first place given the suspicion these entities hold toward the international community. As a way of avoiding these pitfalls, both authors point to the alternative of working with groups in civil society—an approach that has the added advantages of providing direct access to affected populations while offering potential opportunities to build up sources of social power that may hold the leadership of these unrepresentative political entities accountable. These are what Kaldor would call "islands of civility" outside of the reach of the various proto-states.[43]

Channeling the internal dynamics of these incipient political entities away from "killing and stealing" toward "serving" and stabilizing their relationships with the juridical states above them, however, will require more than ad hoc humanitarian interventions. It may also require rethinking the strict adherence to Cold War notions of sovereignty, "breaking the intellectual logjam" that surrounds the issue as Jeffrey Herbst has remarked.[44] What this will mean in practice is beyond the scope of this volume but there is an emerging set of ideas that revolve around the idea of what Kaldor calls "cosmopolitan governance"—combining the development of an international capacity in the enforcement of humanitarian and human rights law with efforts to create the kind of positive space needed for "islands of civility" to reemerge.[45] Referring to the effects of the emergence of the European Union that has facilitated the political expression of subnational identities in ways nonthreatening to sovereignty, Jackson argues in a similar vein for the creation of an "overarching mediating devise" that can act as a neutral arbitrator in situations of state/substate contestation.[46] The key, as Herbst has himself argued, is to create "more space for alternatives than has been the case in the past"[47]— even going so far as to suggest the adoption of the notion of "shared sovereignty."[48] Whatever the case, it is clear that the emergence of greater pluralism in world affairs will require shifts in the practice and theory of international relations. It is our hope that this volume on states-within-states—one example of what is a larger global phenomenon— can contribute to this process of rethinking.

***

The volume is divided into two sections. The first section examines the concept of states-within-states in historical and theoretical perspectives and is structured in the form of a debate. Ian Spears begins the volume by providing an inventory of the empirical elements of these entities, drawing from both the Weberian theoretical literature on states as well as the myriad of current examples of state-like entities that have emerged in many parts of the developing world. This chapter provides the positive case for taking the concept of states-within-states seriously. Scott Pegg (chapter two) takes up the challenge and compares Spears's notion of states-within-states to his previous work on the concept of a more narrowly defined de facto state. Pegg finds problems with the more expansive and inclusive definition of states-within-states of Spears but, by-and-large, argues that, whether narrowly or expansively defined, states-within-states are an important reality for global policy-makers, symbolic of the growing diversity of the international arena. In the absence of an international arena that requires and supports better standards of sovereignty, including the protection of minorities, these substate entities are likely to be an enduring feature of the international system.

The second section brings together the various case studies on states-within-states. While each chapter offers their own unique insights and, hence, stand on their own, there is an implicit logic to the order in which they are presented. The first four chapters, for example, offer insights into the formation of states-within-states, taking as their starting context the weakening if not collapse of the existing juridical state. William Reno's chapter is the most extreme in this regard, painting a picture of the proliferation of various non-state actors in the face of state collapse, very few of which (save the "bush governments" of the Community Defense Leagues (CDL)) offer any sign of a more public-oriented inclination. John Young's chapter on Sudan's South Blue Nile region—a contested region in Sudan's long-standing civil war that possesses some of the identity prerequisites for an autonomous existence yet lacks any of the needed institutional foundations—provides an interesting example of the difficulty in consolidating distinct and autonomous political projects. Chapters five and six move the debate out of the African context and into that of the Middle East and Latin America. Kingston's and Zahar's chapter on the rise and fall of "militia cantons" in Lebanon, likewise, focuses on the difficulties in consolidating these separate political projects, even in the face of a collapsed Lebanese state. Rather than filling the vacuum created by its demise, these entities found themselves unable to overcome not only their own incoherence—especially with respect to the issue of territorial contiguity—but also their own interdependence. Finally, in the case of Colombia, Bejerano and Pizarro argue convincingly and passionately that Colombia's various "proto-state" actors fail to pass Spears's inventory test of state-like elements. While they may be "aspiring state-makers," they lack both the material underpinnings of states-in-the-making, especially with respect to their popular legitimacy. This problem of legitimacy seems to have become particularly acute in the last decade or so as many sub-state entities have been able to cultivate access to sources of revenue outside of the arena in which they operate, separating them from the constituencies upon which more legitimate political entities must be built. All in all, these first four chapters suggest that just as juridical states face enormous difficulties in consolidating their political rule, so too do the substate entities that rise up to challenge them.

The next four chapters offer insights into the role that actors in the international arena can play. The chapters move from the most immediate concerns with respect to the provision of humanitarian assistance to those with the most long-term implications that revolve around issues of recognition. Lauchlan Munro's paper on UNICEF's Eastern Zaire operation in 1996–1998 provides a fascinating firsthand account of the difficulties faced by agencies involved in the delivery of humanitarian assistance in situations of state collapse where substate actors are in their formative—and hence volatile—stages of development. Kenn Crossley's reflective chapter on the workings of UNICEF's Operation Lifeline—Sudan (OLS), on the other hand, examines the dilemmas of working with a more established non-state entity, especially one that, according to Crossley, has predatory political inclinations. Crossley concludes that international humanitarian organizations should not be in the business of supporting substate entities like the Sudan People's Liberation Movement/Army (SPLM/A) but rather the social and community forces over which they rule.

The final two chapters, on the other hand, provide examples of the positive role, both immediate and potential, that international support can have on the development of substate entities. David Romano's chapter on the emergence of the "safe haven" in Iraqi Kurdistan and of the indigenous political development that has ensued thereafter suggests that international support can play a crucial role in protecting populations at risk. Matt Bryden's chapter on the consolidation of the Somaliland project in the 1990s, by and large an indigenous undertaking out of sight of most in the international arena, likewise points to ways in which the "international community" can lend a supporting hand. However, what is interesting about both chapters is that they fall short of advocating outright recognition. Certainly, both entities face internal constraints to the consolidation of their political projects—Somaliland due to the absence of abundant internal resources and Kurdistan due to its history of factional divisions. Yet, the most severe constraints in the move from autonomy to independence—from de facto state-within-a-state to juridical state—remain the regional and international political environment in which they exist. Given the overwhelming advantage that existing juridical states continue to possess in the present international arena, both chapters suggest that the most realistic solution for both state and substate is to reestablish some kind of mutually beneficial relationship, albeit one mediated and facilitated by actors within the international arena. This volume concludes with an essay that builds on theoretical and practical insights of the various chapters by providing a tentative list of recommendations to policy-makers pondering over how to integrate state-within-state entities into their foreign policy deliberations and calculations.

Notes

1. Joel Migdal, *Strong Societies and Weak States* (Princeton: Princeton University Press, 1988); and Joel Migdal, *State-in-Society: Studying How States and Societies Transform and Constitute One Another* (Cambridge: Cambridge University Press, 2001).
2. Robert Jackson, *Quasi-States: Sovereignty, International Relations, and the Third World* (New York: Cambridge University Press, 1990). See also Robert Jackson and Carl Rosberg, "Why Africa's Weak States Persist: The Empirical and Juridical in Statehood," in *World Politics*, Vol. 35 (October 1982), pp. 1–24; Carolyn Warner, "The Political Economy of 'Quasi-statehood' and the demise of 19th Century African Polities," in *Review of International Studies*, Vol. 25 (1999), pp. 233–255; and A.G. Hopkins's reply to the above article "Quasi-states, Weak States, and the Partition of Africa," in *Review of International Studies*, Vol. 26 (2000), pp. 311–320.
3. John Forrest, "State Inversion and Non-state Politics," in L.A. Villalon and P.A. Huxtable, eds., *The African State at a Critical Juncture: Between Disintegration and Reconfiguration* (Boulder: Lynne Rienner, 1998), p. 46.
4. Robert Kaplan, "The Coming Anarchy," in *The Atlantic Monthly*, February 1994.
5. Chris Allen, "Warfare, Endemic Violence and State Collapse in Africa," *Review of African Political Economy*, No. 81 (1999), p. 369.
6. Michael Ignatieff, "The Seductiveness of Moral Disgust," in *The Warrior's Honor: Ethnic War and the Modern Conscience* (Toronto: Viking, 1998).
7. Susan Strange, *The Retreat of the State: The Diffusion of Power in the World Economy* (New York: Cambridge University Press, 1996).
8. Jackson, *Quasi-States*.
9. Cf. Charles Tilly, "War Making and State Making as Organized Crime" in Evans, Reuschmeyer, and Skocpol, eds., *Bringing the State Back In* (New York: Cambridge University Press, 1985).
10. Migdal, *Strong Societies* and *State-in-Society*.
11. Jackson, *Quasi-States*.
12. See argument made by Hamza Alavi, "The State in Post-Colonial Societies: Pakistan and Bangladesh" in Goulbourne, ed., *Politics and the Third World* (London: Macmillan, 1979).

13. James Scott, *Seeing Like a State: How Schemes to Improve the Human Condition have Failed* (New Haven: Yale University Press, 1998).

14. Jeffrey Herbst, *State and Power in Africa* (Princeton: Princeton University Press, 2000), p. 139.

15. Kal Holsti, *The State, War, and the State of War* (New York: Cambridge University Press, 1996).

16. Francois Debrix, *Re-Envisioning Peacekeeping: The United Nations and the Mobilization of Ideology* (Minneapolis: University of Minnesota Press, 1999), p. 45.

17. Christopher Clapham, *Africa and the International System* (Cambridge: Cambridge University Press, 1996). See also O. Rivero, *The Myth of Development: The Non-Viable Economies of the 21st Century* (New York: Zed Books, 2001).

18. Nazih Ayubi, *Overstating the Arab State: Politics and Society in the Middle East* (London: I.B. Taurus, 1999).

19. Max Weber, *The Theory of Social and Economic Organization* (New York: Oxford University Press, 1947).

20. Leftwich, *States of Development: On the Primacy of Politics in Development* (Cambridge: Polity, 2000), p. 77.

21. Joel Migdal, *State-in-Society*, p. 16.

22. Ibid., p. 14.

23. Ibid., p. 22.

24. Scott Pegg, *International Society and the De Facto State* (Brookfield, VT: Ashgate, 1998), p. 149.

25. Tilly, "War Making."

26. Robert Bates, *Prosperity and Violence: The Political Economy of Development* (New York: W.W. Norton, 2001), p. 51.

27. Karen Barkey, *Bandits and Bureaucrats: The Ottoman Route to State Centralization* (Ithaca: Cornel University Press, 1994), p. 1.

28. Fernando Lopez-Alves, *State Formation and Democracy in Latin America, 1810–1900* (Durham: Duke University Press, 2000).

29. Mary Kaldor, *New and Old Wars: Organized Violence in a Global Era* (Stanford: Stanford University Press, 2001), p. 90.

30. Herbst, *State and Power*, pp. 12–14.

31. Ibid., p. 22.

32. Comments at "States-Within-States Workshop," Munk Centre for International Studies, University of Toronto, October 20, 2001.

33. These include the control over a defined territory, the ability to monopolize and extend the use of force, the existence of internal legitimacy, the strength of extractive, infrastructural, and administrative capacities.

34. See Jean-Francois Bayart, Stephen Ellis, and Beatrice Hibou, *The Criminalization of the State in Africa* (London, James Currey, 1999); Patrick Chabal and Jean-Pascal Daloz, *Africa Works: Disorder as Political Instrument* (London: James Curry, 1999); and Mats Berdal and David Malone, eds., *Greed and Grievance* (London: Lynne Rienner, 2000).

35. See the volume by Franz Schuurman, ed., *Beyond the Impasse: New Directions in Development Theory* (London: Zed Press, 1993).

36. Ann Mason, "Colombia's Conflict and Theories of World Politics," in *Items and Issues*, Vol. 4, No. 2–3 (New York: Social Science Research Council, 2003), p. 11.

37. Robert Jackson, ed., *Sovereignty at the Millenium* (Oxford: Blackwell, 1999), p. 41.

38. James Mittelman, *The Globalization Syndrome: Transformation and Resistance* (Princeton: Princeton University Press, 2000).

39. Mark Duffield, "Globalization, Transborder Trade and War Economies" in Berdal and Malone, eds., *Greed and Grievance*; see also the entire volume by Mats Berdal and

David Malone, eds., *Greed and Grievance*; and David Keen, *The Economic Functions of Violence in Civil Wars* (Oxford: Institute of Strategic Studies, Adelphi Paper 303, 1996).

40. See Hedley Bull, *The Anarchical Society: A Study of Order in World Politics* (London: Macmillan, 1977). See also P.G. Cerny, "Neo-medievalism, Civil War and the New Security Dilemma: Globalisation as Durable Disorder," *Civil Wars*, Vol. 1, No. 1 (Spring 1998), pp. 36–64; and Jackson.

41. Comments at "States-Within-States Workshop," Munk Centre for International Studies, University of Toronto, October 20, 2001.

42. We would like to thank Jonathan Barker for contributing this phrase.

43. Kaldor, *New and Old Wars*, p. 111.

44. Herbst, *State and Power*, p. 262.

45. Kaldor, *New and Old Wars*, p. 147. See also Mary Kaldor, "Reconceptualizing Organized Violence," in Daniele Archibugi, David Held, and Martin Kohler, eds., *Re-imagining Political Community: Studies in Cosmopolitan Democracy* (Stanford: Stanford University Press, 1998).

46. Comments at "States-Within-States Workshop," Munk Centre for International Studies, University of Toronto, October 20, 2001.

47. Herbst, *State and Power*, p. 260. See also J. Herbst, "Responding to State Failure in Africa," in *International Security*, Vol. 21, No. 3 (Winter 1996), pp. 120–144.

48. Ibid., p. 270.

Chapter One

States-Within-States: An Introduction to Their Empirical Attributes

Ian S. Spears

One of the principal problems facing many Third World states has been the inability to consolidate power over a defined piece of territory. This failure has, in turn, led to a disjuncture between international assumptions about how states operate and the reality of how and from where power is exercised. In order to understand this gap, scholars have formulated an array of concepts from "quasi" states to "shadow" states to "collapsed" states and contrasted them with states and processes of state formation in Europe. Quasi-states, for example, exist largely on the basis of their juridical nature. It is the international community's willingness to disregard their empirical qualities (or lack thereof) and instead formally recognize their existence that has allowed them to sustain themselves. As Robert Jackson, Jeffrey Herbst, and Charles Tilly each acknowledge, prior to 1945, these kinds of states—ones with weak administrative structures and divided populations—would have been swallowed up by much stronger powers.[1]

Alternatively, William Reno describes a *shadow* state that "is the product of personal rule, usually constructed behind the facade of de jure sovereignty." In these cases, rulers benefit from either superpower patronage or from foreign investors willing to invest in enclave operations rather than from taxing other domestic groups and producers.[2] Consequently, state elites are less interested in state-building or the well-being of their inhabitants per se than in their own personal gain. In these shadow states, elites exert political control by depriving most other individuals of security and resources and making their provision to a select few conditional on political support. Here, the shadow- and quasi-state are distinct ideas that exist simultaneously and often symbiotically: one is the legal structure that keeps foreign interlopers out; the other is the structure of patron–client relationships and personal rule that operates behind it.

Still others have considered the experiences of state failure and state collapse that had become apparent in the 1990s in part as a result of the processes described here. These are states where the respective governments have not only failed to meet a criterion of performance with regard to the most basic needs of their citizens but in some cases have ceased functioning altogether.[3] In one extreme case, Somalia, there has been no central internationally recognized government for over a decade.[4] It is this failure of new states emerging from decolonization that has, in fact, set the stage for groups to organize themselves along bases that reflect more viable alternatives. To this extent, the apocalyptic literature that speculates on the prospects of state breakdown and collapse may be misplaced.[5] While quasi-states break down, these changes do not necessarily have to entail anarchy. On the contrary, the breakdown of large, arbitrary state units may eventually give way to more coherent and viable (though not always benevolent) political entities.

Indeed, the purpose of this volume is to explore an additional concept: that of a *state-within-a-state*. States-within-states contrast with each of the preceding notions of the state in important ways. States-within-states have imposed effective control over a territory within a larger state and may have an impressive array of institutional structures that, among other things, allow taxes to be collected, services to be provided, and business with other international actors to be conducted. Yet they lack the very thing that quasi-states do possess: juridical status. In other words, within the juridical shells of the quasi-state there often exists other more rational, if also more fleeting, political structures that satisfy many of the empirical criteria normally associated with statehood. While the quasi-state has everything but a substantive state, this volume examines political subunits that have many substantive attributes of statehood, that may in fact be more viable than the quasi-state itself, but that for other reasons do not enjoy formal recognition from the international community.

While they might seek control of the larger formal state, states-within-states also remain, at least conceptually, distinct from Reno's *shadow* state. In one extreme, the government of the shadow state and the state-within-a-state are engaged in violent conflict with each other. Indeed, to the extent that they may deprive them of access to valuable resources, elites in shadow states resent the challenge posed by states-within-states and seek to suppress them. States-within-states are also distinct from shadow states insofar as while elites in the latter seek to reduce state bureaucracies (and thus the size of the patronage network) and to increase instability in order to boost the dependence of others on these elites, some states-within-states seek to create a viable political structure that actually benefits the citizenry within. Alternatively, elites in less corrupt but weaker governments of the type that have been cobbled together in peace processes or following state collapse, also resent the challenge posed by states-within-states. States-within-states may appear to be significantly more coherent and viable and may, by their very presence, reflect the weakened position of the putative (and perhaps more legitimate) central government.[6]

The concept of the state-within-a-state has intentionally been left imprecise and the range of state-like structures considered here is broad. Cases could include Eritrea, which has gone on to receive international recognition, to Somaliland, which (despite its efforts to date) has not, to Tigray, Biafra, and localities in Lebanon where aspirations of formal statehood have either been put into abeyance or never existed.[7] In many cases, these political subunits are recognized in journalistic accounts and by scholars, variously noted as "de facto states,"[8] "states-within-states," "fiefdoms," or "mini-states."[9] Alternatively, the name of the principal leader or the movement itself is often incorporated into a name such as "Taylorland" (in Sierra Leone and Liberia), "Savimbiland" (in Angola) or "FARClandia" (in Colombia), and in at least one case, a territory has been associated with a major multinational oil corporation (the "Republic of Chevron" in Nigeria).[10] The concept of states-within-states is also sufficiently broad as to include secessionist movements and warlord states as well as more benevolent indigenous subunits that actively solicit the support of their inhabitants in return for the provision of key services such as protection. Of course, the benevolence or public-mindedness of these entities is very much a matter of perspective. Indeed, a larger objective of this volume is to explore how these political subunits behave and why they select some political routes and options and not others. The only criteria for states-within-states is that they do not, or did not, receive recognition from the international community but that they do exhibit key elements of a Weberian definition of statehood. It is to this latter issue that we can now turn.

Defining the State

The academic literature emphasizes two approaches to defining the state: the empirical, and the legal or juridical. In Weber's classic definition, a state must, at the very least, "successfully uphold . . . a claim to the *monopoly* of the *legitimate* use of physical force in the enforcement of its order."[11] Charles Tilly also emphasizes this empirical aspect of statehood, noting that nation-states are "relatively centralized, differentiated organizations the officials of which more or less successfully claim control over the chief concentrated means of violence within a population inhabiting a large, contiguous territory."[12] But as others have observed, many states in the contemporary developing world fail this test of statehood because their respective national governments cannot lay claim to a monopoly of force over all the territory under their assumed jurisdiction.[13] As a result, the international community has increasingly come to accept a legal approach of statehood that usually includes a former colony's *right* to self-determination (though, importantly, not an ethnic group's right to self-determination).[14] This is because to rely on a strictly Weberian interpretation of statehood would disqualify a large number of states in Africa and elsewhere. A juridical approach to statehood allows one to overlook empirical aspects of statehood that are clearly deficient in much of the developing world.

Carl Rosberg and Robert Jackson note, on the other hand, "[i]f some external or internal organization can effectively challenge a national government and carve out an area of monopolistic control for itself, it thereby acquires the essential characteristics of statehood."[15] Indeed, while central governments may continue to make *pro forma* claims to all their territory, there are instances in the developing world where entities *within* these states come much closer to satisfying the Weberian definition of statehood. Inverting the arguments of Jackson, Herbst, and Tilly, in any other era when the juridical nature of statehood did not have the prominence it has today, it would be these more logical and viable subunits that would form the community of states. After a brief discussion of the role of violent conflict in the emergence of states-within-states, the remainder of this essay will examine previous experiences of these political subunits not in terms of their juridical status—which is clearly lacking—but in terms of their empirical elements including the extension of force, territory, national identity and internal legitimacy, capacity to generate revenue, and finally, in terms of their administration and infrastructure. This chapter concludes with a discussion of the *raison d'etre* of states-within-states in the post–Cold War world and their significance in the political science literature.

States-Within-States and the Significance of War

It has been argued that the viability of European states was very much tied to violent conflict. In his oft-cited statement, Charles Tilly claims, "War made the state, and the state made war."[16] Among other things, war forced states to become more efficient at generating revenue and in creating more durable bureaucracies for administrating resource extraction. Warfare also tended to generate domestic solidarity insofar as otherwise diverse groups within the state tended to overlook their own differences for the purposes of defeating a common external enemy. In this way, the environment of ongoing warfare strengthened state structures and allowed the weakest political entities to be consumed by more powerful political states.

Alternatively, Jeffrey Herbst has argued that the *lack* of interstate war has been central to the fact of state weakness in Africa (and, I might argue, elsewhere in the developing world).[17] War has not been foreign to Africa but war specifically *between* independent states has been rare. Many governments have had difficulty controlling all of their own territory let alone threatening a neighbor. During the Cold War, both the United States and the Soviet Union provided large quantities of military aid to client regimes in the developing world in an effort to compensate for this weakness and to allow them to fend off or put down domestic threats. The superpowers were willing to regulate arms shipments in order to prevent a client-state from projecting power abroad but they rarely had inhibitions about supplying them with weapons sufficient to counter internal dissent.[18] Client regimes did not have to work especially hard to develop a military capability since they had few neighbors interested in conquering their territory (and less imperative to project power of their own) and since most of them received military hardware and training in exchange for basing rights rather than money or commodities.[19] In short, having been born into a relatively benign international environment and provided with superpower-supplied weapons before they encountered external threats, few states in the developing world have faced the war-induced development imperative European states did. Elites, in turn, had more opportunities to enrich themselves even as they failed spectacularly at state-making and institution building.

Tilly argues that the European experience of state formation is unique and is not likely to be repeated in the developing world.[20] Nonetheless, the processes that Tilly describes with respect to Europe were very much at work in creating and strengthening the *substate* units that are the focus of this volume. These states-within-states may have been hard-pressed to overthrow a well-armed, if still inept, client of a superpower. But, not unlike the experience in Europe, the process of constant warfare forced some of them to become stronger and more efficient. While some scholars have noted that few Soviet-supported regimes were overthrown, this was no longer the case by the late 1980s when a budget-conscious Moscow sharply reduced aid to its clients.[21] In the post–Cold War era many of these substate units found themselves to be relatively powerful since both superpowers had by now abandoned most of their clients leaving a suddenly emasculated regime, which had until recently grown fat on superpower patronage.

No doubt processes of state formation in Europe and the developing world are quite different. There are few indications that weak states in much of the developing world are about to embark on a long process of interstate conflict that would strengthen them in the way states in Western Europe were. To the extent that the international community prefers to emphasize juridical rather than empirical criteria of statehood, the existing states that emerged from former colonial states will persist and, within them, states-within-states will remain somewhat obscured, if still sometimes formidable, powers. Nonetheless, if the experience of Eritrea is any indication, under certain conditions some of these substate units—some of which are forged through processes similar to those that occurred in Europe—may be allowed to become full and perhaps more viable members of the international community of states.[22]

The Question of Territory

Central to most definitions of the state is some element of territoriality. Indeed, the fact of states-within-states is an acknowledgment that there is a disjuncture between the territory that is ostensibly under a state's *jurisdiction* and that which is effectively *controlled* by the state. This disjuncture has been sustained because of a well-justified reluctance to create a more rational basis of statehood on the part of organizations such as the Organization of African Unity (OAU) and its successor, the African Union (AU) and the international community in general. Evidently it is preferable to aspire to the development of states as they currently exist than to redraw state borders in a dubious attempt to create more ethnically homogenous states. Prior to 1945, the geographic size of states was more fluid and the fact of both centripetal and centrifugal forces tended to lead to an optimal size of efficiency. As Richard Bean noted, "States larger than the optimal range tend to disintegrate, and those smaller tend to be absorbed."[23] Technology was central to this process that traditionally involved a state's ability to project power in an effort to acquire more territory. More recently, however, states have less often felt the need to expand their geographic size and the international community has been less tolerant of threats to territorial integrity.[24] In the contemporary developing world, many governments have already failed to generate statewide infrastructure even when they do not face a determined challenger within their borders and rarely consider territorial acquisition in other states. In the developed world, the relationship between size and technology has even been reversed. Indeed, as Juan Enriquez has established, governments that control large tracts of territory may be less relevant today than a state that invests in its citizenry.[25] An extreme view is that technology has now made territory irrelevant and some recent scholarship has even emphasized the rise of the "virtual" state.[26] There is a certain irony, then, that at the moment technology has reduced the importance of territory, international law continues to uphold the boundaries of existing—and sometimes very large—states.

While territory remains a central aspect of states-within-states, the extent of territorial control has been more reflective of state capacity than the quasi-states in which they are located. Some scholars have argued that a fixed territory is not always central to "warlordism" or to the operation of "war economies."[27] But many of these warlords do in fact hold large portions of territory. Liberian warlord Charles Taylor, for example, controlled 95 percent of Liberia from his capital in Gbarna. This control allowed him to grant concessions to foreign interests to exploit commodities such as diamonds, gold, ore, rubber, and timber contained within.[28]

While the borders of states-within-states may not be very precise or may shift over time, the area they contain is often more permanent and larger than the territory under the effective control of the central government. Prior to the fall of Mengistu Haile Mariam in Ethiopia in 1991, rebels in Eritrea and Tigray controlled virtually all of their respective provinces even though they were often unable to hold the towns and cities. And while the Somali National Movement (SNM) restricted its control to northern Somaliland, the man who was ostensibly the president of Somalia until his regime collapsed in January 1991, Siyad Barre, was jokingly referred to by many Somalis as only the "Mayor of Mogadishu." At the height of his power as a rebel in 1992, Charles Taylor's territorial control extended across state borders to include most of Liberia, parts of Guinea, and one-quarter of Sierra Leone. The Interim Government of National Unity, by contrast, tended to be restricted to the capital of Monrovia.[29] Despite the fact that Taylor was incorporating ever larger portions of resource-rich land into his commercial network, his ability to maintain territorial control required only that he allow his National Patriotic Front of Liberia (NPFL) fighters the opportunity to loot conquered areas.[30] Taylor's own ruthlessness and the NPFL's use of terror minimized the challenges to his control. There are also instances where rebel control over a fixed territorial boundary is recognized by both the rebel movement and the central government. For example, while Colombian rebels enjoyed de facto control over much of what is admittedly sparsely populated territory in southeastern Colombia, in November 1998 the government of President Andrés Pastrana ceded four counties—territory the size of Switzerland—to the FARC, and a smaller region to a second group known as the National Liberation Army (ELN). While the move was initially meant to be seen as short-term goodwill gesture on the part of the government in Bogatá, the rebels sought to increase their grip on this territory and took measures to ensure that they could not be expelled if the peace process broke down.[31]

In other cases, the end of the Cold War forced long-established groups to strike out from their state-like strongholds. In the case of Jamba, the portion of southeastern Angola that was controlled by rebels associated with the *União Nacional para a Independência Total de Angola* (UNITA), the objective had long been to stay out of the reach of government airstrikes and in close proximity to South African protection and support. But this locale also made it much more difficult to attack government installations or hold positions beyond Jamba. As one visiting journalist put it, "Jamba was a long way from anywhere that mattered. . . . [T]he strategic government installations— the diamond mines, the oil fields of Cabinda, the capital itself—lay far to the north, beyond the reach of an army that boasted a few trucks, one tank, no airforce." As the war in Angola extended beyond the end of the Cold War (and South African and American patronage), however, UNITA leader Jonas Savimbi could no longer afford to confine himself to Jamba but had to find new ways to fund the war effort. This involved redoubled efforts to exploit Angola's vast mineral resources well beyond Jamba.[32]

The Extension of Force

The ability to project power or to have a legitimate monopoly on its use within a territory is obviously a central element in the Weberian definition of statehood. States-within-states are important indications of the inability of many central governments in the developing world to meet this basic criteria. The cession of territory to FARC rebels in Colombia, for example, is a de facto acknowledgment that the government in Bogatá did not exercise full sovereignty over all of its territory. Within states-within-states themselves, however, we often see a more comprehensive monopoly of power both in terms of the ability to reduce nonrebel-related criminal activity and to eliminate rivals for regional power. In Colombia, in the weeks and months after FARC rebels took formal control, crime—including murders, robbery, and rape—dropped significantly.[33] In Tigray, the activities of *shifta* or bandits was inversely related to the strength and effectiveness of the central government. But as the Tigrean People's Liberation Front (TPLF) grew in strength and sophistication, peasants increasingly looked to it to provide them with effective protection from *shifta*. Significantly, the ability to provide greater security against *shifta* activities demonstrated the TPLF's interest in the well-being of ordinary Tigrayans and further endeared peasants to the liberation movement.

John Prendergast and Mark Duffield note further how the strength derived from a long struggle with other rival movements pushed the TPLF ever closer to a Weberian power monopoly—one that would not allow for two concurrent forces to preside over one territory and population either then or now. They write,

> From its inception, the TPLF undertook mass mobilization based on competition. In this atmosphere—which lasted more than fifteen years—there was little room for compromise. Victory went to the strongest, the best organized. "Darwinian socialists" might be one way to characterize the leadership of the Front . . . . It is no surprise then, as we fast forward to the present, that when people do not play by the TPLF rule book, they are "expelled" from the game one way or another. "They're in a race, a competition to win over the country" described one sympathetic outsider . . . In the main, they do not accommodate different visions. There is little space given because it is felt there is none deserved.[34]

Additionally, the "victory" over the Ethiopian government in 1991 and the sacrifices it required from the TPLF and Tigreans in general provided a convenient justification for a disproportionate amount of resources subsequently directed toward Tigray and the north for reconstruction. War, then, not only strengthened the TPLF itself, but allowed its region to benefit in a developmental sense—and often at the expense of other regions of Ethiopia.[35]

As with conventional ideas of how states operate and survive, military assets are also acquired by the substate to attack or defend against external challenges. In the Angolan case, South Africa and, at various times, the United States provided weapons and support to UNITA, which precluded the ruling *Movimento Popular do Libertação de Angola* (MPLA) from consolidating its support across the country. Alan Cowell interprets the significance of UNITA's ability to deny Luanda control over Jamba:

> Without UNITA's constant military harassment of the authorities, Jamba would have been an irrelevance, as threatening as some obscure religious sect that had hidden away in the wilderness seeking solitude and redemption. But the military campaign demanded attention. Lodged like a bone in the throat, it offered a permanent challenge to Luanda's authority, to its ability to implant policies that might ordinarily have improved the lives of Angola's people. It denied the very title that MPLA had won for itself as the Government of the People's Republic of Angola. Savimbi's campaign—and South African strategy—meant that the MPLA did not, could not, govern the country.[36]

Not all states-within-states, however, were the direct beneficiaries of the externally supplied patronage that UNITA enjoyed. Nonetheless, insofar as they could successfully seize these weapons from their opponents, liberation fronts almost always benefited from the largesse of outsiders. Since there were virtually no external suppliers willing to provide arms directly to the Ethiopian liberation movements, the capture of weapons was the central means by which this weakness could be overcome. From the beginning of its insurrection, TPLF fighters had attacked government supply lines north to Eritrea. These tactics, in turn, led to the development of a more formidable conventional TPLF force which, by the mid-1980s, allowed the TPLF to go on the offensive. Indeed, much to the distress of Soviet officials, the rebels often made better use of Soviet equipment that they had captured from *Derg* forces than did the Ethiopian army itself.[37] In one account, a former Ethiopian government official, Dawit Wolde Giorgis, acknowledged,

> Today the Eritrean and Tigrayan movements do not have to go looking for armaments. They are supplied by the Ethiopian army. Ethiopian troops are so heavily armed, so immobile, so conventional in unconventional warfare, that whenever units retreat they leave behind enormous amounts of weaponry and *materiel*—tanks, heavy artillery, guns, munitions—to be seized by the rebels. The secessionist movements have become the most sophisticated and well armed guerilla movements on the continent. These are realities.[38]

Instead of being "born arming"—an expression used to characterize the patronage supplied to some newly independent governments in the Third World—the armies of some states-within-states evolved into formidable forces because they were the only force that stood between the people and the central government. Years of warfare against a much larger army in Addis Ababa had the effect of disciplining the armies in what would become independent Eritrea and post–Mengistu Ethiopia.[39]

"National" Identity and Internal Legitimacy

Of course, territory and a monopoly of force are not the only indications of a state-within-a-state. In many cases, it is also possible to discern a *social* identification with the substate. Indeed, the process of extending state power at home and abroad and the establishment of a more-or-less common identity are similar and mutually reinforcing processes.[40]

Many states in the developing world, however, are deficient in both these dimensions. As is often noted, states in much of the developing world were created arbitrarily by outsiders, imperial powers, who frequently overlooked the diversity of peoples within the territories they were colonizing. Colonialism aside, however, the diversity that is found in states in the developing world is not without precedent. It is often forgotten that nationhood defined in terms of ethnicity and its accompanying attributes of common history and language did not emerge in Europe until the late nineteenth century. France, for example, emerged out of the old Frankish kingdom (Paris, Loire Valley, and the north) but later came to include—by force of arms—other nations of Bretons, Basques, Alsatians, Occitanians, Catalans, Corsicans, and Flemings. At the time of the French Revolution in 1789, half of France's citizenry did not speak French. And even fewer spoke any sort of standardized French. In other words, France was a multiethnic state in the way that some Third World countries are today. The same was true with Italy. During unification of Italy's numerous states in the mid-nineteenth century, only about 3 percent of the population spoke a standardized Italian.[41] Scholars who have examined early immigration records to the United States also note that European immigrants had little sense of being Italian, or Ukrainian, or Croat. Rather, their identities were defined in more local terms to rivers, villages, and regions.[42]

But while some degree of regional affiliation almost always remains, a central factor in uniting these otherwise diverse peoples is war. According to Jeffrey Herbst, "the presence of a palpable external threat may be the strongest way to generate a common association between the state and the population."[43] In other words, when faced with an external threat individuals are inclined to focus their attention on their survival rather than to worry about less critical differences between them.

Similar processes occur in states-within-states. In Europe, territory was conquered and a common identity was consolidated across a diversity of groups through subsequent exposure to other outside threats. In Africa and some other places in the developing world, states were created arbitrarily through colonialism and decolonization and, consequently, there was less sense of a common identity except in the rare instance of threats emanating from outside the formal state. Within the quasi-state, however, a common identity was consolidated within particular regions or territories on the basis of a conflict with, and the resulting fear of, an oppressive central government. "It is these fears," noted the Tanzanian government when it recognized the independent state of Biafra, "which are the root cause both for the secession, and for the fanaticism with which the people of Eastern Nigeria have defended the country they declared to be independent."[44] Obviously, there are important differences in terms of the sequence of state formation. Nonetheless, whether emotional attachments are created as a result of threats from outside or inside the state, the processes of identity formation are largely similar.

In some cases, liberation movements have sought to win local support by demonstrating to their own people that the war was being fought with their interests at heart and that they were worthy challengers to state power. In the early days of the struggle for Tigray, for example, TPLF personnel endeared themselves to the peasantry by traversing the countryside carrying sticks wrapped in plastic to look like guns and providing basic services to those in need.[45] Locally run schools are also principal means by which young people can be indoctrinated into the war movement. As Cowell notes regarding Angola, in UNITA's Jamba "the children went to class under the shade of trees, 4500 of them chanting their way through a little math, a little geography, a lot of propaganda. 'UNITA, the guide; UNITA, the people.' At the roadsides they were taught to snap to attention when trucks of visitors or dignitaries sped by in billows of dust."[46]

War, then, has had a significant role in overcoming diversity and creating a common identity within states-within-states. Eritrea, for example, has more than a dozen ethnic, religious, and linguistic groups. But it has also had much to unite this diversity, including a common history under Italian colonial rule and British administration. More recently, its avoidance of an external benefactor has also generated a sense of isolation and self-sufficiency that has become central to Eritrean identity. Most importantly, however, Eric Garcetti and Janet Gruber note that "a crucial element of Eritrean national identity was shaped by the image of the Ethiopian 'other,' which served to unite the diverse Eritrean population."[47] In particular, prior to its independence in 1993, Eritreans endured 30 years of civil war with the Ethiopian government from which few Eritreans emerged unaffected.[48] The consequence, according to the authors' surveys, was a degree of "national" affiliation that is remarkable for Africa or anywhere in the developing world. Most notably, while ethnic pride remained strong, almost 70 percent of Eritreans preferred to identify themselves in terms of their national identity ("Eritrean" or "more Eritrean") rather than their ethnic identity (7.1 percent).[49] Indeed, if there was any doubt about a commitment by Eritreans to independent statehood that transcended ethnicity, it was removed following the 1993 referendum in which 98.3 percent of Eritreans voted "yes" to independence. "The outcome of a conflict that began on a parochial basis," writes John Markakis, "is a new state with a multi-ethnic population whose 'national' (Eritrean) consciousness was forged in a bloody struggle that lasted three decades."[50]

Of course, this forging of a common identity through war with a common enemy would appear to have important exceptions. Despite a war with a common enemy, the

Nuer and the Dinka of southern Sudan have continued to see each other as adversaries and have engaged in ongoing violent conflict—one that has been encouraged by the various regimes in Khartoum. But when considered in the longer-term context, this problem is not incompatible with the argument that external threats generate a shared sense of identity. The process of state formation also involves the extension of power outward and the pacification, inclusion, or elimination of other challengers for power within a territory. Certainly the Eritrean People's Liberation Front (EPLF) and the TPLF in Ethiopia could not succeed in their own political objectives until they had successfully eliminated challenges from other groups in their respective provinces, notably the Eritrean Liberation Front (ELF) in Eritrea, and the Ethiopian People's Revolutionary Party (EPRP), and Ethiopian Democratic Union (EDU) in Tigray.[51] Not surprisingly, in the case of the TPLF, the struggle against other provincial rivals was won by gaining the support of local peasantry through appeals to Tigrayan nationalism, something the other nonexclusively Tigrean movements operating in Tigray could not do.[52] Similarly, in Eritrea, the EPLF prevailed over its rival ELF.[53] With the elimination of the ELF as a rival, the EPLF continued to focus on nationalities, defined by language, rather than religion—an emphasis that reduced the significance of the Christian–Muslim cleavage between the EPLF and the ELF. Even in southern Sudan during the early 1980s, the mainly Dinka SPLA succeeded in consolidating its grip on much of the south. As it did so, increasing numbers of Nuer defected to it so that by late 1987 many of the so-called *Anyanya 2* had joined the SPLA.[54]

Revenue Generation

Revenue generation remains an essential aspect for the survival of states-within-states. As one senior UNITA official remarked, "You cannot survive as a political party if you do not have funds. Most of the political opposition parties in Africa die of financial asphyxiation before they die of political asphyxiation. That was key for UNITA."[55] In Europe, the raising of sufficient revenue was essential if states were to avoid military defeat. According to Michael Mann, between 1688 and 1815, England experienced six major increases in state revenues and all of these corresponded with the beginning of a war. "State finances," he observers, "were dominated by foreign wars."[56] In light of these findings Jeffrey Herbst notes, "fighting wars may be the only way whereby it is possible to have people pay more taxes and at the same time feel more closely associated with the state."[57]

During the Cold War, however, some states-within-states did survive on remarkably small sources of income. Some movements such as the TPLF in Tigray made poverty a virtue in their dealings with the local peasantry and were almost entirely dependent on weapons captured from the government to carry on the struggle. Unlike some more predatory states-within-states such as "Taylorland" in Liberia, the TPLF generally did not derive income from foreign sources, local crime, or coercing peasants. Instead, it financed itself through taxation in the liberated areas, and voluntary contributions from local businesses, Tigrean expatriates, and companies created by the TPLF.[58] In neighboring Eritrea, the EPLF claimed that it could finance its war with the governing *Derg* on the relatively small £11 million it received each year from Eritreans living in the diaspora—a paltry sum considering the Ethiopian defense budget was estimated to be £951 million.[59] Indeed, perhaps had it not been for the ineptitude of most African armed forces, the quantity of what was often totally unsuitable military equipment provided by the superpowers, and the effectiveness of the guerrilla tactics employed by the fronts themselves, some states-within-states could not likely have survived the Cold War era.

Elsewhere guerrillas movements have generated more significant profits from kidnapping and drug trade operations. In FARC-controlled territory in Colombia, for example, U.S. State Department officials regard the rebels in terms of a "narco-government" running a "narco-empire."[60] Not surprisingly, there is an important link between the weak central government in Bogatá and the ability of rebels to generate income for itself through the drug trade. Guerrillas and drug traffickers have been able to operate in and profit from remote areas of Colombia—some of which is prime coca growing territory—precisely because the central government has never been able or willing to provide basic infrastructure and services and local peasants feel little connection with it. Estimates of the profits generated by the coca trade range from US$100 million to over ten times that amount.[61] Colombian rebels have benefitted from taxing the coca-producing fields and, more recently, FARC rebels planned a "peace tax" to be imposed on the wealthy and companies operating in the zone. Kidnapping in Colombia has soared in recent years and rebels often do not deny that its purpose is economic rather than political.[62]

The end of the Cold War had a dramatic impact on some states-within-states. Not surprisingly, there was an expectation that many rebel movements were too dependent on their own outside sources and would not survive the end of the superpower patronage.[63] But many of those groups actually became more adept at finding other sources of revenue that allowed them to sustain themselves. Now external support tends not to be restricted to a single (or very few) sources but may involve a number of different state and non-state actors. By linking themselves directly to the global economy, many local actors have become extremely effective at making this transition from reliance on a single source of support.

As a result, there has been a contradictory impact on the issue of territoriality of states-within-states. To the extent that the end of the Cold War forced groups such as UNITA in Angola from being mere recipients of foreign assistance to exploiting resources under their control, territory becomes increasingly important. Territorial control not only allows groups to exploit natural resources but also to benefit financially from all other economic activities taking place within. Indeed, a report prepared for the United Nations acknowledged that while Angolan diamonds continued,

> to be the main source of UNITA's wealth and the primary source of its funding, . . . significant amounts of money were made by UNITA in the form of landing fees charged for aircraft bringing in food, medicines, clothing, mining equipment and other commercial commodities. These "taxes" ranged from US$2,000 to US$5,000 and were collected from the crews on the spot. In 1996–97 when commercial activity was probably at its peak, UNITA may have earned as much as US$5 million per month from taxes and other commercial levies collected within its areas.[64]

Indeed, rebel movements have become ever more possessive of territory under their control and have lashed out at efforts to encroach upon these revenue-generating regions. In Angola in the late 1990s, UNITA became more intransigent (and eventually returned to war) when government forces moved into diamond-rich territory under its control—even though it had agreed to an extension of central government administration—because it feared that it would lose the revenue-generating potential of these regions. Similarly in Sierra Leone, in May 2000 RUF rebels took 500 UN peace-keepers hostage when pro-government forces threatened to move into lucrative rebel-held diamond fields.

On the other hand, a lack of external patronage has meant that elites in states-within-states have had to be ever more innovative in developing commercial interests. In Angola, for example, UNITA became more assertive in expanding beyond the confines of Jamba to include diamond-territory in the center and north of Angola, but also to aggressively solicit the purchasers of diamonds and suppliers of weapons outside of country. Indeed, according to Mark Duffield, UNITA "developed a ferocious independence based upon a shifting pattern of regional transborder and international commercial linkages." Duffield adds, "Today's so-called warlords or failed states may act locally, but to survive they have to think globally. In this respect, a high level of complicity among international companies, offshore banking facilities, and Northern governments has assisted the development of war economies . . . Without this help, war economies would find it difficult to survive."[65]

So while the governments of states-within-states do not generally enter formal diplomatic relations with other states, they do often fund themselves by engaging in economic relations with other international actors: in Angola, UNITA continued to help meet the global demand for diamonds, and in Liberia during the 1990s, Charles Taylor supplied one-third of France's tropical hardwood requirements.[66] Indeed, by essentially forcing foreign interests into dealing through his capital in Gbarna—thereby collecting the associated taxes and export duties from timber, rubber, and mining operations—Charles Taylor's predatory state-within-a-state continued to grow and be strengthened to the detriment of the interim government in Monrovia.

Infrastructure and Administration

Warlords and rebel movements in some states-within-states have at times been heavily engaged in, and effective at, activities such as the development of roads, policing, and even telecommunications. In a remarkably short two-and-one-half years, Charles Taylor's state-within-a-state, among other things, managed its own currency and banking system and operated an international airfield and a radio and television network, all of which contrasted sharply with the efforts of the aid-dependent and ineffective interim coalition government in Monrovia.[67] As one journalist noted in 1992, "the Taylor government, which now calls itself the National Patriotic Reconstruction Assembly, has spent lavishly to create a vision of a well-planned bureaucracy. On nearly every corner, signs direct visitors to ministry offices."[68]

In Colombia, roads and airstrips that were built or repaired ostensibly with military objectives in mind also had benefits for farmers and ranchers who previously had difficulty getting their crops to market. In place of a cash-strapped central government's inability to administer a meaningful legal system, FARC rebels imposed "revolutionary justice," which was regarded as swift and uncompromising. While an agreement between the Bogatá government and the FARC rebels required army soldiers and police to be withdrawn from the "zone of disarmament," in practice the rebels drove mayors, judges, priests, and tax collectors out of the region and replaced them with its own authority.[69] At "border" crossings and airports, visitors must have their passports and luggage inspected by rebels. As one FARC commander observed, "In 90 percent of cases, people resolve their problems by calling the guerrillas. . . . FARC is another government."[70]

In Angola, UNITA attempted to reduce its dependence on South African assistance in part through the creation of "Resistance Farms," which were expected to make UNITA-held territory self-sufficient in food. In UNITA's austere educational system, students were taught essential skills in agricultural science, vehicular repair, or were given clerical and linguistic skills.[71]

Perhaps the most direct relationship between the war effort and development can be seen in the Horn of Africa. Not surprisingly, as the struggle against the Ethiopian *Derg* and the liberation movements continued and became more intense, substate structures in both Tigray and Eritrea became increasingly more sophisticated and effective. In a recently published account, Robert Kaplan notes his observations of Eritrea,

> In the 1980s, I saw Eritrean guerrillas build trench warrens lined with slate and sandbags, convert cluster bomb parts into flywheels for trucks, use the tips of spent tank shells for rain gauges in their desert agricultural stations, make wash basins out of exploded MIG shells, and store blood in refrigerators powered by wind and solar energy. In a mountain-side hut, I saw amputees operate an Italian-made machine that produced 10,000 sanitary napkins per hour for women guerrilla fighters at the front. Decades of conflict in their sun-blistered moonscape of a country have raised Eritreans' resourcefulness to levels rarely seen elsewhere. While I watched guerrillas produce chloroquin tablets to fight malaria, the pharmacist in charge told me that he planned to start producing materials from which chloroquin is composed, "since we can't depend on anyone." Even with satellite photographs, in the 1980's it was difficult for Western intelligence agencies to estimate Eritrean battle losses because of the Eritreans' ability to get their dead and wounded off the field more quickly than all but the most sophisticated armies. War has engendered a monastic approach to existence in Eritrea, where people have raised deprivation and absolute self-reliance to the status of religion, even as both Orthodox Christianity and Islam have been de-emphasized.[72]

In Tigray, as increasing numbers of skilled personnel joined the movement, the TPLF launched its own business operations that not only contributed to the war effort and met local needs but served as the basis for reconstruction and development in Tigray and elsewhere in Ethiopia following the fall of Mengistu in 1991. Indeed, John Young connects the sophistication of many of these activities in different regions of Ethiopia to the exposure to the war, saying, "As would be expected, where the anti-*Derg* revolution had the deepest roots among the peasants is where the most effective local governments are found, which in descending order are Tigray, much of the Amhara regions, parts of the south, much smaller areas in Oromia, and bringing up the rear the eastern and western lowland states."[73]

Political Objectives

States-within-states are often simply an empirical fact. Prior to the death of Jonas Savimbi in February 2002, UNITA officials spoke of Angola having "de facto two countries."[74] But beyond being observable realities, states-within-states also have certain purposes or a *raison d'être*. First and perhaps most obviously, states-within-states offer means of protection against a hostile "foreign" government (which may in fact be the central government itself) or alternatively, in the case of extreme state weakness or collapse, as meeting social welfare needs of individuals. In the first instance, states-within-states can offer the promise of a refuge or escape from further state-sponsored violence. "In such a case," noted the Tanzanian government upon its recognition of secessionist Biafra, "the people have the right to create another instrument for their protection—in other words, to create another state."[75] In the case of Tigray, the establishment of an indigenous relief and aid-delivery organization such as the Relief Society of Tigray (REST) served as an important (perhaps the only) survival strategy for Tigrean peasants during the miserable famine years of the mid-1980s.[76] For the international community, such organizations also provided possible mechanisms to help stabilize difficult situations or for the delivery of foreign aid when there were few other organizations who are sufficiently familiar with local conditions.

Second, states-within-states are often way-stations to some other political goal. In this sense, states-within-states are a fleeting or temporary phenomena. Cowell notes, for example, that in Angola, Jonas Savimbi's "entire fiefdom was, indeed, little more than a summer camp forced into a reluctant semi-permanency. Jamba was called the 'provisional capital,' pending his arrival in Luanda, located in terrain that did not favor long tenure."[77] In the case of both Northern Somaliland and Eritrea, the state-within-a-state has provided a vehicle for the preparation and organization of future statehood. States-within-states, then, can provide elites with a platform for carrying out warfare against the central government for some longer-term purpose such as the achievement of political independence or the taking over of power in the state capital.

The political objective of states-within-states, however, is not always greater substate autonomy or independence even if the opportunity presents itself. As Cowell notes, "Savimbi's aim was not secession—for the creation of a separate state of southern Angola would have left him with little more than a great, barren tract of bush. Rather his intention was to ensure that his adversaries could never forget his demand to enter the kraal in Luanda in triumph." In Tigray, the TPLF merged with other ethnically based movements (most of which it had a hand in creating) and, following the defeat of Mengistu Haile Mariam in May 1991, assumed power in Ethiopia's capital, Addis Ababa. Indeed, as John Young writes, "One of the early effects of the EPRDF's victory was a *loss* of some of Tigray's highly prized autonomy as it again assumed the status of a province—if not quite like the others—within Ethiopia."[78] As would undoubtedly be the case with UNITA and Jamba, the TPLF found solace in governing a country that was larger and more prosperous than the notoriously poor Tigray.

Third (and relatedly), states-within-states serve as showpieces used to persuade the outside world that the movement is capable of governing competently. Deliberately contrasting the central government's own secretive attitude toward the international community, leaders in some states-within-states have invited and escorted international media through rebel-held territory for the specific purpose of demonstrating its state-like qualities and their effective leadership. In Savimbiland, in addition to the normal formalities associated with statehood including the examination and stamping of passports and immigration forms, visitors encountered signs proclaiming them to be "Entering Free Angola."[79] Indeed, UNITA leader Jonas Savimbi was skilled at finding ways to appeal to the international media and, by having a territory that was secure from government attack, UNITA could invite VIPs and journalists to demonstrate his competence as a political leader to both international and domestic audiences with little risk that the event would be interrupted by government attack. As Cowell notes, "Savimbi greeted visiting reporters and offered thatched huts, a tour of Jamba, and a military parade in which we, the foreign reporters, were the ones being paraded before his followers, filling the makeshift benches of the reviewing stand as if we were dignitaries or envoys, come to offer gifts and pledges from distant chancelleries."[80]

Fourth, states-within-states can be important vehicles for resource realization and the accumulation of personal wealth. A number of scholars have recently argued that instability and warfare provide important opportunities for elites to enrich themselves.[81] From this perspective, elites in some states-within-states engage in war not for the sake of achieving victory or greater ethnic or regional autonomy per se but because the state of war provides unparalleled opportunities to exploit resources for one's own benefit. Both Charles Taylor in Liberia and UNITA in Angola showed the kind of multimillion dollar wealth that a war economy can generate for these elites. In this sense, war should be seen not as an irrational and destructive struggle between opposing groups; rather the state-within-a-state is a war-making vehicle and warfare is manipulated for the personal benefit of local elites.

Finally, acknowledgment, toleration, or even encouragement of states-within-states can be a valuable interim strategy in the management of civil conflict.[82] Recent literature on conflict resolution emphasizes the difficulties associated with finding settlements in civil wars claiming that, unless they involve partition, peace settlements require the disarmament and demobilization of at least one of the disputants.[83] But most participants in civil wars cannot trust their adversaries enough to implement provisions on disarmament because of the high risks associated with them (i.e. if their opponents cheat and do not disarm) and therefore hedge their bets either by not coming to an agreement or by keeping some of their fighters and weapons outside of the peace process. Recognition or acknowledgment of a state-within-a-state by the central government offers a way around this problem because it avoids or delays the issue of disarmament and does not threaten a rebel movement's other most sensitive security interests—those that are usually associated with territorial control and self-governance. Examples of such arrangements include India and Pakistan, Ethiopia and Eritrea, and Bosnia. Alternatively, states-within-states can provide an important foundation on which a broader regional peace can be built. In some cases, such as Somalia, existing local administrative bodies and "zones of recovery" such as the Puntland in the Horn of Africa serve as "building blocks" which may or may not be used subsequently to rebuild a larger national political structure.[84] While partition introduces risks of secession, it may be the only option for a weakened and besieged central government, and may only require the recognition of the facts on the ground. In at least one, albeit unsuccessful, case, that of the FARC in Colombia, the recognition of a rebel movement's control over a territory has been used as a confidence-building measure.

Conclusions

States-within-states are remarkable not only by their similarities but also their diversity. Some movements have terrorized local populations and provided a minimum of social services (Sierra Leone), while others have sought to endear themselves to peasants by meeting their most basic needs (Tigray and Eritrea). Some states-within-states have displayed considerable longevity while others are more transient. What is clear, however, is that many of these substate units do exist and they often look and act more like states than do the so-called quasi-states that currently receive recognition from the international community. It is worth paying attention to these political units because they may eventually form the basis of future states. As is clear from the discussion here, states-within-states are often incomplete insofar as they do not have all the substantive attributes of statehood. Moreover, not all states-within-states are eager to secede from the existing state structure. But given their viability and the comparative weakness of many existing states in the developing world, the international community may have little choice but to consider them as alternatives for the future.

Notes

1. Robert H. Jackson, *Quasi-States: Sovereignty, International Relations and the Third World* (Cambridge: Cambridge University, 1990), p. 23; Jeffrey Herbst, "War and the State in Africa," *International Security*, Vol. 14, No. 4 (Spring 1990), p. 124; Charles Tilly, "War Making and State Making as Organized Crime," in Peter B. Evans, Dietrich Rueschemeyer, Theda Skocpol, eds., *Bringing the State Back In* (Cambridge: Cambridge University Press, 1985), p. 184.

2. William Reno,"Shadow States and the Political Economy of Civil Wars," chapter 3 in Mats Berdal and David M. Malone, eds., *Greed and Grievance: Economic Agendas in Civil Wars* (Lynne Rienner and International Development Research Council: Boulder and Ottawa, 2000), p. 45.

3. See, e.g., I. William Zartman, ed., *Collapsed States: The Disintegration and Restoration of Legitimate Authority* (Boulder: Lynne Rienner, 1995); and Gerald B. Helman and Steven R. Ratner, "Saving Failed States," *Foreign Policy*, Vol. 89 (Winter 1992–1993), pp. 3–20.

4. See, e.g., *Report of the Secretary-General of the United Nations on the Situation in Somalia*, November 16, 1999.

5. See, e.g., Robert Kaplan, "The Coming Anarchy," *The Atlantic Monthly* (February 1994), pp. 44–76.

6. The distinction between the shadow state and the state-within-a-state may not always be so sharp. Local strongmen (i.e. including those who control a state-within-a-state) may rely on a central ruler to settle conflicts among themselves. Alternatively, shadow state regimes may encourage its soldiers to pay their own way—a directive that often turns soldiers into rebels or "sobels" who may in turn control a portion of territory for their own benefit. See Reno, "Shadow States and the Political Economy of Civil Wars," p. 50.

7. For a discussion that compares the experiences of Eritrea and Somaliland, see Hussein M. Adam, "Formation and Recognition of New States: Somaliland in Contrast to Eritrea," Review of *African Political Economy*, No. 59 (1994), pp. 21–38.

8. Jeffrey Herbst, "Challenges to Africa's Boundaries in the New World Order," *Journal of International Affairs*, Vol. 46, No. 1 (1992), pp. 27–28.

9. Alan Cowell, *Killing the Wizards: Wars of Power and Freedom from Zaire to South Africa* (New York: Simon & Schuster, 1992), pp. 105–106.

10. See Norimitsu Onishi, "Deep in the Republic of Chevron," *New York Times Magazine* (July 4, 1999), pp. 26–31.

11. Max Weber, *The Theory of Social and Economic Organization*, Talcott Parsons, ed. (Glencoe: Free Press, 1947), p. 154.

12. Tilly, "War Making," p. 170.

13. Robert H. Jackson and Carl G. Rosberg, "Why Africa's Weak States Persist: The Empirical and the Juridical in Statehood," *World Politics*, Vol. 35, No. 1 (October 1982), p. 2.

14. Jackson, *Quasi-States*, p. 40.

15. Rosberg and Jackson, "Why Africa's Weak States Persist," p. 2.

16. Charles Tilly, "Reflections on the History of European State-Making," in Charles Tilly, ed., *The Formation of National States in Western Europe* (Princeton: Princeton University, 1975), p. 42. Huntington also considers processes of "defensive modernization" in some

non-Western societies whereby "the need for security and the desire for expansion prompted the monarchs to develop their military establishments, and the achievement of this goal required them to centralize and rationalize their political machinery." Samuel P. Huntington, *Political Order in Changing Societies* (New Haven: Yale University, 1968), p. 123.

17. Herbst, "War and the State in Africa."

18. The Soviet Union abruptly abandoned Somalia, e.g., when Mogadishu invaded Ethiopia's Ogaden desert in 1977. On the other hand, it subsequently provided millions of dollars in military hardware to the Ethiopian government in a failed effort to contain rebels in the northern provinces of Eritrea and Tigray.

19. A.F. Mullins, *Born Arming: Development and Military Power in New States* (Stanford: Stanford University, 1987), p. 95.

20. Tilly, "War Making," p. 169.

21. Steven R. David contends that of the 15 major recipients of Soviet bloc military aid (over $400 million) only in Indonesia was a pro-Soviet regime replaced by a pro-Western military government. See Steven R. David, *Third World Coups d'Etat and International Security* (Baltimore: Johns Hopkins University, 1987), p. 79.

22. For a complete discussion of the processes of war and state formation in Ethiopia and Eritrea, see Christopher Clapham, "War and State Formation in Ethiopia and Eritrea and Ethiopia," paper presented at the Colloquium La guerre entre le local et le global, Centre d'Etudes et de Recherches Internationales, Paris (May 29–30, 2000).

23. Richard Bean, "War and the Birth of the Nation State," *Journal of Modern Economic History*, Vol. XXXIII, No. 1 (March 1973), p. 204.

24. In a speech to the University of Witwatersrand, e.g., U.S. Secretary of State, Colin L. Powell, remarked: "And I want to state very clearly to the people of the Congo that the United States will not support any outcome that does not preserve the territorial integrity and sovereignty of Congo. Partition will not bring lasting peace, and we will not support it." Remarks at the University of Witwatersrand, Johannesburg, South Africa, May 25, 2001.

25. Juan Enriquez, "Too Many Flags," *Foreign Policy* (Fall 1999), p. 38.

26. See, e.g., Richard Rosecrance, "The Rise of the Virtual State," *Foreign Affairs*, Vol. 75, No. 4 (July/August 1996), pp. 45–61.

27. Mark Duffield, "Globalization, Transborder Trade, and War Economies," in David M. Malone and Matt Berdal, eds., *Greed and Grievance: Economic Agenda in Civil Wars* (Boulder and Ottawa: Lynne Rienner and IDRC, 2000), p. 75.

28. See Kenneth B. Noble, "In Liberia's Illusory Peace, Rebel Leader Rules Empire of His Own Design," *New York Times*, April 14, 1992, p. A3.

29. See William Reno, "Reinvention of an African Patrimonial State: Charles Taylor's Liberia," *Third World Quarterly*, Vol. 16, No. 1 (1995), pp. 112–113.

30. Reno, "Reinvention of an African Patrimonial State," p. 116.

31. Larry Rohter, "Colombian Rebels Reign in Ceded Area," *New York Times*, May 16, 1999, Sec. 1, p. 14.

32. Hannelie de Beer and Virginia Gamba, "The Arms Dilemma: Resources for Arms or Arms for Resources?" in Jakkie Cilliers and Christian Dietrich, eds., *Angola's War Economy: The Role of Oil and Diamonds* (Pretoria: Institute for Security Studies, 2000), p. 78.

33. Rohter, "Colombian Rebels Reign in Ceded Area."

34. John Prendergast and Mark Duffield, *Liberation Politics and External Engagement in Ethiopia and Eritrea*, Horn of Africa Discussion Paper Series #8 (Washington: Center of Concern: April 1995), pp. 10–11.

35. Prendergast and Duffield, *Liberation Politics and External Engagement*, p. 14.

36. Cowell, *Killing the Wizards*, pp. 106–107.

37. Reported in "Ethiopia: US Peace Talks Go Ahead," *Africa Research Bulletin*, Vol. 26, No. 8 (September 15, 1989), p. 9385A; and by Jane Perlez, "On the Ethiopian Front, Rebel Confidence Rises," *New York Times*, February 14, 1990, p. A15.

38. Dawit Wolde Giorgis, *Red Tears: War, Famine, and Revolution in Ethiopia* (Trenton: Red Sea, 1989), p. 111.

39. See, e.g., comments by the former American Assistant National Security Advisor, Anthony Lake, in Ian Fisher, "Ethiopians and Eritreans Sign Cease-Fire," *New York Times*, June 19, 2000, p. A8.

40. Barry Posen, "The Security Dilemma and Ethnic Conflict," *Survival*, Vol. 35, No. 1 (Spring 1993), p. 30.

41. On France and Italy, see E.J. Hobsbawm, *Nations and Nationalism Since 1780: Programme, Myth, Reality*, 2nd ed. (Cambridge: Cambridge University, 1990), pp. 60–61.

42. K.J. Holsti, "Armed Conflicts in the Third World: Assessing Analytical Approaches and Anomalies," paper prepared for the Workshop on Grand Strategy and International Security, McGill University, March 5, 1993, p. 6.

43. Herbst, "War and the State in Africa," p. 122.

44. "Tanzania Recognizes Biafra," statement by the Government of Tanzania, April 13, 1968, in A.H.M. Kirk-Greene, *Crisis and Conflict in Nigeria: A Documentary Sourcebook, 1966–1970*, Vol. II (London: Oxford University, 1971), p. 207.

45. John Young, *Peasant Revolution in Ethiopia: The Tigray People's Liberation Front, 1975–1991* (Cambridge: Cambridge University, 1997), pp. 97, 103. Significantly, not all movements seek to win the support of locals. Mark Duffield notes, e.g., that clearing people *off* the land can be essential if the movement's objective is the exploitation of local resources. "Hence, post–nation-state war economies often involve campaigns of immiseration and violent population displacement as an essential precondition of asset realization. Such developments therefore are not an unfortunate but indirect consequence of conflict; they are usually its intended consequences." See, Duffield, "Globalization," p. 81.

46. Cowell, *Killing the Wizards*, p. 106.

47. Eric Garcetti and Janet Gruber, "The Post-War Nation: Rethinking the Triple Transition in Eritrea," in Michael Pugh, ed., *Regeneration of War-Torn Societies* (New York: St. Martin's, 2000), p. 219.

48. The authors note, "Before the war, the population numbered perhaps 2.3 million; it is estimated that at least 200,000 died, of whom 65,000 were combatants. Some 90,000 children were orphaned, and 70,000 suffered injury or permanent disability. A full third of the Eritrean population was uprooted or dislocated as refugees, internally displaced persons, or fighters, resulting in family disintegration and disruption." See Garcetti and Gruber, "The Post-War Nation," p. 221.

49. Garcetti and Gruber, "The Post-War Nation," p. 224.

50. John Markakis, "Ethnic Conflict and the State in the Horn of Africa," in Katsuyoshi Fukui and John Markakis, eds., *Ethnicity and Conflict in the Horn of Africa* (London: James Currey, 1994), p. 229.

51. On the struggles between the TPLF, the EDU, the TLF, and the EPRP during the 1970s, see Young, *Peasant Revolution in Ethiopia*, pp. 101–117.

52. Young, *Peasant Revolution in Ethiopia*, p. 117.

53. David Pool, "The Eritrean People's Liberation Front," in Christopher Clapham, ed., *African Guerrillas* (Oxford: James Currey, 1998), p. 27.

54. Peter Woodward, "Conflict and Federalism in Sudan," in Peter Woodward and Murray Forsyth, ed., *Conflict and Peace in the Horn of Africa* (Aldershot: Dartmouth, 1994), pp. 90–92.

55. Jardo Muekalia, former UNITA representative to Washington, interview with the author, July 7, 1999.

56. Michael Mann, *The Sources of Social Power, Volume 1: A History of Power from the Beginning to A.D. 1760* (Cambridge: Cambridge University, 1986), p. 486.

57. Herbst, "War and the State in Africa," p. 122.

58. Young, *Peasant Revolution in Ethiopia*, p. 17.

59. Andrew Buckoke, "Rebels' Cocktail of Socialist Theory and Self-Reliance Keeps them Ahead," *The Times* (London), November 29, 1988, p. 10. Given the quantities of fuel and ammunition the war effort required, however, Buckoke remained skeptical that the EPLF could survive on such small quantities of cash.

60. Larry Rohter, "Suddenly, Two Parts of a Nation That Aren't There," *New York Times*, May 14, 2000, Sec. 4, p. 4. See also Eric Semple, "The Kidnapping Economy," *New York Times Magazine*, June 3, 2001, pp. 46–50.

61. Diana Jean Schemo, "A Coca-Trade Jungle Town Trapped by Colombia's Strife," *New York Times*, October 11, 1998, p. A3.

62. After a 1999 hijacking of an Avianca aircraft, the chief military strategist for the rebel National Liberation Army, Antonio García, acknowledged that the hostage-taking was not for political purposes but to collect a ransom, noting, "When it comes to financing a war declared by the Government, we think that is legitimate." Cited in Larry Rohter, "A Colombian Rebel Group Gains Notice, Loses Sympathy," *New York Times*, June 21, 1999. Half of all reported kidnappings in the world take place in Colombia; 1693 occurred in 1997 alone. Foreign businesses are particularly vulnerable; See Diana Jean Schemo, "Risking Life, Limb and Capital," *New York Times*, November 6, 1998, p. C1. In the case of the hostage-taking of Canadian businessman, Norbert Reinhart, it was estimated that a US$500,000 ransom was paid to FARC rebels. At the time, a Colombian newspaper even speculated that Reinhart was trying to persuade the guerrillas to take control of a gold mine in the region so it could hand it over to him. See, Charlie Gillis and Richard Foot, "The Price of Freedom a Murky Issue," *National Post* (Toronto), January 11, 1999, p. A3.

63. Regarding UNITA, e.g., Cowell notes, "it was impossible to escape the conclusion that without South African support and smuggled ivory, Jamba would barely have existed. The diesel for trucks and the ceremonial tank and the four-wheel-drive pickups that passed as staff cars all came from South Africa. So did most other things. The lines of communication ran south to South Africa and north to the war." Cowell, *Killing the Wizards*, pp. 104–105.

64. Report of the Panel of Experts on Violations of Security Council Sanctions Against UNITA, United Nations Security Council, March 10, 2000, para. 117.

65. Duffield, "Globalization," pp. 84–85.

66. Duffield, "Globalization," p. 84.

67. Even prior to his formal and internationally recognized election to Liberia's presidency in 1997, Charles Taylor insisted on being called "president," claiming that he would only participate in elections if he was seen as Liberia's incumbent head of state, and refused to acknowledge Liberia's interim government of Amos Sawyer. After moving his administrative and military headquarters to the town of Gbarna, Taylor repeatedly refused to disarm his troops and allow a 7,000-member peacekeeping force to enter his territory. See Noble, "In Liberia's Illusory Peace," *New York Times*, April 14, 1992.

68. Notably, the author adds, "But often these are little more than one-room shacks staffed by untrained and illiterate people." See, Noble, "In Liberia's Illusory Peace," *New York Times*, April 14, 1992.

69. In particular, FARC rebels have insisted on the expulsion of individuals who have opposed or criticized their presence. One of the priests sought to be expelled by the FARC from its territory, Miguel Ángel Serna, told a *New York Times* correspondent, "We are not in Colombia right now, but in something that is a prelude to an independent state." He added that the FARC had "imposed its law" on local Colombians and created its own militia, called Citizen Vigilence, to "spy on civic, religious and business groups," while "accusing anyone who does not agree with them of being an enemy of the peace." Cited in Rohter, "Colombian Rebels Reign in Ceded Area," *New York Times*, May 16, 1999, Sec. 1, p. 14.

70. Martin Hodgson, "Colombian Rebels Impose Law of the Gun," *Globe and Mail* (Toronto), July 19, 1999, p. A15.

71. Bridgland notes how UNITA was forced to kidnap government-trained surgeons in order to meet their needs in bush hospitals. See Bridgland, *Jonas Savimbi: Key to Africa* (Edinburgh: Mainstream, 1986), pp. 319–325.

72. Robert D. Kaplan, "Fate and War in Eritrea," *New York Times*, May 23, 2000, p. A25. See also, Andrew Buckoke, "Rebels' Cocktail of Socialist Theory," *Times* (London), November 29, 1988, p. 10.

73. Young, *Peasant Revolution in Ethiopia*, p. 17.

74. Interview with the author, July 7, 1999.

75. "Tanzania Recognizes Biafra," in A.H.M. Kirk-Greene, *Crisis and Conflict in Nigeria: A Documentary Sourcebook, 1966–1970*, Vol. II (London: Oxford University, 1971), p. 210.

76. Notably, as John Young notes, REST "served both to ensure the effective distribution of foreign and locally provided aid and to reap the political benefits of providing grains directly to those to whom the movement was appealing for support." See *Peasant Revolution in Ethiopia*, p. 17.

77. Cowell, *Killing the Wizards*, pp. 104–105.

78. John Young, "Development and Change in Post-Revolutionary Tigray," *Journal of Modern African Studies*, Vol. 35, No. 1 (1997), pp. 82–83; italics added.

79. Bridgland, *Jonas Savimbi: A Key to Africa*, p. 322.

80. Cowell, *Killing the Wizards*, p. 104.

81. See, e.g., the contributions in Berdal and Malone, eds., *Greed and Grievance: Economic Agendas in Civil Wars*.

82. Fred Tanner, "Bargains for Peace: Military Adjustments During Post-War Peacebuilding," in Michael Pugh, ed., *Regeneration of War-Torn Societies* (Houndsmill: Macmillan, 2000), pp. 75–76.

83. See, e.g., Barbara F. Walter, "The Critical Barrier to Civil War Settlement," *International Organization*, Vol. 51 (Summer 1997), pp. 335–364.

84. See, e.g., "Somalia: Are 'Building Blocks' the Solution?" *Integrated Regional Information Network*, July 19, 1999.

Chapter Two

From De Facto States to States-Within-States: Progress, Problems, and Prospects

*Scott Pegg**

My own initial concern for the subject matter of this book developed out of a prior interest in the rapid expansion of UN peacekeeping operations in the late 1980s and early 1990s. States-within-states first entered into my academic radar screen after reading Barry Posen's observation that because cease-fires favor the party that has had the most military success, UN peacekeeping "protects, and to some extent legitimates, the military gains of the winning side . . . ," even if that winning side has no juridical status in the international system.[1] Subsequently, an offhand question by my Ph.D. dissertation supervisor Kal Holsti asking what sort of precedent a UN peacekeeping force that facilitated the creation of new sovereign states in what is now former Yugoslavia might set for Northern Cyprus peaked my curiosity and turned my research toward the potentially negative consequences of the classic peacekeeping mission of territorially separating warring parties.[2] Ultimately, I became far less interested in UN peacekeeping per se and far more interested in the Turkish Republic of Northern Cyprus (TRNC) as a distinct type of actor in the international system. This single case study soon gave way to a comparative and theoretical examination of what I subsequently labeled de facto states.[3]

As so little academic attention had been directed toward de facto states, one of my primary concerns was defining and delineating the subject matter. In addition to a paragraph-long working definition, I also identified ten theoretical criteria that would distinguish the de facto state from other actors in international relations.[4] While I remain proud of that work and stand behind it, I was also keenly aware of both how new the subject matter was and how particular my own take on it had been. In that regard, I explicitly stated, "it is not claimed that the work done here will serve as a definitive statement on this subject. Rather, it is to be hoped that it will serve as a starting point and that future scholars following on from it will seek to add to, modify or challenge its various premises."[5] After briefly highlighting some of the areas of basic agreement that Ian Spears[6] and I share here, this chapter notes our two main areas of disagreement or divergence. The rest of the chapter then assesses how, and in what ways, the shift from my conception of de facto states to Spears's conception of states-within-states represents progress or creates problems. My conclusion evaluates the empirical and theoretical prospects for states-within-states.

Similarities and Differences

Minor differences in interpretation or emphasis aside, Spears and I share broad areas of general agreement with one another. We are both investigating empirically viable state-like entities that do not enjoy either any or widespread juridical recognition as sovereign states. We both agree and the contributions to this book certainly demonstrate that this general category of de facto states or states-within-states comprises a wide variety of diverse entities. We also strongly believe that this is an important subject matter within international relations that has not, to date, received sufficient attention from either scholars or policymakers.[7]

In terms of the international system as a whole, we both agree that existing juridically sovereign states or what Robert Jackson has termed "quasi-states"[8] continue to face a daunting set of problems that includes solidifying their rule and achieving "empirical" statehood. Correspondingly, we both agree that whatever damage was done to it by the forcible or nonconsensual dissolution of Yugoslavia, the international normative consensus on the desirability of fixed territorial borders and the need to preserve territorial integrity remains strong. This remains true even in today's era of globalization, when borders are said to be increasingly porous. Indeed, as Kal Holsti points out, if one adopts a longer-term historical perspective, there is little doubt that "territoriality has become increasingly institutionalized." In his words, "whatever the effects of revolutions in communications or the dramatic increase in international trade and travel, contrary to many recent assertions there is little evidence to suggest that boundaries are 'eroding' or that the institution of territoriality has become an artifact of a bygone era."[9] Obviously, the existence of states-within-states testifies to the fact that many "weak" or "failed" states are unable, in Naaem Inayatullah and David Blaney's terminology, to "realize" their sovereignty substantively.[10] The fact that these states continue to stumble on while sometimes far more viable states-within-states remain juridically unrecognized demonstrates the importance international society continues to place on territoriality and, more specifically, the sanctity of recognized boundaries. Putting the problems faced by quasi-states together with the continued strong international consensus in favor of maintaining existing territorial borders leads both of us to conclude that states-within-states will remain a part of the international system for some time to come.

In terms of how these entities relate to international society, Spears and I both agree that sovereign state weakness or collapse does not necessarily lead to chaos but can instead lead to the emergence of other, more viable (albeit nonjuridically recognized) alternatives. We both argue that, in some cases, states-within-states are more effective entities and have done a better job of state-building than their juridically sovereign parent states have. Finally, we both argue that states-within-states should not be seen in solely negative terms and that they can potentially make positive contributions to the larger international society.[11]

Again leaving aside minor differences in emphasis or interpretation, there are two main areas in which Spears's work on states-within-states and my work on de facto states substantively differ. The first concerns the purpose or goal these entities have. My conception of a de facto state requires that the entity's ultimate end goal must be secession or, in Alan James's terminology, sovereignty defined as constitutional independence from any other state.[12] In this sense, I distinguished the de facto state from other entities that might exercise functional control over a given piece of territory but that either did not have political goals or had political goals different from secession and sovereign statehood. Thus, my conception of the de facto state did not include drug lords, non-secessionist entities like the Eastern Kasai region of Congo, or movements like the Sendero Luminoso (Shining Path) in Peru, or the Faribundo Martí National Liberation Front (FMLN) in El Salvador, which had the revolutionary goal of seeking to capture control of the existing sovereign state rather than the secessionist goal of trying to create a new one.[13] Spears imposes no such requirement on his states-within-states. According to Spears, the political objective of states-within-states "is not always greater substate autonomy or independence even if the opportunity presents itself."[14] Beyond this, one of the larger objectives of his work "is to explore how these political subunits behave and why they select some political routes and options and not others."[15]

Our second major difference of opinion is basically an enlargement or amplification of this first difference. This difference revolves around how broadly or narrowly these entities should be construed. In this regard, my work represents an attempt to define precisely and narrowly a very specific category of international actor while Spears opts for a looser, broader, and less restrictive approach. My working definition of the de facto state comprised four or five different elements and the concept also had to meet ten specific theoretical criteria that spoke to such things as the entity's capacity or ability, its goals or motives, its distinctions or differences with other related yet, in my opinion, distinct entities, and its legitimacy or likelihood of acceptance by the international society.[16] Spears, on the other hand, notes, "the concept of the state-within-a-state has intentionally been left imprecise" in order to facilitate consideration of a broad array of "state-like structures."[17] Thus, his only criteria for states-within-states is that they exhibit key elements of a Weberian definition of statehood but have not received international recognition.

Progress

There are a number of ways in which this volume represents progress beyond my original work. First, and perhaps most obviously, the sheer fact that it presents a diversity of voices and contributions is, in and of itself, a good thing. The editors have assembled an interesting mix of scholars and practitioners and simultaneously granted them substantial autonomy and kept them focused coherently around a larger central concept. The different array of perspectives offers added value that no one single author can match. The symphony, even if it occasionally strikes a discordant note, sounds sweeter than the soloist. Second, and related to the above, the inclusion of chapters by field practitioners brings something to the study of states-within-states that simply was not represented in my work on this subject. International relations scholars frequently talk about "bridging the gap" between scholars and practitioners,[18] but few of us actually manage to pull it off. The inclusion of practitioner perspectives here is not just a novelty or a gimmick, but something that adds real value and brings a unique perspective to the nascent study of states-within-states. Third, my work focused in detail on four case studies: Eritrea before it won its independence from Ethiopia, the Republic of Somaliland, Tamil Eelam, and the TRNC. Only one of those cases (Somaliland) overlaps at all with this book (see Bryden, chapter ten for more on Somaliland). The combination of new case studies, more case studies, and case studies based on extensive fieldwork is a substantive contribution to the literature.

In terms of the two major differences between Spears's work and my own, an argument can be made that each of these differences represents progress. With the benefit of hindsight, Spears is probably right to drop my earlier insistence on secession or sovereignty as constitutional independence as the ultimate goal.[19] While secessionist entities like Eritrea or Somaliland can easily be distinguished from revolutionary groups like the FMLN or the late Jonas Savimbi's UNITA movement in Angola that seek to take power within the framework of the existing state and its territorial borders, dropping the secessionist goal as a requirement for inclusion makes sense for a couple of reasons. First, while the EPLF and UNITA had different end goals, their similarities in terms of Spears's basic criterion of demonstrating some degree of viable empirical state-like characteristics without (at least until 1993 in the Eritrean case) securing international recognition are equally clear. Second, and perhaps more importantly, goals shift and change over time. At various points in time, the southern Sudanese (see Young, chapter four for more on this) have had both explicitly secessionist and non-secessionist goals. The TRNC proclaimed its sovereign independence on November 15, 1983, but its independence declaration specifically asserts that Turkish Cypriots can again exercise their right of self-determination to join the Greek Cypriots in a federal republic of Cyprus.[20] Even long-term explicitly secessionist movements like the Tamil Tigers are now starting to use the language of autonomy.

Beyond this, states-within-states now arguably have a serious incentive not to proclaim secessionist goals even if they actually harbor them. The Kurds in northern Iraq (see Romano, chapter nine) are probably the best current example here in that almost everyone believes their ultimate end goal is sovereign independence but their political leaders are now studiously avoiding those words in favor of regional autonomy so as not to arouse hostility from suspicious neighboring powers like Iran and Turkey. Indeed, if I were a consultant to one of these movements, one of my first pieces of advice to them would be to get on with state-building, focus on creating empirical facts on the ground, and avoid drawing unnecessary antagonism from the international community by explicitly proclaiming secessionist goals. There are clear advantages to staying below the international radar screen in this regard. Domestically, proclaiming secession risks provoking a harsh response from sovereign authorities who might pay less attention to a "quieter" bid for de facto autonomy. Internationally, states facing explicitly secessionist challengers are generally able to count on strong diplomatic support and frequently substantial economic and military assistance from other members of international society. As Kal Holsti puts it, "We have seen a great deal of 'ethnic politics' in the world in the last 200 years, but in the vast majority of cases where ethnicity and traditional state territoriality clashed, the latter prevailed largely thanks to the policies of the international community."[21] Additionally, in some cases it is extremely difficult to discern what a movement's true goals really are. For all of these various reasons, Spears's decision not to focus exclusively on secessionist entities is probably a good one.

By extension, one could probably make a similar argument in terms of the larger issue of tighter or looser definitions and more or less stringent criteria for inclusion as a state-within-a-state. My categorization of de facto states perhaps suffers from excessively strict definitional criteria that has the unfortunate side-effect of potentially limiting the relevance or applicability of the category to just a small handful of cases.[22] In that sense, Spears's looser conceptualization of states-within-states seemingly offers a more flexible and open approach to the subject that has the advantage of broadening rather than limiting the scope of the analysis. While there is probably a good argument to make here,

I am much less willing to concede this larger point with respect to criteria for inclusion as a state-within-a-state than I am to concede the smaller point about relaxing the secessionist criteria. Indeed, this open-ended conceptualization of states-within-states is arguably the most significant flaw in Spears's work. It is to this that we now turn our attention.

Problems

My own work in this area was perhaps colored by the fact that it originated out of my Ph.D. dissertation research. It is quite possible that I was initially so concerned with precisely delimiting what exactly a de facto state was and was not because I felt that my dissertation committee would not look sympathetically on vague or imprecise research. The result, as noted earlier, was a working definition comprising four or five different elements and ten distinct theoretical criteria to distinguish de facto states from similar yet distinct phenomena such as isolated rebellions, peaceful secessions, prematurely recognized colonial liberation movements, puppet states, and revolutionary movements. In this sense, I can readily acknowledge that any one of my specific criteria (the secessionist goal, e.g.) might deserve to be jettisoned or that the combination of all of them might be unnecessarily limiting. There is a big difference, however, between acknowledging that and intentionally pursuing deliberate imprecision.

Let me illustrate this difference by reference to a comparison between my own work and Charles King's more recent work on the four Eurasian states-within-states of the Republic of Nagorno-Karabakh in Azerbaijan; the Dnestr Moldovan Republic or Transnistria in Moldova; and the Republics of Abkhazia, and South Ossetia in Georgia. King, like Spears and myself, discusses how wars have helped create unrecognized independent state-like entities.[23] In my case, one of my criteria specifically distinguishes the de facto state from peaceful secession movements. In other words, Catalonia and Quebec might both contain substantial secessionist sentiment within them, but they are clearly different entities or phenomena than the Republic of Somaliland or Tamil Eelam in Sri Lanka.[24] King limits his study to "instances in which local armed forces, often with substantial assistance from outside powers, effectively defeated the armies of recognized governments in open warfare."[25] This criteria is obviously drawn more restrictively than mine. King, for example, notes that it would exclude Chechnya and the TRNC, both of which would qualify as de facto states under my criteria.

The point here is not that King's criteria is better than mine or vice versa. Rather, the point is that some kind of definitional criteria going beyond deliberate imprecision is required—not necessarily my criteria, not necessarily King's criteria, but arguably something more detailed and substantive than Spears's relatively open-ended criteria. In this sense, Spears is arguably taking the easy way out by not having to make the hard decisions on whether Northern Cyprus, for example, qualifies as a state-within-a-state by meeting or not meeting specific definitional criteria. By abdicating the need to delineate or specify his concept of states-within-states more precisely, Spears gains some flexibility and inclusiveness. This flexibility, however, is purchased at the cost of a concept that risks becoming so broad that it degenerates into almost anything with the end result that it signifies or distinguishes almost nothing.

One other minor critique worth noting concerns Spears's conception of the longevity or perseverance of states-within-states. Spears correctly points out that states-within-states can often be way-stations on the road to some other political goal.

His subsequent conclusion, however, that "In this sense, states-within-states are a fleeting or temporary phenomena"[26] does not withstand careful scrutiny. In spite of its inherent juridical uncertainty and problematic standing in international society, states-within-states have actually proven to be quite durable entities. The four case studies (Eritrea before independence; Somaliland; Tamil Eelam; and the TRNC) covered in my book averaged 15.25 years of duration at the time of publication in 1998.[27] Extending the calculations forward to 2003 would produce an average 19 years of duration. Even if you argued that a Tamil Eelam de facto state ceased to exist in 1995 after the fall of Jaffna to the Sri Lankan army (an argument I would not make), the average lifespan of these four entities would still be 17 years.[28] The comparable figure for the four post–Cold War era Eurasian de facto states in Charles King's study would be 12.75 years.[29] Some states-within-states like Biafra during the Nigerian civil war or the Serbian Republic of Krajina in Croatia may indeed prove to be relatively fleeting or temporary phenomena. There is, however, compelling evidence that states-within-states can survive for extended periods of time. Although Spears's conclusion might be off here, this only increases the larger importance of the work being done in this volume.

Prospects

In regard to the future empirical prospects for states-within-states, my original assessment was that the safest prediction one could make would be "an approximate continuation of the status quo in terms of the numbers of *de facto* states present in the international system."[30] Given my tighter definitional criteria, this implied more or less a handful of these entities in the international system at any given time. My original prediction was based on a number of different factors. On the systemic level, I argued that the international consensus on juridical statehood, fixed territorial borders, and a narrow interpretation of self-determination had not been fundamentally undermined by developments in the post–Cold War era. On the demand side of the equation, the persistence of weak, ineffective, dysfunctional, and corrupt states along with the continued substantive benefits offered by sovereign recognition[31] would likely lead to future secessionist attempts. The potential growth in the number of these entities would, however, be held back by the sheer difficulties inherent in the state-building process. Some of the same factors that make state-building difficult for juridical or quasi-states also make it difficult for would-be states-within-states to solidify their rule successfully. Finally, the record of sovereign states in successfully addressing challenges from these entities was not good. While some former states-within-states were successfully reincorporated (Biafra) or eradicated (Krajina), there are many other cases like Abkhazia, Chechnya, Nagorno-Karabakh, Somaliland, Tamil Eelam, and the TRNC where governments have not been able to resolve the states-within-states challenge either with the carrot or the stick.[32]

Arguably, the first three of these factors still remain in place today. There is some evidence, however, that the last of these factors, the inability of sovereign states to address these challenges successfully has started to change in a positive direction. Using data from the Minorities at Risk project, Ted Robert Gurr argues that ethnopolitical warfare increased throughout the Cold War period and peaked in the early 1990s but then decreased sharply. From the late 1960s through the end of the 1980s, new wars in each five-year period substantially outnumbered wars contained or settled during the period.

Since 1990, however, the number of wars contained or settled has increased sharply. At the end of 1999, according to his figures, only 18 ethnonational wars were being waged—the lowest number since the early 1970s. Perhaps more importantly, two-thirds of negotiated settlements of ethnopolitical wars in the past 40 years have been concluded since the end of the Cold War. According to Gurr's figures, between 1960 and 1990, only eight ethnopolitical wars were ended by negotiated settlements. Since 1990, however, settlements have ended or led to the de-escalation of 16 wars. Gurr's essential conclusion here is that the brutality of some conflicts obscures a larger shift from confrontation to accommodation. In his view, the trends are clear: a sharp decline in new ethnic wars, the settlement of many old ones, and proactive efforts by states and international organizations to recognize group rights and channel disputes into conventional politics.[33] Assuming Gurr's figures are right and his trends hold, this would arguably reduce the number of states-within-states for two reasons: first, better sovereign state behavior and treatment of minorities would likely reduce future demand for states-within-states and, second, better sovereign success at negotiating agreements providing for greater autonomy or accommodation of some grievances would likely reduce the already-existing supply of states-within-states. The anecdotal evidence, however, remains mixed in this regard. While Tamil Eelam and the TRNC have probably edged closer to negotiated settlements than they have ever previously been, both situations remain unresolved at present. Other cases like Chechnya, King's four Eurasian examples and Somaliland have seen little, if any, serious progress toward negotiated settlement.

While Gurr's work has the compelling advantage of being backed by large-scale quantitative research, a different picture emerges from some of the recent literature on "new" wars. Indeed, one of the biggest issues affecting the empirical prospects for states-within-states is the whole question of whether or not "new" wars are really so different from "old" wars. One of the main distinguishing features of so-called new wars revolves around the level of popular support that the insurgent or rebel movements enjoy. A dichotomous distinction is usually made here between guerrilla or revolutionary war on the one hand and new wars on the other hand. Mary Kaldor observes, "The central objective of revolutionary warfare is the control of territory through gaining support of the local population rather than through capturing territory from enemy forces."[34] The guerrilla's desire to win the "hearts and minds" of the local population was perhaps most poignantly illustrated in Mao Tse-tung's famous dictum that the guerrillas should operate amongst the local population "like fish in the sea." Kaldor, however, argues that the hearts and minds/popular support method of control (which she acknowledges also included a healthy dose of fear and terror as well) is no longer a favored tactic of rebel movements. With today's new wars, in her words, "the main method of territorial control is not popular support, as in the case of revolutionary warfare, but population displacement—getting rid of all possible opponents."[35] Population displacement ultimately depends on the deliberate creation of fear through the imposition of high levels of violence in order to scare people off their lands. While Kaldor's argument focuses on the Balkans, Thandika Mkandawire finds similar dynamics in recent African conflicts. According to Mkandawire, "In the African case, over and over again, armed movements in the post-colonial period have appeared in the water as anything but fish. There can be no doubt that the violence has not been aimed merely at punishing offending peasants but also at sowing fear among the whole peasant community."[36] Employing Mancur Olson's distinction between stationary versus roving bandits, Mkandawire argues that the new wars tend to produce roving bandits that "merely extract resources from areas and move on. They will therefore tend to be extremely predatory and destructive."[37]

If contemporary wars are no longer producing liberation movements that earn popular support through the services they provide but instead are producing predatory and vicious resource extractors with little or no concern for winning hearts and minds, then the prospects for establishing viable states-within-states would certainly be poor. If war is not leading to state-building but to fear-driven population displacement, we would not expect a bright future for states-within-states. A more critical review of the literature by Stathis Kalyvis, however, calls into question the related ideas that old wars were characterized by popular support while new wars are characterized by a lack of support and that old wars featured controlled violence while the violence in new wars is gratuitous and senseless. In terms of popular support, Kalyvis points out that, in old civil wars, "popular support was shaped, won, and lost during the war, often by means of coercion and violence and along lines of kinship and locality; it was not purely consensual, immutable, fixed and primarily ideological."[38] Thus, there is not that much difference between new and old wars in this respect. In terms of the level and types of violence in civil wars, Kalyvis argues, "both the perception that violence in old civil wars is limited, disciplined, or understandable and the view that violence in new civil wars is senseless, gratuitous, and uncontrolled fails to find support in the available evidence."[39] If Kalyvis is correct and the supposed distinction between new and old wars is overblown and needs to be seriously qualified, the future prospects for states-within-states are probably much closer to what they always have been.

In terms of Spears's work on the future prospects for states-within-states, we generally share similar views on both the continued persistence of territoriality and the continued persistence of juridically recognized yet empirically unsuccessful states. Following from our different definitional criteria, however, we see different numbers of entities currently in existence and would expect different numbers in the future. My stricter definitional criteria leads me to see fewer de facto states in the world today while Spears's looser criteria leads him to see more states-within-states. Related to this, my stricter definitional criteria will exclude more such potential entities in the future while his more open criteria will allow for their inclusion.

Our other difference of opinion concerns the likelihood that these entities will successfully graduate to sovereign statehood. According to Spears, "if the experience of Eritrea is any indication, under certain conditions some of these substate units . . . may be allowed to become full and perhaps more viable members of the international community of states."[40] My own assessment was and is much more pessimistic: "The overwhelming probability is that most *de facto* states will never attain widespread recognition as sovereign states."[41] States-within-states do not fail here because they cannot provide effective governance or they lack popular support. Rather, they fail because the normative international consensus against secessionist self-determination and in favor of preserving existing territorial boundaries remains strong and nearly universal. Spears is probably right that "under certain conditions" successful graduation to sovereign statehood is possible. Those certain conditions, however, are seldom met and are unlikely to be met with any great frequency in the coming years. In 1998, I speculated that the two most interesting cases to watch in this regard were "Chechnya and Somaliland—Chechnya because the attempt at a military solution so obviously failed; Somaliland because of the bankruptcy of its sovereign parent, its former colonial status, and its high comparative levels of legitimacy, efficiency, and democratic accountability."[42] In the first case, the Russians took another whack at an anachronistic military solution and are still trying to solidify their rule in Chechnya. In the second case, all the factors identified still remain in place and Somaliland still remains a state-within-a-state with little prospect of emerging from its juridical never-never land anytime soon (for more on Somaliland, see Bryden, chapter ten of this volume).

In terms of the academic prospects for states-within-states, the publication of this volume will hopefully stimulate renewed interest in what remains a grossly under-researched subject matter. While further and more in-depth case study research is clearly needed, this chapter will conclude by highlighting three broad-based areas where further theoretical or conceptual research on states-within-states would be particularly beneficial.

First, there is a need for further research on what might, to borrow from Christopher Clapham, be called "the degrees of statehood question." Focusing specifically on Africa, Clapham argues that the post–Cold War global order is not "crisply divided into entities which do and do not count as 'states.' It consists instead of a mass of power structures which, regardless of formal designation, enjoy greater or lesser degrees of statehood."[43] In a variety of ways, my work, Spears's work, and the various contributions in this volume all highlight the tremendous diversity within the category of states-within-states. What arguably has not been done yet is coming up with quantitative measures or indices that can assess the "degrees of statehood," which different entities possess in various areas.[44] This question will probably remain unanswered for some time to come. One obvious difficulty is that it is very difficult to measure state-building to begin with, let alone in cases where scholarly access is problematic and reliable data is nonexistent. This is arguably also a two-part problem. In the first instance, it is a theoretical problem—what should be measured and how can it be measured. Second, if and when there is some agreement on those points, extended and detailed fieldwork in various states-within-states would be required to generate the actual data that could make the development of future contingent generalizations possible.

Second, there is a real need for more work on the political economy of states-within-states. Spears touches on this and the economics of new wars,[45] warlord states,[46] and the privatization of security[47] have all received some study but much of this work has focused on active conflicts. Yet, as Charles King points out, in the case of many states-within-states, disputes have moved from armed engagements to a more or less stable equilibrium.[48] Although the political economy impact of states-within-states is relatively modest in terms of the international system as a whole, they regularly generate millions of dollars of business with a variety of partners in both legal and illegal industries. The comparative political economy of different states-within-states is one area where further research is desperately needed. The respective costs and benefits of sovereign and nonsovereign status is another area that merits further study.[49] The ethical and normative implications of conducting or embargoing commercial relations with state-within-state entities also needs exploring.

Finally, there is a more general need to assess the respective costs and benefits of states-within-states for the international system as a whole. My work and Spears's work suggest that these entities should not be viewed solely in negative terms. Spears argues that "acknowledgment, toleration or even encouragement of states-within-states can be a valuable interim strategy in the management of civil conflict."[50] My own work suggests that states-within-states can sometimes provide "messy solutions to messy problems" and ad hoc ways to reconcile irreconcilable principles.[51] I have also suggested that the "Taiwan model" of nondiplomatic yet substantive economic and trade relations may offer a template for dealing with other questionably sovereign or nonsovereign entities like Kosovo.[52] States-within-states can also be vital conduits for international relief assistance. Charles King, on the other hand, tends to view states-within-states in much more negative terms. In particular, he sees them as major obstacles to negotiated settlements.[53] For the most part, the larger international society of states has three choices in terms of how it chooses to deal with states-within-states: actively oppose them through the use of sanctions, embargoes, and support for the parent state's government; generally ignore them; or reach some sort of limited accommodation with them.[54] Both the costs and benefits of states-within-states for the international community and the costs and benefits of the different ways in which the international community can engage (or not engage) them, merit further study.

Notes

* I would like to thank Paul Kingston and Ian Spears for their helpful comments on earlier versions of this chapter.

1. Barry R. Posen, "The Security Dilemma and Ethnic Conflict," *Survival*, Vol. 35, No. 1 (Spring 1993), pp. 33–34.
2. Scott Pegg, "Interposition and the Territorial Separation of Warring Forces: Time for a Rethink?" *Peacekeeping and International Relations*, Vol. 23, No. 3 (May–June 1994), pp. 4–5.
3. Scott Pegg, *International Society and the De Facto State* (Aldershot, UK: Ashgate, 1998).
4. Pegg, *International Society*, chapter two.
5. Ibid., pp. 246–247.
6. Ian S. Spears, "States-Within-States: Incipient Political Entities in the Post Cold War Era," chapter one of this volume.
7. The importance of the subject matter is also asserted in Christopher Clapham, "Degrees of Statehood," *Review of International Studies*, Vol. 24, No. 2 (April 1998), pp. 143–157.
8. Robert H. Jackson, *Quasi-States: Sovereignty, International Relations and the Third World* (Cambridge: Cambridge University Press, 1990).
9. Kalevi J. Holsti, "The Changing Nature of International Institutions: The Case of Territoriality," working paper No. 32 (Vancouver: Institute of International Relations, University of British Columbia, November 2000), p. 25.
10. Naeem Inayatullah and David L. Blaney, "Realizing Sovereignty," *Review of International Studies*, Vol. 21, No. 1 (January 1995), pp. 3–20.
11. A more pessimistic and generally negative view of these entities' role in international society can be found in Charles King, "The Benefits of Ethnic War: Understanding Eurasia's Unrecognized States," *World Politics*, Vol. 53, No. 4 (July 2001), pp. 528, 535, and 550–551.
12. Alan James, *Sovereign Statehood: The Basis of International Society* (London: Allen & Unwin, 1986), p. 24.
13. Pegg, *International Society*, pp. 32–35.
14. Spears, "States-Within-States," p. 28.
15. Spears, "States-Within-States," p. 17.
16. Pegg, *International Society*, chapter two.
17. Spears, "States-Within-States," p. 16.
18. See, for an influential discussion, Alexander George, *Bridging the Gap: Theory and Practice in Foreign Policy* (Washington, DC: United States Institute of Peace, 1993).
19. For an interesting argument to the contrary that the secessionist goal fundamentally distinguishes these entities and substantively affects the prospects for conflict resolution, see

Dov Lynch, "Separatist States and Post-Soviet Conflicts," *International Affairs*, Vol. 78, No. 4 (October 2002), pp. 831–848.

20. Pegg, *International Society*, p. 105.

21. Holsti, *The Changing Nature of International Institutions*, p. 25.

22. I am grateful to Paul Kingston for first drawing my attention to this criticism.

23. King, *The Benefits of Ethnic War*, p. 525. The classic statement on war's role in state-building remains Charles Tilly, "Reflections on the History of European State-Making," in Charles Tilly, ed., *The Formation of National States in Western Europe* (Princeton: Princeton University Press, 1975), pp. 3–83.

24. Pegg, *International Society*, pp. 36–37.

25. King, *The Benefits of Ethnic War*, p. 526.

26. Spears, "States-Within-States," p. 28.

27. Pegg, *International Society*, pp. 116, 251, and 257. This calculation was based on a Turkish Cypriot de facto state from 1975 to 1998 (from 1975 to 1983 as the Turkish Federated State of Cyprus and 1983 to 1998 as the TRNC), an Eritrean de facto state from 1977 to 1993, a Somaliland de facto state from 1991 to 1998, and a Tamil Eelam de facto state from 1983 to 1998.

28. The 19-year figure is based on Northern Cyprus from 1975 to 2003, Eritrea from 1977 to 1993, Somaliland from 1991 to 2003, and Tamil Eelam from 1983 to 2003. The 17-year figure is based on reducing the Tamil Eelam figure to 1983–1995.

29. This figure is based on Nagorno-Karabakh existing from 1991 to 2003 and the Dnester Moldovan Republic, Abkhazia, and South Ossetia existing from 1990 to 2003. See King, *The Benefits of Ethnic War*, pp. 530–531 for more on this.

30. Pegg, *International Society*, p. 252.

31. For an interesting example of how one small African country benefited from transforming "the trappings of sovereignty" into hard currency earnings by selling flags and passports of convenience, commemorative postage stamps, policy promises to the World Bank, and diplomatic recognition to Taiwan, see Jedrzej George Frynas, Geoffrey Wood, and Ricardo M.S. Soares de Oliveira, "Business and Politics in São Tomé e Príncipe: From Cocoa Monoculture to Petro-State," *African Affairs*, Vol. 102, No. 406 (January 2003), pp. 57–60.

32. Pegg, *International Society*, pp. 252–256. See Lynch, "Separatist States," pp. 843–844 for an illuminating discussion on how post-Soviet states have failed to become sufficiently attractive places to persuade states-within-states to seek further cooperation with them.

33. Ted Robert Gurr, "Ethnic Warfare on the Wane," *Foreign Affairs*, Vol. 79, No. 3 (May/June 2000), pp. 52–64. Gurr's findings are elaborated upon in greater detail in Ted Robert Gurr, *Peoples Versus States: Minorities at Risk in the New Century* (Washington, DC: United States Institute of Peace, 2000).

34. Mary Kaldor, *New and Old Wars: Organized Violence in a Global Era* (Stanford: Stanford University Press, 2001), p. 97.

35. Kaldor, *New and Old Wars*, p. 98.

36. Thandika Mkandawire, "The Terrible Toll Taken by Post-Colonial 'Rebel Movements' in Africa," in Gilles Carbonnier and Sarah Fleming, eds., *War, Money and Survival* (Geneva: International Committee of the Red Cross, 2000), p. 33.

37. Ibid., p. 34.

38. Stathis N. Kalyvis, " 'New' and 'Old' Civil Wars: A Valid Distinction?" *World Politics*, Vol. 54, No. 1 (October 2001), p. 113.

39. Ibid, p. 116.

40. Spears, "States-Within-States," pp. 18–19.

41. Pegg, *International Society*, p. 223.

42. Ibid., p. 255.

43. Clapham, "Degrees of Statehood," p. 157.

44. Lynch, "Separatist States," pp. 836–837 does not offer any quantitative measures but does make an initial effort at answering this question in regard to four Eurasian states-within-states.

45. David Keen, "The Economic Functions of Violence in Civil Wars," Adelphi Paper no. 320 (London: International Institute for Strategic Studies, 1998); Mats Berdal and David M. Malone, eds., *Greed and Grievance: Economic Agendas in Civil Wars* (Boulder: Lynne Rienner Publishers, 2000); Kaldor, *New and Old Wars*, chapter five.

46. William Reno, *Warlord Politics and African States* (Boulder: Lynne Rienner Publishers, 1998).

47. P.W. Singer, "Corporate Warriors: The Rise of the Privatized Military Industry and Its Ramifications for International Security," *International Security*, Vol. 26, No. 3 (Winter 2001/2002), pp. 186–220.

48. King, *The Benefits of Ethnic War*, pp. 525 and 550.

49. Christopher Clapham, for example, points out that the international narcotics trade is one "in which *not* being a formally recognized state confers substantial market advantages." See Clapham, "Degrees of Statehood," p. 151 for more on this.

50. Spears, "States-Within-States," p. 29.

51. Pegg, *International Society*, pp. 192–200.

52. Scott Pegg, "The 'Taiwan of the Balkans'? The *De Facto* State Option for Kosovo," *Southeast European Politics*, Vol. 1, No. 2 (December 2000), pp. 90–100.

53. King, *The Benefits of Ethnic War*, pp. 550–551. See Lynch, "Separatist States," p. 832 for a similar argument.

54. Pegg, *International Society*, pp. 177–181.

Chapter Three

The Collapse of Sierra Leone and the Emergence of Multiple States-Within-States

William Reno

> Though in a sense the diamond areas were lawless, in another they were a law unto themselves in that a considerable organizing capacity was shown by the illicit miners in the conduct of their affairs. This included the *ad hoc* "bush governments," with courts, recognized headmen and messengers, and scales of fines and punishments for infringement of rules and conventions.[1]

A UN report links competition to control alluvial diamonds, Sierra Leone's main source of foreign exchange earnings since the start of the Second World War, with a brutal civil war that started in March 1991 and ended only in early 2002. This and later reports also link Charles Taylor, president of neighboring Liberia, to this violence and to the commercial network operated by Lebanese, Israeli, Russian, Liberian, and other traders.[2] This conflict came on the heels of a prolonged collapse of formal state access to domestic revenues, which had generated about $250 million annually during the mid-1970s, plummeting to $10 million in 2000. Meanwhile the GDP declined to $636 million, 57 percent of its 1980 value.[3] During a peak in fighting in 1999, about 600,000 of Sierra Leone's five million people sought refuge in neighboring countries and two-thirds were displaced inside their own country.[4] Violence and predation continued despite internationally mediated peace agreements in 1996, 1997, 1999, and 2000, winding down only in 2002.

The distribution of natural resources, refugee movements, and the breakdown of state capacity to generate revenue and command a bureaucracy point to general causes of violence, but this is only half of the story. The collapse of formal state institutions does not translate into violent conflict in the same pattern everywhere. The destruction of old institutional orders can lead to novel arrangements, some of which may propagate violence, others of which may stabilize intergroup relations. Hence, conflict is not necessarily a priori bad for societies. As Albert Hirschman has noted, new social mechanisms for dealing with conflict may signal a redefining of the social rules, which play a key role in legitimating what become new institutions for organizing society.[5]

In the context of Sierra Leone, for example, some of these new institutional arrangements emerged to shield populations from the violence of armed groups that exploit the collapse of centralized hierarchies. It is these kinds of arrangements—however informal—that correspond with Douglass North's definition of an institution as "the rules of the game in a society or, more formally, the humanely devised constraints that shape human interaction."[6]

In Sierra Leone this institutional pluralism stretches back to at least the country's colonial history. Natural resources, especially diamonds, have been a long-term point of contention between administrators in Freetown, the country's capital, local officials, populist politicians, landowners, and gangs of armed youth. The country's longest serving president, Siaka Stevens (1968–1985) managed to wrest control of some of these informal institutions to consolidate his power in parallel structures alongside formal institutions of state power. Some groups maintained a degree of autonomy in response to the predations of Stevens's rule, some of which survived to become important in the 1991–2002 war. Other groups, including members of the Revolutionary United Front (RUF) and groups opposed to them, developed locally distinct methods for mobilizing violence and to oppose it.

What follows is a survey of alternative configurations of power alongside the collapsed formal institutions of Sierra Leone. I will start by providing a framework to identify which institutional arrangements promoted or controlled violence. Some of these tend to resemble shadow states insofar as they maintained their informal connections with the broader political arena.[7] Others resemble the states-within-states described elsewhere in this volume insofar as they develop their own independent logic and forms of protection. Whether shadow state or state-within-state, not all of these alternative configurations of power are self-serving to those who organize them. Thus this chapter looks not only at the process of state collapse itself but also looks at the varied social and political responses that occur as a result.

The Argument

Violence is not organized in the same way everywhere in Sierra Leone, despite the widespread prevalence of risk factors such as social tensions related to insecurity, the emergence of predatory groups, complex patterns of ethnic intermingling, and histories of mutual grievances. An overview of conflict in Sierra Leone shows clusters of armed clashes between gangs of diamond miners and government agents stretching back to the 1950s, clashes that government officials in the capital and locally have exploited in their political strategies. This political entrepreneurship that has often led to the establishment of paramilitaries, which sometimes ally themselves with politicians and at other times freelance (such as in the 1990s), has led to the emergence of what might be called a "market of violence" in Sierra Leone. The appearance of the RUF in 1991 has only reinforced this dynamic leading to the instrumental uses of violence as a means of making profits.[8]

Many authors accurately identify these underlying conditions as increasing the risk of violence.[9] When states collapse, entrepreneurs take center stage as people come to believe that their only viable option for protection from anarchy is to attach themselves to kin or ethnic group leaders. This rationality of fear strengthens the hand of radical leaders who can offer protection. It attracts opportunists who use violence to increase their own political standing and personal wealth through fielding private armies to exploit business opportunities that local conflict and predation create.[10] This process militarizes and radicalizes other groups, since their members have difficulty distinguishing between their neighbors' offensive and predatory, versus strictly defensive moves in times of disorder. Some authors have applied this security dilemma, a concept originally used to explain conflict between states, to explain why the cessation of hostilities and widespread cooperation is so difficult to achieve in internal conflicts that follow the collapse of centralized hierarchies like the state.[11]

This approach explains the rise of leaders such as Charles Taylor in neighboring Liberia. Taylor exploited fears of retribution and desires for vengeance to consolidate his position. Most other armed groups in Liberia during its 1989–1996 civil war used similar strategies to mobilize fighters. This dynamic allowed opportunists to exploit disorder given that organizers of predatory gangs are as concerned with looting as with fighting rivals. It also goes far to explain conflict in Sierra Leone, especially since the RUF's appearance in 1991. The state's centralized hierarchy broke down, in part because high government officials controlled people through informal means of coercion at the expense of the capacity and viability of formal state institutions. Some of these officials teamed up with private businessmen and used armed gangs to control diamonds, the country's main source of income. They dominated this and other avenues of commerce, doling it out to associates in exchange for support. Taylor used this disorder to extend his influence to Sierra Leone through close coordination with rebels there to exploit predatory opportunities for mutual political gain and wealth.

Thus, in the context of state collapse, Sierra Leone saw the rise of a variety of alternative movements and political entities, some related to RUF rebels, some linked to Charles Taylor in neighboring Liberia, others linked to predatory groups in the army or to the so-called West Side Boys, and still others linked to more publicly oriented groups such as the Civil Defense Forces (CDF). To get at the causes of this variation this chapter examines underlying institutional frameworks of state collapse and the organization of violence. These political entities develop alongside the collapsing formal administrative structure of the state, and then occupy the political space left by the recession of formal state authority.

These divergent outcomes amidst state collapse permit the formulation of three hypotheses. First, some unofficial non-state institutions, including those organized around clandestine economic activity that might otherwise incite groups to engage in predation, in fact reduce risks of fragmentation that attend state collapse. Groups that pursue inclusive and integrative projects of creating public order can be explained with reference to these informal mediating institutions and circumstances that diffuse intergroup security dilemmas. Second, informal institutions that favor old networks and economic interests over new ones reduce the influence and opportunities for entrepreneurs of violence, limiting predatory behavior. Third, new institutions and channels for resources such as peace conferences, NGO aid, and outside military intervention can increase security dilemmas and offer new niches for entrepreneurs of violence, thus increasing the risk of political fragmentation. The course of conflict in Sierra Leone examined later illustrates these bases for variation in outcomes.

Gangs, Guns, and Diamonds

Since the discovery of alluvial diamonds in 1930, Sierra Leone's diamond industry has played a major role both in the prosperity of the 1950s and 1960s and in the devastation and war of more recent years. Initially, the state and/or private corporations were able to exercise reasonably effective control over proceeds from diamonds. This early state control of resources helped finance rapid increases in state capacity. In the late 1950s, officials complained that institutions of higher learning were expanding too fast to absorb new spending, but lauded the greater frequency and punctuality of government bus service to rural communities and looked forward to the arrival of daily newspapers from the capital in time for officials' lunch breaks, courtesy of expanded domestic flight service.[12] Yet, by the 1980s, frustrated civil servants had to make do with sporadic salary payments. Television broadcasts ended in 1987 when the Minister of Information sold the transmitter to a "Kuwaiti investor." The radio broadcast tower fell over in 1989, halting Sierra Leone broadcasting service's programming outside the capital. By 1993, only 3 percent of the (drastically reduced) official budget was spent on education, leaving a meager 4 percent for other social services.[13] By then, the battle against the RUF absorbed 75 percent of official spending, forcing the government to layoff a third of its employees.[14]

The initial cause of this radical recession of state capabilities is rooted in difficulties state officials faced in controlling diamond exploitation from the outset. The discovery of alluvial diamonds occurred in a colonial legal context that distinguished between recently arrived immigrants or "strangers" and "natives" of chiefdoms, of which Sierra Leone had 148 at independence in 1961.[15] Previous to this codification, land use rights theoretically were subject to review each year by local chiefs and headmen. In fact, strangers often married into local lineages and exploited social obligations of their local patrons to protect them in hard times and serve as an advocate for them in local disputes.[16]

Along with the discovery of diamonds came the start of clandestine mining, centered on Kono and Kenema Districts. This opportunity attracted large numbers of young men from all parts of Sierra Leone and neighboring West African territories. Large numbers of people, mostly single young men, arrived causing considerable consternation among colonial officials who feared negative political and social consequences of the appearance of "rootless, detribalized natives." These new arrivals also helped create cross-border clandestine trade networks that would play important roles in supplying arms and military support to RUF fighters in the 1990s. A Mines Department official highlighted these networks in his report in 1955:

> A large number of Protectorate natives resorted to the illicit mining of diamonds, apparently due to some bad crop years, and although many were failures, there were also quite a number who did very well and a few who made large sums of money and became rich. This attracted Africans from French territory and Liberia, some of whom come to mine and others to buy diamonds to smuggle away from Sierra Leone.[17]

An estimated 35,000 strangers settled in Kono to mine diamonds each year during the 1950s and 1960s, while the colonial government estimated that 75,000 people were engaged in mining in the whole country in 1956, the majority of them illegally in what came to be known as IDM, or illicit diamond mining.[18]

These new strangers had to make arrangements with local authorities not only to gain access to diamonds, but also to protect them from the authorities based in Freetown. Furthermore, chiefs in the primary mining districts had to contend with huge influxes, amounting to 43 percent of Kono's people in 1963, and 48 percent by 1970.[19] More enterprising chiefs and headmen found that they could use their offices to extract informal "license fees" and "fines" from gangs of young men in return for protection for their IDM activities. Willing chiefs also could benefit from widespread sentiments among local people "that the diamonds were in reality their property . . . . This feeling also seems to have been prevalent in the rank and file of both the police and [mining company] security force."[20] The colonial government, on the other hand, preferred that a large foreign firm mine the diamonds, thus ensuring regular payments of royalties and taxes, and after 1956, that local mining take place under the rubric of a government-run licensing system. A similar debate would reemerge in the 1990s, with Sierra Leone's foreign creditors preferring a large company for familiar reasons.

Corporate control did not resolve the conflict of interests in mining areas. Indeed, it created more conflict. "Mr. Carter, Assistant Superintendent of Police, Special Constabulary, raided an area near Yomandu and was captured by illicit miners, and they, the illicit miners threatened to cut his throat," reported a local Mining Department official in 1957. "Some of the African employees were man-handled, and Mr. Carter was lucky to be allowed to go free."[21] The coincidence of local interests enabled ambitious chiefs to use local IDM strangers to marshal support for their preferred local headmen candidates and to intervene in chiefdom succession disputes in neighboring areas. The strangers possessed the added advantage of vulnerability. They were reliant on the chief's favor, since the chief could use the illegal nature of their activity to call upon Freetown officials for help if their guests got out of hand.[22] This arrangement represented a fairly efficient form of informal social control over young men and diamond mining. It occurred against the interests and sanctions of the state, yet was legitimate in the eyes of at least some local people and was accepted by a large number of strangers so long as chiefs controlled access to mining opportunities. It was when outsiders emerged such as Freetown officials or agents of the foreign firm, interlopers in the view of strangers and their local patrons, that conflict became more serious in the 1950s.

In order to diffuse local resentment, colonial authorities started licensing local small-scale mining operations in 1956. Officials in Freetown feared that as party politics was introduced in preparation for independence, local and stranger youths demanding a share of diamond resources would end up favoring a radical nationalist party that was gaining support in Kono District on the basis of its criticism of "foreign exploitation" and a seemingly insensitive officialdom in Freetown.[23] The government's response was to legalize small-scale alluvial mining under a licensing scheme that relied upon chief support for applicants and Ministry of Mines approval. However, while appearing to legitimate and strengthen chief control over mining gangs, this started a process of chipping away at the informal structures of chief control over IDM. For example, the dominant moderate political party, the Sierra Leone Peoples Party (SLPP, which enjoyed tacit British support) began to use its growing control over the state administrative apparatus in the late 1950s to distribute mining licenses according to party loyalties. Hence, instead of ending informal local controls over mining, it gave informal political resources to emerging national parties.

In 1968 a new ruling party, the All Peoples Congress (APC) under the leadership of Siaka Stevens was installed in office. Stevens, who had been elected in 1967, then prevented from taking office by a military coup, only assumed the mantle of the presidency when a countercoup enforced the election's result. He thus moved quickly in 1968 to shift the legal right to grant licenses from the chiefs to the Ministry of Mines in order to control directly the awards of mining licenses to the associates of loyal chiefs. A.B. Zack Williams shows how the award of mining licenses in the late 1960s made a radical shift from chiefs who supported the SLPP to a more concentrated group that either switched loyalties or were installed in office by the APC.[24] This tool gave Stevens a more certain means for controlling his associates than the unreliable army that earlier had prevented him from taking office.[25]

Tighter control over regulation of the formal institutional and informal "clandestine" arrangements (but in fact now "official" in the sense of playing a central role in a very real, if informal strategy of rule) of the mining industry also gave Stevens control over armed IDM gangs, which he used to intimidate and attack political opponents. This control was threatening enough to elected APC parliamentarians for some to complain on behalf of constituents that "thugs under the cloak of the youth section of the All Peoples Congress intimidate the inhabitants and extort money."[26]

This forced chiefs in mining areas to make a choice. They could side with Stevens, but at the expense of their direct local control over IDM. They also had to suppress opposition party activity. But not all local authorities faced the same circumstances and choices. The pressure on those in the Kono mining district to come to accommodations with Freetown officialdom was stronger than it was on those further downstream. Both places hosted extensive alluvial mining operations. The upstream (Kono) area, however, also contained deep-rock kimberlite mining and more extensive and deeply buried alluvial deposits away from present river courses. This distribution of resources meant that upstream deposits included diamonds that were difficult to exploit without substantial capital investments and the involvement of technically skilled outsiders. Downstream deposits were readily accessible by mining gangs with hand tools. Conventional wisdom would consider the latter more susceptible to predation and an attraction to armed gangs from outside the region, and thus greater social disruption.

Focusing on resources alone, one might think that Freetown officials would concentrate on co-opting downstream chiefs to organize scattered alluvial deposits, while sweeping aside upstream chiefs to exploit deep deposits directly. In fact, this did not turn out to be the case. Upstream deposits became the subject of a Co-operative Commercial Mining Scheme (CCMS) in 1973 that Stevens advertised as an Africanization of some of the large foreign firm's mining concession. This gave chiefs in the diamond source area access to joint ventures with businessmen and politicians who were more directly tied to Stevens's favor. This further concentrated the distribution of diamond wealth in this area into the president's hands. The CCMS arrangement also gave upriver political cliques more opportunities to make large amounts of money in industrial-scale mining operations. Downstream, chiefs and local officials were relatively less molested, and could maintain some control over IDM gangs provided they showed sufficient levels of loyalty to the ruling party, but they were not as tightly integrated into the president's favored economic circuits. This pattern also mirrors chiefs' social control over violence in the 1990s. In areas where chiefs became more dependent on an "official" clandestine economy before the war, youth, especially in IDM gangs, were more likely to collaborate with the RUF in the 1990s, and outside armed youth gangs (such as army units) also could mine with more impunity. Local authorities further downriver were more successful in channeling youth violence into home guard units to defend communities, control IDM for the benefit of local entrepreneurs and officials, and fending off and controlling the intervention of groups from outside the area.

This contrast appears in the histories of the organization of clandestine business in individual chiefdoms. The chief of the upriver Nimikoro chiefdom moved very quickly into alluvial operations with associates of the president after 1968, then into larger-scale mining operations in joint ventures.[27] The rise of Stevens's APC also resulted in greater Freetown intervention into the politics of choosing new chiefs. One Kono chief who supported the SLPP simply was deposed in 1971 and was replaced with a former guard for the foreign mining company who later became Stevens's bodyguard. The new chief ruled until late 1992, when it became a central area of RUF operations and a major region of contention in the war.

The new chief was unpopular among IDM gangs in the early 1970s. "It was a case of this chief against the (illicit) miners," said the former Provincial Secretary,[28] an unpopularity that remained through the 1980s as the chief favored the business partners of his presidential patron at the expense of the now "unofficial" clandestine economy of small-scale IDM gangs. This may explain the early affinity of IDM gangs in this chiefdom for the RUF when they arrived in this area in 1992. The chief's reliance on his capital-based patrons was also reflected in his relations with local inhabitants. Civil servants in Kono wrote to the capital to warn that the chief's exactions were likely to cause unrest and recommended that he be suspended. Instead, word came from the capital to cease investigation of the chief instead.[29]

This disjuncture between the informal institutions of Stevens's political networks and the remnants of the civil service appeared again a decade later. Prior to an election in 1982, the chief shot a critic of the president who was attempting to contest the nomination of candidates for the (by then) single-party general election. The senior District Officer recommended suspending the chief during the criminal investigation. From Freetown came the word: "I would have suggested that the chief be suspended from office until the case is disposed of, but his opponents may capitalize on his fate and cause chaos and confusion in the chiefdom with a view toward disposing of him."[30] The chief was released and the case dropped.

Stevens had another upriver Kono chief, this one a critic of the president, removed in 1982 when an ethnic Lebanese business partner of the president wanted to set up his large-scale mining operations in the chiefdom. The official justification for removing the chief was the chief's loss of support among his strangers who became violent when they discovered that their former patron could no longer protect them from the business interests of Freetown officials who demanded that IDM gangs be cleared off.[31] Another Kono chief installed in 1981 was chairman of the recently nationalized diamond mining corporation.

Downriver, closer to Kenema, a civil servant responsible for administering this area explained that its chiefs and IDM gangs were "total SLPP," and that this meant that Freetown officials had to tread more carefully. This did not mean that the downriver communities escaped interference. Alpha Lavalie, the founder of a precursor to the CDF in the early 1990s, wrote that the APC "condoned, perhaps even encouraged, chiefdom uprisings which entailed intimidation and coercion" that mobilized otherwise unemployed youths under the supervision of APC stalwarts to intimidate candidates who attempted to contest nominations for single-party elections.[32] He observed that APC organizers recruited youths from outside the area, even though many local "rowdy youths" were idle. Lavalie explains that this recruitment pattern reflected the success that local notables had in "organizing an anti-APC campaign tactic based on the use of Poro," a customary male initiation society. "By this means, the SLPP was able to unify all its supporters in Mende land to drive out from their areas imported APC supporters."[33] A local politician also noted the link between Poro and local defense: "If you see twelve or fourteen lorries with marijuana-smoking people in them coming to cause trouble, people in the South would regard it as an invasion. Even the Poro devil came out sometimes. So they withdrew, or, where they persisted, they were met."[34]

Lavalie's observations point to the importance of the social context of youth violence and the relationship of local leadership to predatory central authorities. Though downriver communities have been well known as IDM sites, local chiefs were more successful in keeping political and social distance between themselves and the emerging APC "official" clandestine economy and political network. They still faced serious challenges in the form of youth violence directed against them. In the long run, however, they maintained greater control over local youth through their capacity to manipulate informal institutions such as the initiation society and serve as patrons to local IDM operations. The former draws from widespread practice, but specific units are limited to youth with local family ties. For IDM, the ability of many local chiefs to preserve some political distance from Freetown politicians and their business partners left these chiefs with less access to large-scale wealth through joint ventures. But they were able to behave in a more legitimate manner as local patrons for "their" IDM gangs, since they did not have to tolerate as much interference from Freetown from large joint ventures that forced IDM gangs off their land.[35] This was not so much because they may have wanted to. Rather, the president was suspicious of them and they had to find alternate local means of defending their privileges.

This mode of community defense became apparent in 1986 when a few local aspirants challenged externally imposed candidates in single-party elections. Poro authorities rounded up local rowdy youth, including seasonal laborers and IDM miners and pressed them into defense of their communities.[36] A precursor of the Kamajor CDF militias emerged when these youth were recruited with the approval and consent of traditional authorities, and organized into bands of "traditional hunters." This practice gave fighters a high level of commitment and a stake in obedience to local social strictures governing the use of violence, thus protecting local communities upon which they relied for support from atrocities.

Urban society in Sierra Leone also shows the consequence of different configurations of social control over resources and youth violence. Armed APC youth and the Internal Security Unit (ISU), formed in 1973 under presidential command, attacked University of Sierra Leone students in 1977. Students were protesting the abuse of power in the president's hands and the start of a precipitous economic decline. In what students would later commemorate as All Thugs Day, the ISU joined with local unemployed youth, known locally as *raray man dem*, not only to repress students, but also to loot. Resembling future RUF operations, the ISU and their collaborators were accused in the government-owned newspaper of "capitalizing on their position to harass innocent traders at night, attempting assault on women, and even going to the extent of store breaking."[37]

All Thugs Day highlighted the difficulties that ideological opponents of the Stevens regime would face in their efforts to mobilize. Some students organized a "people's tribunal" and used the student union to try to build a political alternative to the regime. Some left school to arm themselves and train for insurgency. Yet no ideological underpinnings or move to mobilize social groups for the purpose of fulfilling a revolutionary or reformist vision of the future ever emerged in the RUF. Ibrahim Abdullah, a student during that era, explains that a "lumpen culture" swamped the student movement. His description of the RUF as drawing from "the large unemployed and unemployable youths, mostly male, who live by their wits or who have one foot in what is generally referred to as the informal or underground economy."[38] He explains how the inability of the student movement to channel or exert social control over this violence rendered them irrelevant to the war that would follow. Like youth in parts of the mining districts, urban youth had to calculate whether it was advantageous to ally with politicians whom they considered to be corrupt and vile in order to improve their prospects for survival. Backing opposition figures who did not control resources would leave individuals facing superior firepower of politicians' militias and without opportunities for looting such as those that occurred during All Thugs Day.

The Destruction of the Formal State

The proliferation of paramilitaries and their consequence for local efforts to resist the regime gave Stevens more leeway to manipulate what was left of state institutions to loot the country's resources. He and a Sierra Leone–born Lebanese partner, Jamil Said Mohammed (known locally simply as Jamil) took control of the state diamond marketing monopoly in 1976 as part of a bogus privatization exercise. This left Stevens and his partner in control of as much as $300 million (in 2001 prices) in diamond revenues. Stevens extended his style of privatization to other state agencies responsible for agricultural marketing, road transport, and oil refining. Other deals included schemes to import toxic wastes and to sell an island to the Palestine Liberation Organization (PLO).[39]

The shift of revenues to Stevens's personal control wrecked state agencies as channels for patronage via regular salaries and access to state assets, which made the favor of Stevens, not access to the state, the primary avenue to enrichment. Deficit spending reflected this shift, jumping from about 50 percent of revenues through the 1970s to over 100 percent in the mid-1980s.[40] The subsequent collapse of state services, accelerating inflation (briefly reaching 30,000 percent in 1989), and mass impoverishment reinforced the centrality of Stevens's "official" clandestine market for people's survival strategies.

Stevens retired in 1985 and died soon after. He handed power to his handpicked successor, General Joseph Momoh, the commander of the largely unarmed army. Stevens chose Momoh because his position was too weak to challenge the shadow state that Stevens and his business partners had built around the "official" clandestine economy. Momoh's lack of control was reflected in the near total cessation of official diamond exports by 1989[41] as Stevens's partners expanded their domination of the country's economic resources.

Momoh struggled to build his own political network, a task made more difficult by the near absence of his control over the clandestine, let alone formal, economy. Pressure from international financial institutions worsened Momoh's dilemma. The government's accumulation of arrears led to a break between Freetown and the IMF in 1987 and an end to loans. Shortly after, associates of Stevens were accused of attempting to launch a coup. Momoh's main base of support was in the army of about 3,000 soldiers, many of whom were ghost soldiers who existed only on paper so that commanders could collect additional salaries on the increasingly infrequent occasions when these were paid. Live soldiers attracted names like "One Bullet" from the citizens of Freetown, in reference to the army's low level of training and subordination to armed gangs.

Momoh and the IMF saw solutions to the weak capacity of the government and the country's growing debt in corporate control over diamond mining areas. IMF officials expressed the opinion that a large foreign firm would displace IDM and channel revenue to Freetown without the need to build strong (and expensive) state institutions at the outset. A steady stream of revenues could be used to pay Sierra Leone's debts and to build a smaller, more efficient bureaucracy. From Momoh's perspective, a large mining operation offered him the best chance of chasing off Stevens's business partners, their local strongman allies, and IDM gangs.

Two Israeli firms appeared in succession after 1987, but neither ended up establishing large-scale operations in the country. Instead, they purchased diamonds from local traders. The first firm used Sierra Leone's diamonds to launder money and to finance sanctions-busting trade with the apartheid regime in South Africa. The second firm was alleged to have been involved in laundering drug money. A third firm, a more established joint venture based in the United States, promised to invest in a major mining project on the condition that the Sierra Leone Army clear Kono's mining areas of IDM operations. In mid-1990, the army launched Operation Clean Sweep, then Operation Clear All, forcing as many as 30,000 miners out of the area. The vigor of the soldiers, many of whom did not receive regular salaries, became more understandable when many set up their own IDM operations, or joined those of the former patrons of the miners they chased off.

This episode underlines the extent to which outside intervention influences social control over violence. Both the IMF and the president envisioned the foreign firm's presence as helping to centralize control over coercion and resources. IMF advisors conceived of this as occurring in a formal institutional framework; the president most likely imagined a reconstituted patronage network. Instead, external intrusion and reordering of resources shifted resources to armed groups that were even further divorced from central control. As young soldiers joined IDM gangs they began to take on a strong resemblance to the groups that would fight each other to control diamonds in the war that was soon to come.

War Among Gangs

Soon after the army's invasion of Kono's mining district, RUF fighters crossed into Sierra Leone from Liberia in March 1991 with fighters from Charles Taylor's NPFL. Momoh had little choice but to expand his army to 6,000 men to meet the RUF threat. Momoh's foreign minister admitted that most recruits were "drifters, rural and urban unemployed, a fair number of hooligans, drug addicts and thieves."[42] The more able junior officers among them who actually fought the rebels found that corrupt senior officers in Freetown were stealing supplies meant for frontline soldiers. Sergeant Valentine Strasser and a few other noncommissioned officers, most in their early twenties, marched to Freetown in April 1992, forcing Momoh to flee. Strasser's immediate demand concerned the absence of medical care—he was allegedly injured in a battle with RUF fighters who discovered Strasser and his men mining diamonds. Strasser set up a National Provisional Ruling Council (NPRC) with the promise of defeating the RUF. By 1994, the NPRC had increased the army's enlistment to 14,000 soldiers recruited from the unemployed youth, some of whom had earlier joined armed gangs or earned a living through crime.

Kono's diamond mining areas fell to the RUF in November 1992, and were recaptured by NPRC's soldiers in January 1993, only with the help of Nigerian troops. Meanwhile, many of Sierra Leone's soldiers took advantage of opportunities to mine diamonds, sometimes in collaboration with RUF fighters, while the RUF developed its own diamond marketing links to their Liberian patron. "There developed," wrote a former NPRC minister, "an extraordinary identity of interests between NPRC and RUF. This was partly responsible for the rise of the *sobel* phenomenon, i.e., government soldiers by day become rebels by night."[43] The NPRC became concerned enough about these predations that they warned citizens that they estimated that 20 percent of the army was disloyal.[44]

Despite the success of the April 1992 coup, many in Sierra Leone recognized that old connections between armed gangs and politicians continued to exist, especially in diamond mining and trafficking. A Freetown journalist explained that "bush rebels are made up of young and old people . . . ., all under the influence of hard drugs and always shabbily dressed." He went on to note, however, that armed gangs continued to get backing from what he called "town rebels" that are:

> In constant help and communication with bush rebels. They are always neatly dressed and so are not easily identified. They live in towns . . . They work for the established government. They work in offices close to the seat of the President . . . They are always neatly dressed especially in coats and ties. This class of rebels is responsible for the ugly state (and pleasant state) you are in today . . . With just a signature they robbed your country of billions.[45]

Most of the young officers who took office after the 1992 coup hailed from among the marginalized segments of the population who in other circumstances sought the patronage of strongmen in return for acting as political muscle.[46] The RUF leader, Foday Sankoh, echoed these sentiments in his justification for the RUF's preoccupation for mining diamonds: "They ask us why we mine diamonds. Why didn't they ask Jamil or Shaki [Siaka Stevens] that when the APC was in power? Yeah, we mine! We in RUF believe in wealth, arms and power in the hands of the people . . . We are not going to give up diamonds or our guns to anybody."[47] In this regard, Sankoh and NPRC soldiers shared a similar political analysis of the country's problem—it was potentially rich, but politicians had stolen about anything worth stealing.

A respite from war came in April 1995 when the NPRC government hired Executive Outcomes (EO), a South African private security firm, to fight the RUF, who at that time were 20 miles from the capital. Three months earlier they had seized titanium-oxide and bauxite mines that by then provided almost 60 percent of the government's revenues. By December 1995, the EO had captured the Kono mining area from the RUF, and had supported Kamajor fighters who had managed to keep downriver areas out of rebel hands. The EO reorganized the Kamajors in the formal CDF framework as part of the EO's strategy of training local home guard units to defend communities and track rebels. The RUF appeared beaten on the battlefield, and sought negotiations. This led to the Abidjan Agreement in November 1996 whereby the RUF pledged to transform itself into a political party.[48]

Soon after the agreement was signed, President Amhed Tejan Kabbah, declared that he would reduce payment of the EO's $1.8 million monthly fee to $1.2 million. Kabbah still faced IMF and donor pressure to quit spending the government's meager funds on the EO, so he told the outfit to leave.[49] Not long after, on May 25, 1997, a combined force of rebellious soldiers and RUF fighters battled their way into Freetown. The combined forces formed the Armed Forces Ruling Council (AFRC) with the army's Major Johnny Paul Kromah at its head and the RUF's Sankoh as his deputy.

Human rights abuses, including amputations of the limbs of civilians already prevalent in areas under RUF control, now appeared in the city. Eyewitness accounts tell of instructions to amputees to deliver messages to others that the AFRC would not give up power, even if they faced international pressure.[50] The AFRC urged civil servants to "donate" their efforts in lieu of payment, as fighters looted the city. When faced with opposition from Nigerian soldiers (which still occupied a small corner of the city), AFRC spokesmen announced that they would kill citizens and burn the city in Operation No Living Thing.[51] Elsewhere in Sierra Leone, the regime was accused of mass executions of civilians, including more than 550 found in a mass grave in the town of Bonthe, and over 100 in a grave in the town of Bo.[52]

Nigerian soldiers forced the AFRC out of the city in February 1998 and reinstalled Kabbah as president. Despite their desperate straits, AFRC and RUF fighters made no attempt to appeal to citizens or mobilize followers. One fighter who mutilated a civilian reportedly told his victim "Since you civilians are not here for us, we are here to destroy you."[53] Indeed, during a brief invasion of the city in 1999, fighters kidnapped 2,700 children, some of who were allegedly pressed into service as fighters and porters.[54]

Elements of the army that had joined the AFRC regime now called themselves West Side Boys, and behaved much like the RUF, preying upon local communities for fighters, recruiting youth to loot, setting up roadblocks and collecting "taxes." West Side Boys, like their occasional RUF allies, also incorporated elements of Sierra Leone *rarray man dem* youth culture into their war fighting culture. The name West Side comes from hip-hop music admired by some urban youth. It refers to rivalries between U.S. gangsta rap recording studios located on opposite coasts. This business rivalry led to the murder of Tupac Shakur, the popular "West" artist, and Biggie Smalls (Notorious B.I.G.), the CEO of "East."[55] This association is anti-system in the sense of defying social conventions of more educated and wealthier Sierra Leone society. It reflects positive values for fighters, however, in admiring enterprising and clever drug dealers, who like *rarray man dem* have to live in the informal economy and depend on their wits to survive, and who use violence and business savvy to make a lot of money. Violent enterprise in this context is justified as acts of resistance among these fighters, or at least a rationalization for their crimes against the population.

Other renegade army units that did not affiliate with the West Side Boys, along with some RUF fighters shared a preference for "West." In October 1998, more than 100 army and RUF fighters joined to attack Tonko Limba Chiefdom. They were attired in t-shirts bearing the picture of Tupac Shakur, which were cheap and readily available in Freetown markets. In February 1999, fighters again appeared in Tupac t-shirts, this time during their attack on the provincial capital of Kenema. Rap affiliations also chart the growing fragmentation of these groups. When West Side head Johnny Paul Kromah accepted a government position in 2000, some of his followers criticized him for trading nice suits and an air conditioner for life in the bush. While still "West," this researcher found critical youth adopting names like Two Tech and Master Plan that feature in the Notorious B.I.G. ("East") song "Everyday Struggle."

CDF Exceptionalism

Most civilians recognized little difference between soldiers, West Side Boys, the RUF, or other groups that fought each other on some occasions, collaborated on others, and usually inflicted predatory behavior on civilians. As a current leader of the CDF said: "The situation arose when the nation needed some protection, and protection could not come from the army that had betrayed the people."[56] The alternative was found in the traditional hunting societies attached to initiation societies and local authorities like the earlier anti-APC groups noted earlier.

These groups first appeared in the context of war in several northern chiefdoms in 1993. Dr. Lavalie founded similar groups organized along the lines of conventional military hierarchy to fight in the east, which suffered the worst predations of the RUF. These fighters were not very effective. They lacked the support of local civilians. RUF fighters easily overwhelmed them, but not before local communities under attack formed their own vigilante groups. During the December 1994 RUF attack on the downriver towns of Bo and Kenema, Lavalie and several local chiefs organized these vigilantes under the rubric of traditional authorities and initiation societies that Lavalie championed. These local defense units survived Lavalie's death in late 1994. They came under the leadership of Chief Hinga Norman of Telu Bongor. A former military officer, the Sandhurst-trained Norman was jailed in the 1970s on suspicion of participating in an anti-APC coup plot, ironically sharing a cell with the RUF's future leader. Using this legitimacy as a known opponent to the old regime, Norman coordinated the defense of downriver towns.[57]

The effectiveness of the most powerful of the groups associated with the CDF—the Kamajors—was due in part to fighters' shared Mende ethnic identity. The limited disruption of local customary practices and the relatively greater legitimacy of traditional authorities also helped to make this identity more accepting of participation by outsider youth. The strangers still present in these communities were more easily incorporated into local social structures through customary practices of assimilation. Because chiefs in mining areas had more incentive to try to protect outsiders in the "unofficial" clandestine economy against APC predations, informal institutions such as Poro binding these people to communities still played a large role, in contrast to the social disruption that the Freetown political and business elite's intrusion into Kono politics and business caused. In the context of war, these reciprocal obligations in downriver communities translated into a promise that the warrior chief and his allies guarantee each other's security, what one scholar calls an unwritten constitution of Mende people[58] and a history that Chief Norman actively invoked in controlling local militias.

Although weakened by APC rule and earlier colonial administrative practice, the pressures of wartime and home defense revived a state-within-a-state capable of supplying order, a fundamental ingredient of governance. They overcame the fragmenting pressures of mutual security dilemmas and the self-interest of political entrepreneurs that scholars noted here associate with war involving natural resources and the collapse of state institutions. Within Kamajor units, "Kamajoi Police" enforced discipline, preventing the rise of political entrepreneurs from within the ranks and limiting predatory behavior against civilians. The EO further armed and provided logistics to these fighters in 1995, and by 1996, the RUF was confined to a few sanctuaries.

The CDF record was not without blemishes. Part of the explanation for the 1997 coup lay in president Kabbah's strategy of favoring CDF units in place of the army. Kabbah's fears were reasonable, but they also aggravated army suspicion of the president. Johnny Paul Kromah, head of the AFRC regime justified the coup, complaining: "The SLPP tribal hunter militia, the Kamajors, received logistics and supplies far beyond their immediate needs. This was enough indication of the preference for the private army over our Armed Forces, foreshadowing the ultimate replacement of the Constitutional Defense Forces by Mr. Kabbah's hunters."[59] In addition, once CDF units were deployed outside home areas, they were removed from the social institutions that helped discipline their behavior and limit abuses. CDF attacks on journalists in Freetown earned them the name South Side Boys, amidst numerous reports of CDF abuses of human rights elsewhere in the country. These problems resulted in the appearance of a faction under the leadership of Eddie Massally, who argued that Kamajors should not be deployed outside their home areas, unless they were included in a new constitutional role in Sierra Leone's defense.

The Kamajor and CDF history shows the importance of continuity of informal institutions, including chief control of the "unofficial" clandestine regional economy. This experience belies predictions of standard approaches that link exploitation of easily obtained natural resources with predatory behavior and political opportunism, confirming the first hypothesis posed at the start of this chapter. The second hypothesis finds confirmation in the importance that continuity of authority played in enabling downriver chiefs to organize local "unruly youth" in contrast to APC-imposed Kono chiefs who lacked informal institutional ties to their communities or control over youthful strangers and violence. Local authorities in some downriver communities were able to build upon this institutional legacy to create an effective state-within-a-state that was responsive to popular interests. The third hypothesis, regarding the intermediating role of external intervention is explored in the next section.

The Ambiguities of Outside Intervention

Outside intervention in Sierra Leone's war played a major role in shaping the distribution of social control of violence and resources. Liberia's president Charles Taylor provided direct support of the RUF from the start of the war in 1991. Taylor spent time in prison in Sierra Leone in 1988 after he appeared in Freetown to interest Momoh in a plot to overthrow Liberia's president Doe. Momoh instead tried to sell Taylor to Doe, but Taylor escaped, a feat he had pulled off in 1986 when he was held in a U.S. prison on charges of fraud. Harboring a grudge against Momoh, Taylor threatened to "do a RENAMO" on Momoh; to support a predatory rebel group to wreck the economy, create social disorder, and eventually remove Momoh from power. More immediate motives for Taylor appeared in early 1991 when Momoh allowed an anti-Taylor coalition of West African forces and an anti-Taylor rebel group to use Sierra Leone as a base.

Taylor aided the RUF throughout the war, reducing RUF incentives to rely upon popular support in Sierra Leone to survive. This gave the RUF incentives similar to those that chiefs in Kono found in the 1970s under the APC. They could ally with a distant patron in exchange for access to diamond wealth, and were given military muscle to chase off local people who opposed that arrangement. Much like Stevens and Jamil, Taylor used international business connections to market diamonds and to supply weapons to allied fighters. A UN investigating team revealed that Liberian transshipments of diamonds after Taylor's election as president in 1997 involved sums on the order of $70 million annually, close to the Sierra Leone government's total annual reported expenditures of about $75–80 million.[60]

International recognition of Taylor's election as president of Liberia reinforced his role as an external patron for diamond mining rebels. International organizations, particularly the West African regional coalition of states, negotiated primarily with armed groups while ignoring other more broadly based groups. Negotiators reasoned that they had to talk to people who had guns and who could disrupt any agreement that did not satisfy them. Local organizations like the Liberian Inter-Faith Mediation Committee

(IFMC) complained that external recognition of warring groups weakened the IFMC's ability to use appeals to local religious values and social obligations to rein in fighters and combat factions. This joint Muslim and Christian association had tried to use the moral authority that local religious institutions had accumulated through the health and education services that they offered. Most of Liberia's bureaucrats and officials had benefited from these services in the past and thus generally demonstrated respect for these religious leaders. Unlike comparable authorities in Sierra Leone's downriver communities, these leaders had to contend with large-scale intervention by outsiders who dealt directly with the targets of the IFMC's efforts. In contrast, the EO's intervention in Sierra Leone in 1995–1996 built upon the social control that CDF units already harnessed, and bolstered it with weapons and logistical aid to attack RUF fighters.

Taylor accurately guessed that foreign mediation and eagerness to disengage from the conflict would free him from a need to build new popular bases of support if he wanted to be president. Once he entered Monrovia in 1995 to join a coalition government, his NPFL fighters assassinated opponents and journalists, and even tried to kill the Catholic Archbishop.[61] Even under these conditions Taylor won the 1997 election. More than 75 percent voted for him as he warned that he would go back to war unless the country's people let him be president.[62] As Taylor predicted, international monitors were satisfied that he was the elected civilian president of the country, which was sufficient excuse for them to leave.

Taylor then used his position to support the RUF after it was expelled from Freetown in the February 1998 Nigerian operation. Military setbacks and international pressure forced the RUF into peace negotiations that culminated in the 1999 Lomé agreement. The agreement once again called for the RUF to transform itself into a political party in preparation for elections, and promised Sankoh a position as head of the Strategic Minerals Resource Commission to manage Sierra Leone's diamond resources. The aim was to make Sankoh face popular pressure to use diamond resources for public works and relief, rather than to enrich RUF fighters. The agreement also made provisions for 12,000 UN observers as the United Nations Mission in Sierra Leone (UNAMSIL) to oversee disarmament of all factions in the country.[63]

This international intervention did not resolve Sierra Leone's conflict. RUF fighters resisted entreaties from UN observers to visit areas under their control. When UN observers tried to visit these areas, RUF fighters robbed UNAMSIL convoys. In January 2000, a UNAMSIL convoy was robbed of 500 automatic weapons, armored personnel carriers, and several truckloads of ammunition. Meanwhile, RUF fighters refused to report to disarmament sites.[64] In April 2000 RUF fighters even managed to capture 400 weapons that the UN had collected from other factions. Meanwhile, Sankoh used his official position to market RUF diamonds. Violating a UN travel ban, Sankoh flew to South Africa to visit a business associate in February 2000, allegedly to sell diamonds. He imported eight large dump trucks, explaining: "I want to be adequately prepared for full-fledged campaigning."[65]

The tenuous order erupted into RUF kidnappings of several hundred UN observers in early May 2000. Sankoh was captured and arrested on May 16, 2000 after fleeing his Freetown residence. This marked a shift in the UN's approach to the conflict and provoked a British military intervention into the conflict. Almost a thousand Royal Marines and paratroopers arrived to bolster the vulnerable Kabbah government. With this came a conviction among British planners that Sankoh could no longer figure in negotiations with the RUF. British trainers arrived to retrain and support the

Sierra Leone Army in an offensive against rebels. This succeeded in forcing rebels to hand over weapons to redeployed UN peacekeepers as they sought refuge from military offensives on other fronts. British strategists also coordinated with CDF units to press the offensive against the RUF.[66] By late 2001, UN peacekeepers had access to most of the country, and for the first time in over a decade, the country appeared to be at peace.

Informal Institutions and Diversity of Responses to Conflict

Sierra Leone's experience illustrates the importance of informal institutions, including clandestine economies, in shaping the organization of violence. This presupposes the possibility of a diversity of outcomes that even integrate elements that contribute to predation and fragmentation in other contexts, such as clandestine diamond economies. It also shows the adaptability of some informal institutions—in the cases mentioned earlier, organizations like initiation societies, the non-statutory powers of chiefdom office, clandestine economic channels—to new demands. One finds similar patterns across the country. In Freetown, for example, young community organizers in Freetown's West II constituency revived a decades-old Firestone Society that once harbored criminals and provided them with drugs to reconcile youths from the RUF, the CDF, Sierra Leone Army, and local vigilante groups to a common youth agenda. Now called the Firestone Development Association, it runs a nursery school, training center, and hosts the Union of Sierra Leone Jazz Artists where youth can gather and discuss musical interests (and listen to music—more often than not hip-hop and rap) under a large portrait of Chief Bai Bureh, an icon of the Sierra Leone resistance to the British imposition of control in the interior in the late 1890s.

Similar examples of informal institutional control and syncretic adaptations to manage conflict appear in Somaliland. Unlike the southern part of Somalia, the self-declared independent Republic of Somaliland in the north reworks informal institutional strategies to manage young fighters and control political entrepreneurs. There, clan elders benefited from their marginality to "official" channels of predation in the 1980s, and had to construct their own links to clandestine traders and foreign remittance networks in neighboring Djibouti and Yemen. Elders were then able to couple control, or at least influence over the distribution of resources, with customary claims of reciprocity. As in Sierra Leone, leaders of local home guard units found that this discipline broke down as soon as fighters left their home areas and were free of the social sanctions that elders could wield.[67]

Likewise, one could search for similar states-within-states of the non-predatory sort in places like Transdnestria, base of the Soviet 14th Army, and widely expected in the early 1990s to become a site of major conflict like its former Yugoslav cousins. After initial battles in 1992 and 1993, it did not erupt into further conflict. Elsewhere, while Chechnya's conflict is well known, neighboring republics remained quiet, despite concerted efforts by Chechen fighters to provoke security dilemmas and recruit the interests of would-be political entrepreneurs. Similarly, one wonders why Macedonia (till now, at least) has enjoyed relative peace while neighboring parts of the former Yugoslavia saw numerous political entrepreneurs, predatory groups, and widespread war.

Notes

1. *Report of the Administration of the Provinces for the Year 1955* (Freetown: Government Printer 1956), 4.

2. United Nations, *Report of the Panel of Experts Appointed Pursuant to UN Security Council Resolution 1306 (2000), Paragraph 19 in Relation to Sierra Leone* (New York: UN, December 2000).

3. Figures for the 1970s are adjusted to 2000 real values, and are derived from International Monetary Fund, *Balance of Payments Statistics Yearbook* (Washington, DC: IMF, 1990), p. 243. Year 2000 figures are from Government of Sierra Leone, *Bulletin of Economic Trends* (Freetown, 2001), p. 12. GDP figures from Economist Intelligence Unit, *Sierra Leone* (September 2001), p. 32.

4. International Crisis Group, *Sierra Leone: Time for a New Military and Political Strategy* (London: ICG, April 11, 2001), p. 2.

5. Albert Hirschman, *A Propensity to Self-Subversion* (Cambridge, MA: Harvard University Press, 1995).

6. Douglass North, *Institutions, Institutional Change and Economic Performance* (New York: Cambridge University Press, 1990), p. 6.

7. William Reno, *Shadow States and Warlord Politics in Africa* (Boulder: Lynne Rienner, 1998).

8. Jean Francois and Jean-Christophe Rufin, eds., *Économie des guerres civiles* (Paris: Hachette, 1996).

9. For example, Paul Collier and Nicolas Sambabis, eds., *Special Issue of Conflict Resolution: Understanding Civil Wars*, Vol. 46, No. 1 (February 2002).

10. Rui de Figueirdo and Barry Weingast, "The Rationality of Fear: Political Opportunism and Ethnic Conflict," in Barbara Walter and Jack Snyder, eds., *Civil Wars, Insecurity, and Intervention* (New York: Columbia University Press, 1999), pp. 261–303.

11. Barry Posen, "The Security Dilemma and International Security," Michael Brown, ed., *Ethnic Conflict and International Security* (Princeton: Princeton University Press, 1993); Jack Snyder and Robert Jervis, "Civil Wars and the Security Dilemma," in Walter and Snyder, eds., *Civil Wars*, pp. 15–38.

12. Governor's Office, "Confidential, No. 13383/517" (Freetown, February 12, 1959).

13. John Karimu, *Government Budget and Economic and Financial Policies for the Financial Year 1996* (Freetown, December 29, 1995), p. 12.

14. John Karimu, *Government Budget and Economic and Financial Policies for the Fiscal Year 1995/1996* (Freetown, June 29, 1995), p. 10.

15. *The Laws of the Colony and Protectorate of Sierra Leone* (London: Waterlow & Sons, Ltd., 1925), Cap 170, III, 19.

16. Vernon Dorjahn and Christopher Fyfe, "Landlord and Stranger: Change in Tenancy Relations in Sierra Leone," *Journal of African History*, Vol. 3, No. 3 (1962), pp. 391–397.

17. Department of Mines, *Report of the Mines Department for the Year 1955* (Freetown: Government Printer, 1956), p. 3.

18. The first estimate if from H.L. van der Laan, *The Sierra Leone Diamonds*, (Oxford: Clarendon Press, 1965), pp. 10–11; the latter is from Department of Mines, *Report on the Mines Department, 1956* (Freetown: Government Printer, 1957), p. 4.

19. David King, "Population Characteristics of Diamond Boom Towns in Kono," *Africana Research Bulletin* (1975), p. 62.

20. Chief Inspector of Mines, "Interim Report on the Alluvial Diamond Mining Scheme," June 18, 1956.

21. Letter of Area Superintendent of Mines, Kono, to Area Superintendent of Mines, Kenema, March 6, 1957.

22. Victor Minikin, "Indirect Political Representation in Two Sierra Leone Chiefdoms," *Journal of Modern African Studies*, Vol. 11, No. 1 (March 1973), pp. 129–135.

23. Fred Hayward, "The Development of a Radical Political Organization in the Bush: A Case Study in Sierra Leone," *Canadian Journal of African Studies*, Vol. 6, No. 1 (1972), pp. 1–28.

24. A.B. Zack Williams, *Tributors, Supporters, and Merchant Capital* (Aldershot: Ashgate, 1995), pp. 164–166, 231.

25. After an attempted coup d'etat in April 1971, Stevens limited the army's strength to just 1,500 men. "Sierra Leone: The Brink of a Republic," *Africa Confidential*, April 2, 1971, p. 1.

26. Minute Paper (State House, Freetown), January 14, 1969.

27. David Rosen, "Diamonds, Diggers and Chiefs: The Politics of Fragmentation in a West African Society," Ph.D. dissertation, University of Illinois, Champaign-Urbana, 1974.

28. Interview with former provincial secretary, Eastern Province, Freetown.

29. "District Officer, Letter to Chief," copy sent to Freetown under PF/NA/405/1/2, August 16, 1972. The reply is recorded in Minute Paper [State House, Freetown], November 11, 1972.

30. The District Officer's report is found in "Arrest of Paramount Chief of Gbense Chiefdom, Kono District," PF/NA/405/1/2, July 5, 1982. The reply is found in Sierra Leone Government, Minute Paper (State House, Freetown), July 14, 1982.

31. Interview, Tankoro Chiefdom, March 26, 1990.

32. Alpha Lavalie, "SLPP: A Study of the Political History of the Sierra Leone Peoples Party with Particular Reference to the Period, 1968–1978," M.A. thesis, University of Sierra Leone, 1983, p. 12.

33. Alpha Lavalie, "Government and Opposition in Sierra Leone, 1968–1978," paper presented at Fourth Birmingham Sierra Leone Studies Forum, Birmingham, UK, 1985, p. 80.

34. Quote from Fred Hayward and Jimmy Kandeh, "Perspectives on Twenty-Five Years of Elections in Sierra Leone," Fred Hayward, ed., *Elections in Independent Africa* (Boulder: Westview, 1987), p. 51.

35. Observation of former provincial secretary, Eastern Province, May 7, 2001.

36. Marianne Ferme, "Studying *politisi*: The Dialogues of Publicity and Secrecy in Sierra Leone," in John and Jean Comaroff, eds., *Civil Society and Political Imagination in Africa* (Chicago: University of Chicago Press, 1999), pp. 160–191.

37. "Halt Deteriorating Situation," *Daily Mail* [Freetown], February 4, 1977, p. 8.

38. Ibrahim Abdullah, "Bush Path to Destruction: The Origin and Character of the Revolutionary United Front (RUF/SL)," *Africa Development*, Vol. 22, No. 3–4 (1997), p. 73.

39. "US Dumping Demonstration," *West Africa*, February 25, 1980, p. 377.

40. International Monetary Fund, *Balance of Payments Statistics Yearbook* (Washington, DC: IMF, 1990), p. 173.

41. Government Gold and Diamond Office, *Annual Report* (Freetown, GDO, 1988, 1989, 1990).

42. Quoted in Lansana Gberie, "The May 25 Coup d'État in Sierra Leone: A Militariat Revolt?" *Africa Development*, Vol. 22, No. 3–4 (1997), p. 153.

43. Arthur Abraham, "War and Transition to Peace: A Study of State Conspiracy in Perpetuating Armed Conflict," *African Development*, Vol. 22, No. 3–4 (1997), p. 103.

44. Gberie, "The May 25 coup," p. 154.

45. In Nasralla, "Types of Rebels," *For di People* [Freetown], February 5, 1999, p. 2.

46. Jimmy Kandeh analyzes the social origins of West African junior officer coups in "What Does the Militariat Do When It Rules? Military Regimes: The Gambia, Sierra Leone and Liberia," *Review of African Political Economy*, Vol. 23 (1996), pp. 387–404. See also Ibrahim Abdullah and Patrick Muana, "The Revolutionary United Front of Sierra Leone," in Christopher Clapham, ed., *African Guerrillas* (London: James Currey, 1998), pp. 172–193, and Jimmy Kandeh, "Ransoming the State: Elite Origins of Subaltern Terror in Sierra Leone," *Review of African Political Economy*, Vol. 26 (1999), pp. 349–366.

47. "What Foday Sankoh Really Said in Makeni," *For di People*, February 1, 2000, p. 3 [my translation of text].

48. United Nations, *A Peace Agreement Between the Government of the Republic of Sierra Leone and the Revolutionary United Front of Sierra Leone*, November 30, 1996, S/1996/1034.

49. John Hirsch, *Sierra Leone: Diamonds and the Struggle for Democracy* (Boulder: Lynne Rienner, 2001), p. 40.

50. Human Rights Watch, *Sowing Terror, Atrocities Against Civilians in Sierra Leone* (New York: HRW, 1998),

51. U.S. Department of State, "Sierra Leone Atrocities Against Civilians" (Washington, DC, May 12, 1998), United Nations, *Second Progress Report of the Secretary General on the United Nations Observer Mission in Sierra Leone*, October 18, 1998.

52. U.S. Department of State, *Sierra Leone Country Report on Human Rights Practices for 1998* (Washington, DC: Bureau of Democracy, Human Rights and Labor, February 26, 1999).

53. Human Rights Watch, "Fresh Reports of RUF Terror Tactics," May 26, 2000.

54. United Nations, *Fifth Report of the Secretary General on the United Nations Observer Mission in Sierra Leone* (New York: UN, March 4, 1999), para. 26.

55. This story is recounted in the Sierra Leone press. Osman Benk Sankoh, "Is Tupac Alive?" [two part series], *Concord Times* [Freetown], November 11 and 18, 2000, p. 2.

56. Chief Norman Hinga, transcript of interview on BBC, *Focus on Africa* radio show, October 12, 2001.

57. Patrick Muana, "The Kamajoi Militia: Civil War, Internal Displacement and the Politics of Counter-Insurgency," *Africa Development*, Vol. 22, No. 3–4 (1997), pp. 77–100.

58. Arthur Abraham, *Mende Government and Politics Under Colonial Rule: A Historical Study of Political Change in Sierra Leone, 1890–1937* (Freetown: University of Sierra Leone Press, 1978).

59. Letter from Johnny Paul Kromah to Economic Community of West African States, August 12, 1997.

60. United Nations, *Report of the Panel of Experts Appointed Pursuant to UN Security Council Resolution 1306 (2000), Paragraph 19 in Relation to Sierra Leone* (New York: UN, December 20, 2000), paras. 68–90. Government spending from Economist Intelligence Unit, *Sierra Leone*, September 2001, pp. 22, 32.

61. "Liberia: Threatening Good Order," *Africa Confidential*, Vol. 37, No. 9 (May 10, 1996), pp. 3–4.

62. David Harris, "From Warlord to Democratic President: How Charles Taylor Won the 1997 Liberian Election," *Journal of Modern African Studies*, Vol. 37, No. 3 (September 1999), pp. 431–455.

63. *Peace Agreement Between the Government of Sierra Leone and the Revolutionary United Front of Sierra Leone*, author's copy of original.

64. United Nations, *Third Report of the Secretary General on the United Nations Mission in Sierra Leone* (New York: UN, March 7, 2000), para. 24.

65. Augustus Mye Kamara, "Sankoh's Vehicles Arrive at Quay," *Pool* [Freetown], April 5, 2000, p. 1.

66. United Nations, *Tenth Report of the Secretary General on the United Nations Mission in Sierra Leone* (New York: UN, June 25, 2001), para. 16. The author was able to observe aspects of the CDF offensive in the Daru area in May 2001.

67. For more details, see my "Somaliland: State-Building on the Margins of the Global Economy," presented at Queen Elizabeth House, Oxford University, September 29, 2001.

Chapter Four

Sudan's South Blue Nile Territory and the Struggle Against Marginalization

John Young

Sudan has been beset by conflict from independence in 1956 to the present, with the exception of an 11-year period of peace between 1972 and 1983. Although widely characterized as a struggle of Christian and pagan Africans against a Muslim Arabized north for autonomy or independence, the war has many dimensions. Caught in the middle and reflecting these dimensions is the South Blue Nile (SBN).[1] It bears similarities with the south because its people have been engaged in a struggle against the hegemony of the Sudanese state. But unlike the south, the people of the SBN are predominantly Muslim and Arabic speaking and have strong ties with the north. This complicated mix of identity and politics has resulted in long-standing tension between the peoples of the SBN and the central government.

However, sustained rebellion only took place after the rise to power in Khartoum of the National Islamic Front (NIF) in 1989. Although most postcolonial governments in Sudan pursued programs of Arabization and Islamization, the NIF made this the centerpiece of its government and its implementation was as much directed at border territories like the SBN as southern Sudan with its large pagan and Christian populations. The Sudanese state in the postcolonial era has always been weak and so have the governments that have operated through it, but the NIF represents a new phenomenon: a hard and ideologically driven government embedded in a soft state. As a result, the weak institutions of the state were often supplemented by the ruthlessness of the organs of the party, and this in turn produced resistance from the peripheries. In the case of the SBN, the government's alliance with Arab and Fallata (descendents of West Africans most recently from the Darfur region of western Sudan) pastoralists in their struggles with the largely settled population of the SBN deepened the conflict and strengthened the resistance of the latter.

Since 1983 this resistance has been supported by the SPLM/A, alongside its larger campaign to capture substantial parts of southern Sudan and parts of the northern territories of Abeyei, Nuba Mountains. At the time of writing, the SPLM/A claimed that some 300,000 people were under its control in the SBN. However, despite the assistance of the SPLM/A, it is by no means clear that the inhabitants of the SBN want to break their historical links with the north. Certainly, if given the opportunity to express their views, the peoples of the SBN would most likely demonstrate their distaste with the present regime in Khartoum. It is also clear, however, that rejection of the north could mean much closer relations with south Sudan. This would be an uneasy fit given that the SPLM/A and its intelligentsia, by-and-large Christian, harbor mixed feelings toward Muslims. Although the SPLM/A has endeavored to both break the cultural ties of the SBN with the north and to make it part of "New Sudan," it has largely failed. This is true for two main reasons: first, the identity of the territory is closely bound up with its mixed north–south heritage and the former still predominates, and second, the SPLM/A does not have the commitment, capacity, or vision to carry through such a project. Evidence of the second element is seen in the lack of institutional development within the territory.

In May 2003, the Sudanese territory of the SBN was at the center of peace negotiations sponsored by the Inter-Governmental Authority on Development (IGAD) in Kenya. This followed the signing of the Machakos Protocol by the SPLM/A and the Government of Sudan (GoS) on July 20, 2002. Although this included a cessation of hostilities agreement, there has been no peace and furthermore no sanctioned movement between government and SPLM/A controlled areas of the SBN. Administratively the SBN has been considered part of northern Sudan, but for the past six years a considerable portion of the territory has not been under the control of the GoS. Further complicating the status of the territory, the SPLM/A demands that the region be considered part of the south and that people have the right to self-determination as part of the south, a right, however, which the GoS denies.

The crux of the issue boils down to whether the SBN territory is to be considered part of north or south Sudan for administrative purposes, or whether its people will be given the right of self-determination. The answers to this question is by no means clear. On the one hand, the conflict surrounding the SBN has not resulted in the generation of political institutions that are part of state formation as described by Charles Tilly.[2] Indeed, the SBN has emerged more as a by-product of the process of the disintegration of the Sudanese state than as an explicit desire of the inhabitants for independence or to resurrect the past. On the other hand, the SBN has escaped processes of "state inversion"[3] that have often given rise to anarchic "new violence."[4] Indeed, despite the long-standing endemic resource-based conflicts between pastoralists and peasants and the more recent resistance in the context of the Sudanese civil war, the SBN cannot be characterized as having been particularly violent and is considerably safer than so-called peaceful neighboring Kenya. Moreover, despite the ambiguity of the identity of its disparate peoples, caught as they are between north and south, it nonetheless remains distinct from the two main protagonists in the Sudanese civil war. Hence, while not in existential competition with either the SPLM/A or the larger Sudanese state, there seems to be some basis for the SBN as an autonomous region within postconflict Sudan, however it is governed. Indeed, this analyst predicts that this will be the likely result of the IGAD peace negotiations. It is for this reason that a study of the experience of this territory warrants inclusion in this volume and can contribute to a broader understanding of processes that surround the emergence of these kinds of incipient political entities.

Background

The area of the SBN was once part of the polyglot Funj Kingdom before it successively fell to the Ottoman Empire, the followers of the Mahdi, the British Empire, and to independent Sudan. According to James, the various peoples that inhabit this area "share the peculiar geopolitical situation of being marginal to the processes of state formation in the adjoining regions of the Nile basin and the Ethiopian highlands."[5] While this area and the adjacent Benishangul territory of Ethiopia have been Arabic-speaking and Islamic for at least two centuries, some of its territory was attached to Upper Nile in southern Sudan in 1938 and its people, notably the Uduk, Koma, and Mabaan were exposed to Christianity. When this territory was transferred back to the SBN and northern administration in 1953, the southern type of education and religious exposure these people received became a source of tension.[6] The first civil war from 1955 to 1972 only had a minimal impact on the SBN, but correspondingly the region did not benefit from the various development projects of the south during the subsequent period of peace from 1972 to 1983. Nor did the region receive the promised vote stipulated in the Addis Ababa Agreement of 1972, which ended the first civil war on whether it would be part of northern or southern Sudan.

Beginning in 1983 the second civil war did affect the SBN, and while *Anyanya*, which led the first insurgency, was solely a southern movement, the SPLM/A claimed a national status and struggled for a "New Sudan" that embraced all Sudanese, irrespective of race or religion. In 1984 the SPLM/A launched attacks on the SBN from bases in the Ethiopian border territory of Gambella, and while they were not able to capture the territory, they did start a low-level guerrilla insurgency. In 1986 the Sadig Al-Mahdi government began supporting tribal militias throughout southern Sudan to fight the SPLM/A, and this approach was also used in the SBN, principally with the Rufa'a Arabs and the Fallata. Nonetheless, the SPLM/A was able to gain a measure of support from the local people and to attract recruits from some of the indigenous non-Muslim people, particularly the Uduk. This in turn led the militia and government troops to attack civilians and destroy anything they deemed might be turned over to the SPLM/A. As a result, by the late 1980s most of the Uduk had been displaced from their traditional lands and many had fled to Ethiopia where they took up residence in the UN High Commission for Refugees (UNHCR) camp at Tsore near Assosa in Benishangul.[7] But in this early period SPLM/A efforts were not successful, nor were the attempts to take the region in 1987 and 1989. In each case the SPLM/A received support from the Ethiopian *Derg*, or military government, thus forcing the GoS army to withdraw and permitting the SPLM/A to take possession of the area. On both occasions the GoS retook the lost territory within one month, each time inflicting further damage and forcing the civilian population to flee.

The coming to power of the Ethiopian People's Revolutionary Democratic Front (EPRDF) in 1991 ended Ethiopian support for the SPLM/A and the GoS strengthened its control over the territory thus forcing the dislocation of many of the territory's inhabitants to either government-held Nasir or to Ethiopia.[8] Those who remained were subject to NIF activism as the regime tried to make the region a "model province" for Sudan.[9] Much of the government's focus was on Kurmuk district, which has a large Christian minority as a result of early evangelization. Islamist non-governmental organizations (NGOs) constructed and staffed schools, conducted Islamic re-education campaigns, established student organizations, encouraged Islamic dress for women, and worked closely with the Sudan army garrison and government authorities. De Waal describes the activities of the Islamist NGOs in the SBN and elsewhere in Sudan as being "at the vanguard of the NIF project for the social and political transformation of Sudan to a prophetic society and an Islamic state."[10]

These developments took place in the context of what appeared to be a new era of friendly relations between Ethiopia and Sudan. And for a time this was the case, but an NIF commitment to expansionist political Islam soon soured relations as the regime supported groups wanting to subvert and Islamize neighboring countries. In response the United States attempted to construct an alliance to overthrow the regime led by Ethiopia and including Uganda and Eritrea. As a result, while in 1991 the EPRDF fought with the SPLM/A in the final days of its own liberation struggle, in 1996 the SPLM/A was welcomed back to Ethiopia. And in early 1997 the SPLM/A, with considerable support from the Ethiopian army, attacked and captured a number of towns in the SBN, including Kurmuk, adjacent to Benishangul.

Politics of Identity

Having captured these lands, the SPLM/A is attempting to undermine the cultural hegemony of the riverain Arabs and construct a new identity for the people of the SBN. If Sudan is a transitional zone between an Arab-Muslim north and a Christian-African south as it is sometimes simplistically suggested, then the SBN can be considered one of the cutting edges of that transition. As a result, the area is dominated by the politics of identify formation and manipulation. While the majority of the territory's people are Muslim, their affiliation to the religion is typically not strict and they are not Arabs, and are generally not seen as such, by either themselves, or by most northern Sudanese. Many among the leadership of the initial SPLM/A army were Christian or pagan southern Sudanese, but are little different in color than the local inhabitants, and moreover, are led by Malik Agar, a Muslim from the SBN's Ingessana Hills.

In the SBN most people speak Arabic, but also retain their indigenous languages, and while most proclaim Islam to be their religion, it is clear that Islam adapted to powerful traditional belief systems, rather than the latter to the former. Malik is by no means unique in claiming to have followers of three faiths—Islam, Christianity, and indigenous—in his own family and probably none of those belief systems would be seen as strictly orthodox.[11] But when pressed, most of the local inhabitants I questioned identified themselves as Muslims. They were, however, equally clear in rejecting any Arab identity. Like those in the north, men frequently wear *jalabyas* and women wear *tobes*, but I was repeatedly told these items did not constitute Arab attire, but Muslim clothes.

Although SBN inhabitants usually consider Arabs to be exploiters, since independence Khartoum-based governments have also endeavored to Islamize and Arabize both southern Sudan and the cultural borderlands like the SBN. Governments in Khartoum not only tried to dismiss or play down earlier pre-Islamic civilizations, but also non-riverain, but largely Islamic civilizations, such as the Funj Kingdom of the SBN. And this objective of manipulating or changing the identity of the people of the SBN was intensified after the NIF coup of 1989. Until then, there was a level of religious tolerance and the region had a number of churches led by the Sudan Interior Mission (SIM), recently recast as the Society of Internal Ministries. Upon coming to power, the NIF closed the churches, but they were reopened after the 1997 SPLM/A takeover.

The low levels of development and education and Khartoum's efforts to maintain political and cultural hegemony meant that virtually all leadership and administrative offices were held by riverain Arabs and teachers above primary level were invariably from the state core areas in the north. Economically the regional economy was dominated by the *jallaba*, or northern merchant class, who ran the markets, purchased the gold and surplus fruits and vegetables for sale in the northern towns, and imported the requisite consumer goods. Other northerners, locally called "Arabs," but from the Rufa'a tribe, who were largely pastoralists with cattle and some camels, moved into the area in the mid-nineteenth century. As well, the Fallata moved into the lands between the White and Blue Niles in the 1940s. These people were originally Fulani Muslims from West Africa who pursued pastoralism with their long-horned cattle. Largely beyond the control of local authorities their cattle were held responsible for the spread of many diseases and their introduction disrupted the balanced relations between the nomadic and sedentary peoples of the area.[12] And perhaps because they were late-comers, they have tended to look to the government of the day for security and under the present regime many have joined the Islamist Popular Defense Forces (PDF) or established government-supported militias.

As well, the SBN became a focus for large-scale capital investment from the north, particularly mechanized farms and this too increasingly became the source of conflict because of the damage this form of agriculture is deemed to cause the environment. The introduction of the Arabs and Fallata, the economic dominance of the Jallaba, and the political hegemony of the riverain northerners was fiercely resented by the local inhabitants. And it is not surprising that the SPLM/A used this resentment to mobilize opposition to the regime and solidify its position in the region. A few *Jallaba* remain in the region, but they have married local women, focus their activities on Ethiopia rather than northern Sudan, and appear to be accepted by the indigenous population. The riverain administrators, together with the teachers, Arab nomads, and Fallata followed the retreating government of Sudan army north after the SPLM/A occupied the area in 1997, although the Arabs and Fallata continued to be critical to Khartoum's security in areas adjacent to the SBN.

While most of the people of the SBN are Africans, the question remains as to whether they are able to identify with southerners, give allegiance to the largely Christian-led SPLM/A, and endorse the movement's notion of New Sudan. There were clearly problems of adjustment in the period immediately after the arrival of the SPLM/A in 1997. In one celebrated case, Christian SPLM/A fighters took shots at the mosque in Kurmuk. Yet, on the other hand, *Omda* Debeid, who joined the movement as a traditional chief of a section and briefly served as the deputy to the governor of the region after defecting from the GoS, left the SPLM/A when he disagreed with Malik over the dominant role of southerners in the SPLM/A's SBN administration. Despite these cases, however, the prevailing view in the towns of the region that I visited was that there was little tension between Christians and Muslims. Moreover, the majority of the SPLM/A soldiers are now local residents, and in any case as noted earlier, most inhabitants are very relaxed in their approach to religion.

Because the attitude of southerners in the SPLM/A-held territories to Islam is mixed and it is not uncommon to hear anti-Muslim sentiments, the ties between the peoples of the SBN and southern Sudan will remain tenuous and this will also impact on the formation of identity and the politics in the region. Indeed, while northern governments have attempted to force a particular Arab-Muslim identity on the people of this region, it is not inconceivable that a politically powerful south would press an African-Christian identity on them. Malik acknowledges this, but considers association with the south as "the lesser of two evils."[13] His reasoning is that northern efforts to manipulate identity formation in the SBN have always had a political strategic character, while the south would not have this imperative.

With the expulsion of the imposed northern political class, a local SPLM/A-dominated elite is emerging. Malik is of course the focal point of the new administration, but there was a concerted policy to move quickly to ensure that the majority of the SPLM/A soldiers are from the SBN and that appears to have been achieved. However, while indigenous soldiers now figure among the officers, the top military leadership remains overwhelmingly from outside the region and this is not likely to change in the near future given the low levels of education of the local inhabitants. In the early period tribes exposed to Christianity clearly formed the majority of SPLM/A recruits, but it would appear that the movement is acquiring a broader base, and further, as I witnessed on a visit to Upper Nile in May 2003, forces from the SBN are now being utilized outside the region. On the political and administrative side local cadres are coming to the fore. Most of these people are from, or have had some education in, the Damazin-Rossaires area, which is the major urban core and has been the political center of the region since British colonialism. These cadres are not traditional SPLM/A supporters and have typically only joined the movement in the mid-1990s, in some cases because of local disputes in the GoS-controlled areas over the appointment of NIF officials. They are Arabic-speakers with limited knowledge of English, but could nonetheless broadly be defined as intellectuals. While they do not consider themselves Arabs, they clearly share stronger cultural ties with the north than the south.

How these people adapt to, and are accepted into, the SPLM/A will be a test of the movement's commitment to a multicultural, tolerant, and secular New Sudan. Acceptance of the SPLM/A by the people of the SBN will also depend upon the movement's commitment to the 1994 Chukudum pledge to develop civil society and administration in the liberated territories. Currently civil administration in the SBN is weak because of a lack of human and material resources, but also because the SPLM/A has given priority to the army. Moreover, while many southerners would likely prefer independence if given the option, this is not the prevailing view in the SBN. For all their objections to the policies of successive Khartoum governments, the people of SBN are linked by language, culture, economy, and transportation links with the north. Southern independence would leave the SBN with two untenable options: choosing to be a Muslim minority in a Christian-dominated south, or be an African minority from a traditionally marginalized area in an Arab-dominated north. Further complicating matters, the region is culturally and to a lesser extent economically linked to the Ethiopian state of Benishangul.[14] In such circumstances independence for the SBN cannot be ruled out, as local leaders of the SPLM/A acknowledge, but even more than the other alternatives it would be extremely problematic. The best option would be for a reconstructed united Sudan where the marginalized people of the south and the north were given their full rights.

Questions of identity and the receptivity of local inhabitants to SPLM/A direction in this area also depend upon the makeup of the movement and the tribal loyalties it gains. The fact that Malik is from the area and a Muslim clearly gives him and the SPLM/A a measure of legitimacy. But to some extent this is undermined by the fact that the people of his home area of the Ingessana Hills have not demonstrated much commitment to the struggle to date as evidenced by the lack of local recruits in the movement. Unlike the Ingessina, because of circumstances considered earlier the largely Christian Uduk were the movement's strongest supporters in the early period and at that time were estimated to have composed 90 percent of the SPLM/A's forces. But their numbers are now much reduced and many Uduk are currently living in refugee camps in Ethiopia.

The Muslim Berta, who reside on both sides of the border, are now reckoned to make up the largest number of SPLM/A soldiers and are joined by Jum Jum and Mabaan people dislocated from neighboring Upper Nile, although again these tribes stand out for their exposure to Christianity in a region where Muslims form the majority. There are also Dinka and Nuer soldiers assigned to the territory.

Recognition of a sort has sometimes been acquired by territories like the SBN and the associated rebels by the United Nations, international agencies, and the NGOs involved in humanitarian disasters. Recurring famines in southern Sudan and international pressure on the GoS led to the establishment of Operation Lifeline Sudan (OLS) in 1989, which made both Khartoum and the SPLM/A partners to the agreement and gave the latter a measure of recognition. But the GoS never agreed to the SBN being covered by the OLS and this not only weakened any juridical identity of the territory, which was the major concern of Khartoum, but also deepened its isolation. As a result, only a handful of small NGOs operating outside the OLS consortium have carried out activities in the SBN. This, however, is changing and as a result of progress in the IGAD-sponsored peace talks, the World Food Programme for the first time delivered food to the region in April 2003.

SPLM/A in the South Blue Nile

The SPLM/A takes pride in the capture and holding of the SBN although, as noted, Ethiopian support was crucial in the early period. Unlike parts of southern Sudan, the war in the SBN has mostly been of a conventional character. This is because the terrain is largely featureless and flat and thus for both the SPLM/A and the GoS the most active fighting period is during the dry season. The GoS broadly defended positions a little to the south of the Blue Nile and east and parallel to the White Nile. It should also be noted that the SBN is not only a transitional zone in a cultural sense but, militarily, it is—in Malik's words—"a buffer zone" like SPLM/A territories in northeast Sudan and the Nuba Mountains. As such, the SBN draws disproportionate human and material resources of the GoS that would otherwise be directed at SPLM/A positions in southern Sudan. In addition, the SPLM/A in the SBN is strategically well placed to bring pressure on the Rossaires Dam to the north and the oil fields to the west. As a result, the GoS has made these major security concerns and the movement has made little progress in capturing them. Instead, SPLM/A forces from the SBN have attempted to move south into militarily softer areas of Upper Nile.

SPLM/A propaganda justifies its take-over of the SBN because the area was politically, economically, and culturally marginalized by the riverain Arabs that maintained hegemony over the Sudan state since independence. And this is no doubt true, but it cuts both ways. By making the SBN a war zone, the SPLM/A has brought about the almost complete destruction of the territory's infrastructure and much of its once vibrant economy. In addition, the SPLM/A has not had the capacity to provide a fraction of even the limited social services that were previously available to the people of the region. This is due in part to the defection of the educated people and a lack of skills of those available to the SPLM/A. But it is also the result of repeated organizational changes made by the SPLM/A headquarters. Previously the regional governor had complete control over civil and military spheres, but now day-to-day operations of the military are left to the commanders who report directly to the center. Malik has three deputies, the first for the military, followed by civil, and then political affairs in level of importance. This change has clearly undermined Malik's authority in the region and reportedly led to tension with some of his commanders and the transfer of one of them to Bahr El Ghazal.

The SPLM/A has always emphasized the military dimension of its activities and for the most part its resources and talented people are drawn to the army. This in turn limits the prospects of having anything more than a skeletal civil administration, much less mobilizing the inhabitants. Indeed, the SPLM/A does not have the organizational capacity to carry out many development tasks, raise revenues for the movement, nor establish bonds of a revolutionary character between the movement and the people.[15] The SPLM/A sometimes launches public campaigns with the assistance of traditional authorities to raise funds for the purchase of fuel, and has established farms to grow sorghum for its soldiers. As elsewhere in SPLM/A territories, individual soldiers are free to trade in the market and this serves to take the pressure off the limited supplies available to its forces. Ethiopian security personnel also report that SPLM/A fighters have in some cases looted public property and taken it across the border for sale.

Many SPLM/A officials speak of self-sufficiency, but given the limited international presence in the SBN such a view must inevitably be seen as self-serving. In spite of this perspective, a common view of outsiders, including this observer, is that local administrators are reluctant to make decisions and typically defer to Malik. A further weakness is that unlike the revolutionaries of Eritrea and Ethiopia that came to power in 1991 and had strong ideologies, the SPLM/A does not have major convictions. After ascribing to socialism when under the influence of the Derg, the post-1991 SPLM/A does not have an overriding philosophy.[16] Indeed, one observer noted that to the extent that the movement has an ideology it is one of being "Sudanists," in other words, a locally derived perspective that emphasizes the objective of a reconstructed equitable Sudan, rather than any theory or global view.

Despite this, by most accounts the SPLM/A's internal discipline in the SBN has improved and early reports of insecurity in the liberated territories and of abuse of civilians are now rarely heard and any mistreatment of the local inhabitants by SPLM/A soldiers is apparently dealt with quickly and harshly. But the SPLM/A still has to deal with a poor legacy. For example, the town of Ora on the Kurmuk to Yabus road was completely deserted by its inhabitants when the SPLM/A entered the area in 1997 and they have never returned because, as Malik acknowledged, the movement previously mistreated civilians in the area.[17]

South Blue Nile in the Regional Context

The SBN is ultimately a relatively small territory within the wider political configuration of the Horn of Africa and theorizing on such territories should never overreach these contexts. The SPLM/A was ushered into the SBN by the EPRDF at a time when Khartoum was supporting a terror campaign in Ethiopia and relations between the countries were at rock bottom. But by the late 1990s, the NIF had shelved its Islamist designs for the region. Instead, it sought improved relations with Addis Ababa in order to either stop Ethiopian support for the SPLM/A or ensure that it does not resume. With the loss to Addis Ababa of access to Eritrean ports as a result of its war with Asmara, arrangements have been made for Ethiopia to use Port Sudan and to import much of its oil from Sudan at discounted prices. The GoS in turn holds out the prospect of trade beyond present low levels and an oil pipeline to Ethiopia through the "Damazin corridor" that is currently largely controlled by the SPLM/A, thus implicitly suggesting the gains to both countries if the SPLM/A was removed from the SBN. So far, the EPRDF has not taken the bait.

The SPLM/A, as the third element in this triangular relationship, is not without its own cards to play. First, even if the border was completely sealed by Ethiopia, supplies could, at considerable cost, be flown in from Kenya and Uganda. Thus, short of a successful Sudanese army attack or Ethiopian military action—and neither seems likely at the time of writing because of the IGAD cessation of hostilities—the Damazin corridor is not likely to be opened soon. Second, Ethiopia does derive some economic benefits from the present arrangements, in particular the undetermined amount of gold that goes to Addis Ababa. Indeed, a leading EPRDF official told me of Ethiopia's satisfaction at the gold's destination.

But the card the SPLM/A plays, or tries to play, with the government of Ethiopia is that the security threat posed by the GoS remains and could be unleashed again if the movement no longer assumed the function of providing a "cordon sanitare" along the border. Continuing political instability in the Benishangul regional government and attempts by the Eritrean government to infiltrate dissident Ethiopian groups through Sudan and across the Ethiopian border means that the EPRDF cannot feel completely secure on its western frontiers. Moreover, the SPLM/A leadership invariably maintain that they are the frontline against expansionist Islam in Africa that has long targeted "Christian Ethiopia." This is an appeal designed to touch the nerves of many Ethiopians who have for long held their country to be an outpost of Christian civilization surrounded by threatening Muslims. The secular-minded EPRDF does not appear to be receptive to this appeal, but it does face a low-level Islamist threat in the Ogaden to the east and it cannot feel comfortable with a radical Islamic regime in Khartoum.

Beyond the governments of Ethiopia and Sudan and the SPLM/A, there are broader international interests at stake in the SBN. The forces of Malik Agar have reportedly been as close as 25 kilometers from the strategically important Rossaires Dam. This dam provides most of Khartoum's electricity and much of that of the towns north along the Nile to the Egyptian border. It also regulates the flow of most of the water entering the main course of the Nile and thus has a direct impact on Egypt. Indeed, both Malik and Nairobi-based SPLM/A officials have told me that an attack on the dam would involve significant geostrategic considerations and that Egyptian officials have been consulted over such a possibility. In other words, a major attack—or even the real prospect of such an attack—on the dam poses the possibility of bringing an alarmed Egypt into Sudan's civil war. And further, Egypt's troops would be up against the border of Ethiopia and its leaders view that country as its primary strategic enemy in the region. The SBN region is thus a critical element in the wider drama of Nile hydro-politics.

Meanwhile, SPLM/A forces in the west are adjacent to the Adar oil fields that the movement is committed to disrupting, or at least was, until the advent of the Machakos peace process. Discoveries of oil are increasingly moving south and east, while until the recent cessation of hostilities, the SPLM/A had endeavored, albeit with limited success, to move west. But SPLM/A concerns over oil is not simply one of propaganda and Malik told me that if the movement failed to disrupt the oil flow and the Khartoum government was to use this financial windfall for the next three to four years then "the SPLM/A would lose the war."[18] Some hope for the success of the IGAD-sponsored peace talks may reduce these concerns, or alternatively may intensify them if the negotiations drag on and oil revenues continue to flow to Khartoum.

If the SPLM/A in the SBN was routed, the threat to the Rossaires Dam would end and GoS military resources would be freed for deployment elsewhere.[19] Most significantly, defeat of the SPLM/A in the SBN would open wide areas to the east of Upper Nile to oil exploration and development. And if Malik's prognosis is true, this would provide the GoS with the resources to marginalize, if not defeat, the movement and make the war confinable. With the success of the peace process by no means guaranteed, such scenarios cannot be completely dismissed.

But the political fall out from the loss of the SBN would also be significant. Currently the SBN forms the major territorial base held by the SPLM/A in the north and without it Garang's notion of New Sudan would be seriously undermined. Even without a military loss of the territory, it could be lost to the north during the course of negotiations. Many within the SPLM/A, and even more outside who are sympathetic to the movement, have long had misgivings about struggling for a united Sudan. For those of this persuasion the loss of the SBN would be easy to bear and might even be welcome if it led Garang to advocate a clearly stated southern separatist political agenda. That said, few in the international community, and in particular in the Horn, would favor an independent southern Sudan.

Another threat to SPLM/A control of the SBN is a result of the warming of relations between Khartoum and Addis Ababa. Derg and EPRDF support for the SPLM/A has historically been crucial and the security agreements between Sudan and Ethiopia have important implications for the SPLM/A generally and the SBN contingent in particular. For example, Ethiopia has agreed to export electricity from Lake Tana to Damazin, after which it will be sent north to Gederef, Kassala, and Port Sudan. But not only does this agreement provide economic benefits to both countries, it crucially links Ethiopia's security to that of Sudan since an SPLM/A attack on Damazin or the nearby Rossaires Dam would undermine Ethiopia economically. Whether Ethiopia would—as Khartoum clearly desires—assist in the removal of the SPLM/A from the SBN is doubtful at this stage, and even more so because of the advance of the IGAD peace process. But the movement can no longer expect either direct or strategic support from the EPRDF and that must be worrying.

Conclusion

The future status of the SBN is very much undecided, and the only thing that can be said with confidence is that it will be different than it is today. As it stands, and unlike SPLM/A-occupied areas of southern Sudan that have been recognized by the GoS and the international community through the UN relief operations conducted by the OLS, this territory is just beginning to achieve such a recognition as a result of the advance of the IGAD negotiations. The SBN thus has no juridical recognition at the moment. Yet, however, there is something afoot here. While the SPLM/A has done little to promote civil administration and development in the SBN, neither has it acted like an army of occupation, pillaging the local population. Indeed, as we have seen, the movement does have a legitimating philosophy and hence one can argue that state building and identity formation are in fact major interests of the ruling administration of the territory.

At the IGAD-sponsored peace talks at Lake Bogoria, Kenya on September 21–October 4, 2000, the positions of the mediating Sudan Secretariat, GoS, and the SPLM/A could not be at greater variance in their approaches to the SBN. Based on the observation that the SBN (and southern Kordofan) had "raised arms along side the

SPLM/A" the Sudan Secretariat urged that a separate mediator be appointed and a separate forum be organized to resolve the conflict.[20] This position was undoubtedly taken because the Secretariat appreciated that the SBN was not in South Sudan at the time of independence and since the IGAD peace process was restricted to South Sudan, that it did not have the authority to take up the issue itself.

Nonetheless, its advocacy on the SBN raised the ire of the GoS who predictably questioned the intervention of the Sudan Secretariat and the right of the SPLM/A to represent peoples "who are northerners and predominantly muslims."[21] The SPLM/A, meanwhile, held that the IGAD mediation involved "the sum total of their [i.e. the GoS and SPLM/A] respective parts" and therefore it would take up the issue of the SBN (and the other territories of Abeyei and Southern Kordofan where SPLM/A-led insurrections were underway) in negotiations and would include members of these areas on its negotiating team.[22] And indeed, Malik Agar has served on the SPLM/A's negotiating team in recent years. As a result of these divergent positions no progress was made on this issue at the Lake Bogoria talks. As this article is being completed, another round of IGAD-sponsored talks (and parallel to the main talks) that focuses on the border territories is taking place in Kenya, and this must be acknowledged as an achievement. But there is little reason to hope for an early breakthrough on this contentious issue, unless one or both parties is prepared to make major compromises.

What this study suggests is that the SBN was able to sustain a rebellion while other areas of Sudan that were equally marginalized could not because of specific conditions. This was first due to the political decision by the SPLM/A to open a military front in this area and that in turn depended on it sharing an international border and gaining the support of two successive Ethiopian governments. Rebellions might well have flared up in the area because of local grievances, but it is unlikely that they could have produced a sustained rebellion without support from Ethiopia, at least in the formative stage of the revolt. Second, while this area nursed grievances with a number of Khartoum-based governments, it reached a crisis under the NIF because of its aggressive pursuit of an Islamist-Arab agenda that challenged the mixed and laissez-faire culture of the local people in general and a handful of Christian tribes in particular. The latter in turn supplied the SPLM/A with its first and crucial recruits. Added to this was the attempt by Khartoum to overcome local resistance by encouraging Arab pastoralists and Fallata to move into the territory, and later to establish government-supported militias. This served to intensify conflict with the local sedentary population and encourage them to accept the SPLM/A as protectors. Third, government encouragement of the Arabs and Fallata and the resulting intensification of the struggle over resources, together with the age-old, albeit weak, identification with the Funj Empire, produced the basis for a regional identity that the SPLM/A could nourish and use as a justifying ideology. The regional identity that the movement attempted to foster did not develop deep roots because of countervailing tribal and religious identities, but it has served to gain its recognition as a "marginalized territory" in the context of the IGAD peace negotiations.

Interestingly, Johnson makes the argument that it was precisely the SPLM/A's retention of local civil administration, custom, livelihood, and the fact that it did not attempt to introduce revolutionary, but alien, systems of administration, in areas like the SBN that accounts for the movement's ability to build a basis of support.[23] No doubt this pragmatic approach has its advantages, but it has been pursued at the cost of sustaining a very weak local administration in the SBN. Moreover, the lack of a developed administration of any character has less to do with any philosophy as such than with a lack of resources and the priority given by the SPLM/A to war and not civil administration.[24] The SPLM/A has to some extent raised the consciousness of the indigenous people of the area and further developed their collective sense of identity. But it has been at a tremendous cost in human lives and destruction of the economy and at the end of the day it is by no means apparent that the people of the region fully embrace an African south Sudanese identity that would support separation from the north.

Ultimately the example of the SBN would suggest that the state-within-states thesis has more resonance at the height of a conflict when all options appear possible, than when a viable peace process is underway (as is now the case in Sudan) and the options are more limited, but also more realizable. Moreover, the ties between revolutionaries (assuming that they are revolutionaries and not mere warlords) and local inhabitants have a particular and intense character during the course of a war when survival is a collective affair, than during peace when a broader scope of interests and loyalties come into play. During war the SPLM/A is the state, but in times of peace the movement is likely to quickly become another interested party open to challenge. In time of war, the stateness of the SPLM/A administration depends crucially upon both a monopoly over the organs of violence, and that these organs be used to defend the citizenry. But the defense of the citizenry fades as an element of the legitimacy of the SPLM/A in times of peace. Increasingly the concern of the inhabitants will be for development and the SPLM/A has largely proved ineffective in meeting these demands. Moreover, it was the IGAD cessation of hostilities agreement of October 2002 that for the first time in six years provided the citizenry of the SBN with a measure of security, and not the SPLM/A.

Ironically, peace will mean the end of the isolation of the SBN occupied by the SPLM/A and also acquisition of its long sought recognition by the international donor community. But SBN's recognition will be as a component of a broader unit of Sudan, or less likely, as part of southern Sudan. In addition, under a regime of peace the failure of the SPLM/A to establish workable institutions of civil administration or resurrect a functioning economy will make the movement's weakness clear. Trade and the movement of people will inevitably follow the patterns of the past and that will mean a shift to the north. To its credit the SPLM/A in the SBN has ended the cultural assault of the NIF and provided a space in which the people can, and in their own ways, define themselves.

While the people of the SBN have rejected the civilizational project of the NIF, they have not given up on the Sudanese state. The SBN may have given the appearance of a state within a state during the years of struggle and isolation, but with the war winding down and the isolation ending, it increasingly looks like it will resume its former position as a province, albeit probably through the auspices of the IGAD negotiations, one that has an acknowledged constitutional status within the Sudanese state. But the SBN definitely will remain a component within a broader political formation defined by Sudan. After 20 years of Sudan's second civil war, the loss of two million lives, regional marginalization, an assault on their culture by the NIF, and the displacement of more than five million people (including a substantial number from the SBN), this is remarkable and speaks to the resilience of the state, even a demonstratively failed one like that of Sudan's.

Notes

1. South Blue Nile (SBN) is a large area south of the Gezira, west to the Blue Nile, east to the Ethiopian border, and south to Upper Nile. It broadly corresponds to the southern part of the historic Funj Empire. The area is considered woodland savannah and the rainfall varies from 400 mm in the north to 700 in the south. According to the 1956 Government of Sudan (GoS) census the province of the SBN had a population of 1.2 million. For further details about the historical roots of the SBN, see Abdel Ghaffar, "Nomadic Competition in the Funj Area," *Sudan Notes and Records*, Vol. 54 (1973).

2. C. Tilly, "War Making and State Making as Organized Crime," in Evans, Reuschmeyer, and Skocpol, *Bringing the State Back In* (New York: Cambridge University Press, 1985).

3. J. B. Forrest, "State Inversion and Nonstate Politics," in L.A. Villalon and P.A. Huxtable, eds., *The African State at a Critical Juncture: Between Disintegration and Reconfiguration* (Boulder: Lynne Rienner, 1998), p. 46.

4. Chris Allen, "Warfare, Endemic Violence and State Collapse in Africa," *Review of African Political Economy*, No. 81 (1999), pp. 367–384.

5. Wendy James, "War & Ethnic Visibility: The Uduk on the Sudan-Ethiopia Border," in K. Fukui and J. Markakis, eds., *Ethnicity & Conflict in the Horn of Africa* (London: James Currey, 1994), p.140.

6. Ibid., p. 144.

7. Ibid.

8. Wendy James, e-mail correspondence with the author (16-05-01).

9. Alexander De Waal, *Famines Crimes: Politics and the Disaster Relief Business in Africa* (London: African Rights & the International African Institute in association with J. Currey and Indiana University Press, 1997).

10. Ibid., p. 234.

11. Interview with Malik Agar, 13-03-01.

12. Abdel Ghaffar, "Nomadic Competition."

13. Interview with Malik Agar, 06-11-00.

14. John Young, "Along Ethiopia's Western Frontier: Gambella and Benishangul in Transition," *Journal of Modern African Studies*, Vol. 37, No. 2 (1999).

15. Please see chapter eight by Kenn Crossley in this volume.

16. John Young, "The SPLM/A and Governance in South Sudan," *Politique Africaine* (Paris: December 2002).

17. Interview with Malik Agar, 18-03-01.

18. Ibid.

19. At the time of writing, the major GoS security concern is not the south, but a growing insurrection in Darfur.

20. IGAD Secretariat on Peace in the Sudan, "Proposed Settlement on the Issue in Southern Kordofan and Southern Blue Nile" (unpublished and undated).

21. GoS delegation to the IGAD Peace Talks, "GoS Response to the Draft Proposal on the Issue of Abeyei, Southern Kordofan and Southern Blue Nile" (unpublished and undated).

22. SPLM/A delegation to the IGAD Peace Talks, "Proposed Settlement on the Issue of Southern Kordofan and Southern Blue Nile" (unpublished and undated).

23. Douglas Johnson, "Food Aid, Land Tenure & The Survival of the Subsistence Economy," unpublished paper presented at the Money Makes the War Go Round Conference (Brussels: 13-06-02).

24. Young, "The SPLM/A and Governance."

Chapter Five

Rebuilding *A House of Many Mansions*:[1] The Rise and Fall of Militia Cantons in Lebanon

Paul Kingston and Marie-Joelle Zahar

L ebanon provides a good opportunity to consider both the characteristics and trajectories of the concept of state-within-states. It is a country that has been described as "extremely plural";[2] it is a country whose state has always been "weak," debilitated by a confessional power-sharing agreement that has periodically kept the peace but which has never allowed for a concentration of political power at the center; and it is a country that, during its 16-year-long civil war, effectively broke up into several distinct and self-functioning cantons. Yet, Lebanon is also a country whose subsidiary political units, however state-like they may have appeared during the war, were never able to exist separately from the loosely knit Lebanese collectivity. Indeed, there exists a dialectical relationship between Lebanon's various political communities and the state—supported though not determined by international juridical norms— that pushes them toward coexistence rather than dissolution.

This chapter begins with an historical overview of the weak Lebanese state, examining the fragility of the consensus that surrounds its existence, the shallow nature of its penetration into society, as well as the prewar expression of the dialectical relationship between communities and the state. In the second part, we examine the breakdown of the Lebanese state and the emergence of "state-like" cantons during the civil war. We argue that the parasitic destruction of the Lebanese political economy—especially in the latter years of the war—ultimately proved counterproductive to the sustainability of the political subunits. The third section examines the postwar Lebanese period of reconstruction—arguing in this phase for the existence of a paradoxical but positive symbiosis between the rebuilding of the Lebanese political economy and the reinvigoration of institutions and power structures within Lebanon's various political communities. In conclusion, this chapter raises questions as to whether the Lebanese experience points toward a future where states and substates will coexist in symbiotic union characterized by overlapping dimensions of sovereignty and political authority.

Lebanese Politics in a Historical Perspective

Unlike many of the other "artificial" states in the Middle East, the modern Lebanese state has historical roots that predate its formal creation in 1920. Indeed, Lebanon's status as a distinct and autonomous political entity goes back as far as the sixteenth century under the Shihab Emirate that ruled over a mixed feudal community of Maronite Christians and Druze in Mount Lebanon. Lebanon's confessional political system, characterized by a power-sharing arrangement between the two religious communities, has slightly more recent roots being established in 1860 in the form of the foreign-imposed *mutasarrifiyya*. Both this long-standing tradition of autonomy and the more recent experience with confessional politics were inherited by the modern Lebanese state that emerged in 1920 and remain features of the state today. Hence, while definitely a "weak" state, both internally and in relation to its regional neighbors, it is less clear that Lebanon fits into Jackson's definition of a "quasi-state."[3]

The general explanation for the weakness of the Lebanese state revolves around the resilient strength of Lebanon's sectarian communities and the nature of the relationship between communities and the state. All of Lebanon's religious communities are guaranteed representation in the Lebanese Assembly, at a 5:5 ratio between Christians and Muslims since the signing of the Ta'if Accord in 1989, and this confessional distribution of power reaches the very height of the Lebanese state with the office of president, the prime minister, and the speaker of the Assembly being allocated to a Maronite Christian, a Sunni Muslim, and a Shi`a Muslim respectively. This confessional distribution of power has had two very limiting effects on the process of state formation. First, it has made agreement on the very rules and boundaries of the Lebanese polity difficult to reach and uphold—especially in times of regional tension and nationalist fervor. Moreover, it has enabled the various communal authorities, eager to preserve their status as mediators, to restrict the degree to which the Lebanese state penetrated and directly regulated Lebanese society. As a result, many of the functions increasingly provided by states in the modern world, from social welfare, health, and education to even the provision of basic security, have either remained the preserve of the various communities or have been shared with the state performing a facilitative and distributive role. In this sense, the Lebanese state shares the components of an "ideal-type" Weberian state, including the ability to control the means of violence, with its constituent communities.

However, while arguing that the Lebanese state is of limited strength and coherence, it would not be correct to assume that Lebanon's constituent sectarian communities are more so. Historically, this has certainly not been the case—be it from the point of view of their identity, social cohesiveness, or institutional foundations. Before examining the rise and fall of Lebanon's states-within-states in the war and postwar period, it is important to also place them in a historical perspective.

While religious identities have always been an important component of social life in Lebanon, they have not necessarily been the primary political identity—nor are they necessarily today. Indeed, much modern scholarship is critical of the unqualified use of the term "primordial" to describe the political salience of confessionalism in modern Lebanon. In a penetrating examination of social violence in Lebanon in the early to mid-1800s, Ussama Makdisi argues that Lebanon underwent a process of "sectarianization" in which "religion was detached from its social environment and treated as a cohesive, exclusivist and organic force."[4] Because they interpreted the violence as purely "sectarian" instead of being the result of more complex social and economic forces,

European consuls and Ottoman bureaucrats imposed a religious power-sharing formula on Lebanon that, in effect, introduced the notion of a "pure communal actor" where it had never existed before. As Makdisi writes, "[w]hereas religion had once been an integral part of an elaborate nonsectarian order . . . ., it now constituted the basis and raison d'être for communal segregation."[5] Thus, Lebanon's system of confessional power sharing is not the result of an organic political relevance of religion in defining political community. Instead, as Makdisi argues and as we shall see, by channeling politics in sectarian ways, European and Ottoman statesmen fostered the creation of political subunits in Lebanon that were "inherently unstable and highly ambivalent."[6]

This instability and ambivalence becomes evident when examining the partial and unevenly distributed material underpinnings of Lebanon's sectarian communities. First, Lebanon's religious communities have never been defined territorially even though specific communities have been historically associated with certain geographic locales (e.g. the Druze and the Shouf mountain, the Shi`a and the South). Rather, the tradition has been one of intermingled populations. Indeed, increased rates of rural–urban migration leading to the dramatic growth of Beirut in the latter half of the twentieth century resulted in an increase in the degree of social interaction and integration. Hence, despite a partial process of territorialization that occurred during the war, it has never been an easy proposition to define clear territorial boundaries for any particular religious community in Lebanon.

Second, it would also be difficult to describe any of the religious communities of Lebanon themselves as socially cohesive. Each is led, for example, by a highly heterogeneous and often fragmented elite base. Power within the various communities is often locally rather than communally based with the latter affiliation often being used by local elites to bolster local power. This often leads to situations of intense conflict between families of the same sect for hegemony over a particular region—consider, for example, the enduring conflicts in the Zghorta region between the three Maronite families contending for power, notably the Franjiehs, the Duweihis, and the Maouwads. The result is the often-cited observation in Lebanon that intra-sectarian conflicts are more severe than ones between sects.[7]

Divisions between elites and communal masses also affect the social cohesion of Lebanon's religious communities. Horizontal cleavages within communities can be equally as severe as the above-mentioned vertical ones.[8] While patron–client relationships are the dominant mode of sociopolitical interaction and integration in Lebanon, these relationships are highly unstable, designed to perpetuate systems of social hierarchy and domination yet constantly challenged from below. Indeed, much of the rising instability of prewar Lebanon can be understood in terms of the breakdown of patron–clientelism.[9] Be it migrants from the south of the country escaping the feudal clutches of their sectarian leaders, *qabadays* (clientelist intermediaries) in Beirut challenging the local hegemony of the various urban-based *zu'ama* (communal leaders), or the fast-growing middle-class and professional elements of society promoting the growth of nonsectarian political parties in the hope of promoting a secular future, Lebanon witnessed in the years immediately prior to the outbreak of civil war a dramatic unraveling of its clientelist heritage, one that had been a principal mechanism of maintaining social cohesion, however hierarchical and fragmented. Hence, to the extent that sectarian-based communities existed in Lebanon, they were racked with internal contradictions, cleavages, and porous borders.

What of institutional development within and across communities that could act to compensate for the weak integrating abilities of ambiguous primordial identities and clientelism; in other words, what was the degree of "political development" within these sectarian-based communities? Here, the work of Khalaf and Denoeux[10] that points to the uneven and ambiguous nature of communal institutionalization is instructive. The Maronite community seemed to have gone the farthest in developing community-wide institutions. These included a whole host of educational and social welfare institutions, in addition to the array of religious-based institutions and orders associated with the Maronite church. Perhaps the most important institutional development, however, was the emergence of the Kata'ib Party in the late 1930s that combined ideological goals with personalistic leadership and a militia apparatus. This institutional development contrasted sharply with that of the other communities, especially the Sunni and Shi`a, that lacked sectarian and ideologically based (as opposed to personally based) political parties and where religious institutions were more personalized, decentralized, and indeed competitive. This would make the emergence of wartime states-within-states within these communities a more problematic enterprise.

Nonetheless, in the years prior to the outbreak of the civil war, fueled by the fast pace of economic development yet sparked by its uneven nature, Lebanon witnessed an accelerated pace of factional institutional and political development across all the communities. The Muslim communities, increasingly perceiving the Lebanese state as unable to address their needs and aspirations, began to lay the institutional groundwork for the emergence of substate-like entities and movements. Imam Musa Sadr, the new populist leader of the Shi`a, for example, in taking up the cause of increased social welfare and economic redistribution to the marginalized Shi`a populations of the country, laid the basis for the emergence of the Amal movement with an array of institutions including a militia. The Druze, also battling for sociopolitical reforms to secure "a piece of the pie" commensurate with their historical role as political leaders in Mount Lebanon, established the Lebanese National Movement—a coalition of leftist parties that became increasingly associated with the political and military apparatus of Lebanon's prewar "state within a state"—the PLO. As the legitimacy of the Lebanese state in the eyes of the Muslim population continued to decline in the early 1970s, perhaps epitomized no better than by the army's violent involvement in the quelling of the 1975 demonstration by fishermen in Sidon, this institutionalization continued apace.

Paradoxically, this same dynamic of political development at the substate level also gathered pace within the Christian communities though for the opposite reasons. Initially, Lebanese state institutions were devised to provide Christian communities, more specifically the Maronites, with guarantees that they would not be forced to blend in the larger Arab and Muslim World. However, the state's perceived inability to decisively deal with crises in 1958 and 1969 that challenged this "Maronite vision of Lebanon" led Christian leaders to infer that the state was weak and the army unable to defend the country. Consequently, they embarked on the formation and training of paramilitaries to defend their vision of Lebanon. After 1958, for example, the Kata'ib Party built up its armaments, reorganized, and trained a fighting force that numbered in the range of 3,000 men—the largest militia in the country with the exception of the Palestinian guerrillas that flooded into the country after 1970.

Hence, on the eve of the civil war, Lebanon possessed a weak state characterized both by its limited reach and capacity and by its declining legitimacy. As much as by default as by design, it both delegated responsibility to decentralized actors at the communal and local levels and was finding itself increasingly challenged by them—especially with respect to the provision of security. The stage was set for the emergence of states-within-states. Yet, as is clear from the historically imposed nature of confessional identities and their problematic though developing institutional underpinnings, Lebanon's sectarian communities would not easily step into the political vacuum caused by the disintegration of the state with ease. What we turn to now is an analysis of the emergence of state-within-states in wartime Lebanon with an eye both to their internal development and their symbiotic relationship with a disintegrating but, as we shall see, lingering national Lebanese political economy.

Lebanon's Wartime States-Within-States: The Rise of "Militia Cantons"

There is an interesting literature emerging on the relationship between war and state building. From examinations of the predatory nature of the early stages of state making[11] to the emergence of modern states that channel the use of violence into productive rather than predatory activities,[12] war or its absence[13] has proved crucial in determining the trajectory of state-making efforts and processes. From Tilly's examination of the similarities between organized crime and the early stages of state making, there emerges a synergetic relationship between the perception and/or generation of threats by the community in question and the need to extend control over a widening piece of territory in order both to generate resources for conflict and to build a power base; the longer the conflict, the more this extension of power becomes centralized and routinized. Hence, the very act of building a military machine tends to promote the emergence of Weberian characteristics associated with statehood: territory, taxes, a bureaucracy, and monopoly over the means of coercion.

With the effective collapse of the Lebanese state in 1975 and the descent of Lebanon into a long period of periodic but persistent warfare, one did see the emergence of sub-state entities that drew their power from the act of war making. Indeed, as we have seen, the historical weakness of the Lebanese state meant that much of this process had actually already been underway. While initially only territorialized sanctuaries and enclaves, by the early to mid-1980s, one began to see the crystallization of what we might loosely call states-within-states. Elizabeth Picard, for example, has attempted to draw up a typology for the various militia political economies that emerged during the war.[14] Her four main types neatly fit with the four principal militias in wartime Lebanon:

(i) Authoritarian corporatism—the Lebanese Forces (LF): By the mid-1980s, the LF had established tight control over the territory under its control. It centralized much of the economic activity under the umbrella of a "National Treasury" (*Sunduq al-Watani*) out of which were spawned a number of parastatal enterprises; it also increased its penetration into society under its control—epitomized by both the increase in taxation and by the intensified provision of social welfare goods. Picard writes, "No civil activity, whether lawful or unlawful, could escape the control of the LF."[15] She concludes that the militia was inching toward a governing strategy described as "authoritarian corporatism."

(ii) Autonomous principalities—the Druze PSP: A similar centralization of economic activity took place within the Druze-controlled Shouf region of the country. Facilitated by the creation of "the Mountain Administration" that built on the institutional foundations of the Druze-controlled Popular Socialist Party, the Druze leader,

Walid Jumblatt, gained control over the region's main economic enterprises (ports, cement works, power stations) while also substituting for the Lebanese state through the provision of social welfare. Despite its fundamentally parasitic nature, Picard argues that the Druze region was "the best controlled and best kept in the country." She described this entity as "an autonomous principality."[16]

(iii) Social welfare and self-defense networks—Harakat al-Amal: On the ground, Amal had a much looser institutional structure, originally being made up of an amalgamation of local self-defense and social welfare efforts. In many ways, its strength was based on its networking abilities rather than on its institutionalizing abilities—deriving benefits from its continued connections with the rudimentary Lebanese state (that continued to pay salaries to its civil servants), as well as to the large community of Shi`a expatriates outside the country. Despite its significant military capacity, Amal was the least state-like of all the large-scale militias.

(iv) Organizational autonomy—Hizballah: Perhaps the most interesting substate entity that emerged during the Lebanese civil war has been Hizballah. Competing with Amal for legitimacy among the Shi`a populations of Lebanon, Hizballah developed a strategy of institution building based upon "organizational autonomy."[17] At the forefront was its militia created to resist Israeli occupation in the south. This was joined, however, by an array of increasingly effective charitable, medical, and educational institutions. Financing Hizballah's expansion was a combination of internal finance (religious taxes, involvement in the production and trafficking of drugs in the Beka'a) and external patrons (Iran and portions of the Shi`a diaspora). Picard has described Hizballah as establishing the rudimentary structures for an "Islamic welfare state."

However, while Picard places all these entities on a diverse set of trajectories toward statehood, it is less clear whether these trajectories of state formation could ever have been fulfilled. First, rather than seeking independent statehood, it seems more accurate to argue that the leaders of each of these entities sought to either maintain (Christians) or challenge (Muslims) the status quo. The war was more about control of the state and the reordering of the political relationship between communities. Only the LF ever suggested that their second option would be separation.[18] Second, all factions were equally constrained by three factors that stood in the way of potential attempts at creating their own state-like entities: (1) the problems of securing control over contiguous territory and a homogeneous population; (2) the difficulty of maintaining social and political coherence and unity within the various cantons and communities; and (3) the symbiotic advantage in maintaining some degree of economic cooperation between the various militia enterprises. We turn now to an analysis of each of these factors.

The Ability to Secure Contiguous Territory and a Homogeneous Population

One of the principal features of a Weberian state is to set borders over a defined and relatively homogeneous population. As we have seen earlier, however, defining clear territorial boundaries for any of the religious communities in Lebanon has never been an easy task. Indeed, with the prewar acceleration of migration to Beirut, a city that by the early 1970s accommodated over 50 percent of the Lebanese population, the prospects seemingly became even more remote. Nonetheless, the war brought on attempts both to create rigid boundaries between the different cantons and to homogenize the population within. Perhaps the best example of this is the emergence of the

"Green Line" between Christian East Beirut and Muslim West Beirut. A similar territorialization of confessional control in Beirut took place with the emergence of Shi`a control in the southern suburbs. In effect, Beirut witnessed the hardening of boundaries between the various religious quarters that already had deep historical roots, albeit increasingly porous ones before the war. Outside of Beirut, the LF established territorial control over the northern part of Mount Lebanon, Kisrawan, as well the coastal strip extending from Beirut to the northern town of Jubayl—an area already predominantly Christian. By far the most territorially and religiously coherent canton, however, was the preserve of the Druze, located in the southern parts of Mount Lebanon and the Shouf mountains.

It should be noted, however, that even the most seemingly organic communal canton—the Druze-controlled Shouf region—emerged only following a process of "ethnic cleansing" in the mixed Maronite–Druze areas along the "borders" with Mount Lebanon to the north. None of the other cantons were able to represent all of their co-religionists in a unified, comprehensive, and territorial manner. While the "Christian canton" was the largest and arguably one of the most homogeneous following "ethnic cleansing" of Palestinian camps in its midst, the LF control over Mount Lebanon, Kisrawan, and the coastal strip in between did not include Maronite areas to the north—such as the Zghorta that was ruled by the rival Maronite militia of the Franjieh clan—let alone those in the south of the country. The Shi`a populations of Lebanon were even more dispersed with pockets located in Beirut, in the north of the country near Jubayl, in the hinterland areas of the southern and eastern Beka`a, as well as in the south. Finally, the Sunnis lived predominantly in the cities of Beirut, Tripoli, and Sidon along the coast—areas that proved notoriously resistant to policies aimed at the pursuit of ethnic cleansing.[19]

Maintaining Social and Political Coherence and Unity

One of the interesting aspects of the civil war in Lebanon was the degree to which the fighting was intra-rather than intercommunal in nature. As noted earlier, this has been a long-standing feature of Lebanese politics—one fueled by intra-elite competition that did not diminish with the onset of war. Indeed, with the demise of the minimal regulatory framework provided by the state, intra-elite competition increasingly spilled over into violence. Examples abound, be it the rivalry between Amal and Hizballah for the loyalty of the Lebanese Shi`a or the series of smaller turf battles within Beirut between various Sunni militias. Perhaps the most illustrative case of intra-communal rivalry and dissent, however, came from within the LF for control of Lebanon's largest and most powerful wartime canton.

During the initial stages of the Lebanese civil war, for example, the LF described themselves as the military "arm" of the Christian resistance, a label indicating the existence of other actors claiming political and social representation of the community. By 1979, this began to change with the Joint Command Council of the LF proceeding—often forcibly—to integrate the smaller militias of all Christian parties under its command. The integration process culminated in July 7, 1980 with the destruction of the last independent military units of the National Liberal Party.[20] The dismantling of the smaller militias was instrumental in "reducing the political parties' capacity for independent action outside the framework of the Lebanese Forces."[21] However, while the array of outside autonomous parties and interests were reigned in, the LF remained susceptible to internal divisions and rivalries. The assassination of the newly elected Lebanese president and LF leader, Bashir Gemayel, by a dissident group within the LF in 1982 was a powerful reminder of the enduring centrifugal forces and interests that pulled at the coerced coherence of the LF. Even when in 1985, the militia laid claim to the monopoly of political and military power in the Christian canton, this did not preclude the emergence of challengers to its supremacy, particularly in the person of Army commander Michel 'Awn. The "struggle between brothers," as the nine-month-long internecine fighting between the LF and the Lebanese Army under 'Awn's command became known, was one of the most violent and destructive episodes of the Lebanese civil war.[22]

A further factor that complicated the efforts of those seeking to control wartime cantons was the prior extent of communal organization—what we have labeled here as the degree of "political development." On the one hand, it is clear that the high levels of institutional development and functional differentiation within the various sectarian communities contribute to the social viability of wartime cantons. The various youth leagues of the Maronite Church, for example, provided the LF with a ready-made basis for recruitment. However, it is also clear that these very same institutions also acted as an autonomous source of power, constraining the militia's efforts to monopolize communal representation. Be they cultural, social, or religious, these institutions worked to confine militias to a more narrow security role. The high degree of institutional differentiation within the Maronite community, for example, contributed to the adoption of a style of statecraft by the LF that Picard labeled "authoritarian corporatism"—characterized by political efforts to quell all kinds of internal dissent. Conversely, we would argue that the more unified and uncontested control of Hizballah by religious clerics combined with the relative underdevelopment of social institutions within the Shi'a community effectively gave them a monopoly over their followers—save for the competition from Amal.

The Political Economy of War and the Sustainability of Cantons

Perhaps the most important factor determining the viability of cantons—at least in the short term—was the sustainability of their financial base. The ability to generate resources was important not only to finance the conflict itself but also to offer combatants and their families a range of benefits to offset the dangers associated with membership.[23] Initially, all Lebanese militias offered social services to the populations under their control. For example, the revenue generated by the LF in the early 1980s was instrumental in the provision of collective goods to the population of the Christian enclave. The establishment of a subsidized public transport network, garbage collection, a police force, and a legal system, among others, reinforced perceptions of the militia as "of and for the people." The LF also provided subsidized services—education, housing, medical care, summer camps for war children—which created a network of patrimonial ties between the militia and the population. The success of this policy was reflected in popular perceptions of LF militiamen as *al-shabab*, literally "youngsters" but a term connoting identification and belonging. And while the popular committees of the LF were the most organized and extensive network, the Druze Civil Administration of the Mountain did not lag far behind. Even the more disparate services of latecomers into the game such as Amal and Hizballah met the basic needs of populations under their control.[24]

However, Lebanon's narrow economic base and preponderant service economy was a difficult terrain upon which to build a successful and thriving war economy. Unlike resource-rich African countries where control of diamond mines and other natural resources provides the militias with a relatively autonomous resource base, in Lebanon militia funds initially came from two sources: plunder and revolutionary taxation. In 1975, combatants raided the banking district in downtown Beirut, broke into safe coffers, and stole their contents. The militias collectively partook in ransacking the Beirut harbor. But as lucrative as these acts of looting might have been, they were one-time deals that could not provide a sustained flow of income. In those early days, the only other source of income was revolutionary taxation of civilians. As early as 1976, for example, the Christian militias established the "national treasury," a highly sophisticated internal revenue department in charge of generating revenue for the war effort. The money came from direct taxation of individual households and from ransoms extorted from industrialists and wealthy businessmen.[25] Other factions engaged in similar practices.

The limitations and difficulties of revenue generation caused by the narrow Lebanese resource base also led militias to continue to try and cultivate their external resource base in the form of political and military alliances with regional powers interested in the outcome of the civil war. But it was clear that this came at a cost as the assistance of external funders was often conditional on the adoption of their political agenda. Of note here is the emergence of dissatisfaction between the various Muslim militias and their Palestinian allies when it became clear that the Palestinians were more interested in pursuing the fight against Israel than helping their allies get the upper hand in the struggle to change the status quo in Lebanon. Equally illustrative of the conditional nature of external support was the precipitous falling out between the LF and Israel when LF leader Bashir Gemayel reneged on a promise to deliver a separate peace with the Jewish state if he were elected to the presidency of the Lebanese Republic. The result was a new dynamic whereby militias sought new ways to both generate and diversify their sources of revenue. The establishment of a holding company in 1986 by the LF, for example, led to a situation by the end of the war whereby their reliance on indirect taxation within the canton amounted to little more than 5 percent of the militia's considerable revenue. It is also apparent that much of this economic activity was illicit in nature. Hizballah, for example, in addition to its continued patronage from Iran, generated tremendous revenues from its association with the production and trafficking of hashish in the Beka`a; and Amal funds were generated in part through the traffic of conflict diamonds by Lebanese traders in Africa. Other militias became enmeshed in a variety of global smuggling rings—perhaps the most noted when revealed in the early postwar period in Lebanon, being the selling of rights to dump toxic waste in the country.

What is interesting about this move toward the more autonomous generation of profits and revenues by the various militias was the realization on their part that profits could be maximized if militias entered into a minimum regime of cooperation. Militias on different sides of the conflict, for example, seldom attacked each other's main sources of income. The operations of illegal harbors were rarely disrupted; nor were attacks targeted at the elimination of such vital commercial interests as fuel and petroleum installations. Finally, while some militias attempted to homogenize the territory under their control, they maintained open border posts, allowing the controlled movement of people and goods across the "green lines." Of course, the militias benefited from this scheme by collecting "visa" fees and customs taxes.[26]

This (covert) cooperation, however profitable economically, ultimately weakened the militias in two ways. First, as militias became richer and more "profitable," internal struggles over the control and distribution of resources fed into the problem of intra-group unity. From the mid-1980s onward, the LF, the Progressive Socialist Party (PSP), and Amal emerged as the three major warring factions in Lebanon and their relations could best be described as a precarious balance of power. However, within each community, contenders for power emerged who targeted the economic assets of the militias in their strife for control of the group. Once again, the most telling example comes from the Christian canton where in the 1989 and 1990 confrontations between the LF and General 'Awn, control of the fifth basin of the Beirut harbor (one of the nerves of LF economic power) became a major bone of contention between the two sides. In 1990, the forces loyal to 'Awn targeted the economic foundations of LF power in what would become the most violent, destructive, and costly episode of the civil war.

Second, and in a paradox of sorts, the more militias moved toward state-like functional differentiation the more their popular legitimacy dwindled. The case of the LF is particularly indicative in part because of the path of corporate authoritarianism that the group elected to pursue. For the LF, things began to change in the second part of the 1980s. The growing financial empire of the militia created a psychological distance between the "faceless bureaucratic monster" and the population of the Christian enclave.[27] Moreover, transgressions committed by militiamen—in spite of efforts by the leadership to punish transgressors—reinforced the brigand stereotype. In 1985, as economic conditions deteriorated and resentment started to grow among the population, the LF dropped direct taxes on households and businesses. In 1989, the militia stepped up its involvement in social services and the provision of collective goods to shore up declining popular support. However, mounting popular exasperation with the LF outweighed potential patrimonial benefits in the decision of many Christians to join the campaign of General Michel 'Awn to "restore the rule of law."[28]

Hence, during the 16-year-long civil war in Lebanon, militia enterprises developed a number of state-like features and capacities. This usually started with the creation of a unified security apparatus and was followed subsequently by the emergence of administrative capacity with respect to both fiscal and social activities. War certainly seems to have contributed to the emergence of routinized political entities in Lebanon. However, for a variety of reasons that affected the militia enterprises to different degrees, the consolidation of control over populations and territories proved an elusive process. Borders between most of the cantons, for example, were fluid, subject to contestation, and/or impossible to create given the scattered and intermingled nature of much of the Lebanese population; the institutionalization of a political process that contained both intra-elite and elite–mass relations also proved difficult and, paradoxically, seemed to have been made more complicated in cantons with a high degree of social complexity; and finally, the search for political autonomy was compromised by the realization that some degree of cooperation provided better advantages. The result was a system of cantons in wartime Lebanon that were riddled with contradictions and inconsistencies.

From "Cantons" to "Shadow States": Political Reconstruction in Postwar Lebanon

Postwar Lebanon has witnessed the dismantling of the various militia enterprises and cantons and the reemergence of the state as the central focus of Lebanese political life.

This process is symbolized by a number of factors—the catalyst being the reconstitution of Lebanon's elite social compact, the Ta'if Accord in 1989, backed up by the coercive support of the Syrian government. Out of Ta'if has flowed a number of other centralizing processes, among them being the demilitarization of most of the wartime militias, the emergence of a large-scale program of national reconstruction, and the revival of activism from Lebanon's quieted civil society calling for the strengthening of a socially conscious and more universalist public sphere in the country. All provide hopeful signs of the reintegration of Lebanon's national political economy. Yet, below the surface lies a more ambiguous and fragmented political reality. After examining the various centripetal forces in postwar Lebanese politics, this chapter will turn to an analysis of how these centralizing processes have also provided increased opportunities for the renewal of predatory practices by Lebanon's political elite, practices that have led to the strengthening of the institutional foundations of micro though not necessarily state-like power in the country.

The Ta'if Accord was the watershed event in Lebanon's 16-year civil war, providing a political framework for the reconstitution of the Lebanese consociational republic. Like other compacts before it—notably the 1926 Constitution—Ta'if encompassed two seemingly contradictory main elements: an agreement on an adjusted power-sharing formula that divided power on an equal basis both between Christians and Muslims and between the three main religious communities (Maronite, Sunni, and Shi'a); and a commitment to move toward the de-confessionalization of the political system. Parliamentary elections have now been held on three subsequent occasions (1992, 1996, and 2000) and with increasing degrees of legitimacy and these have been supplemented by municipal elections (1998) and the parliamentary election (albeit constitutionally delayed) of a new president (1998). While elections have certainly been open to manipulation, fraud, intimidation, and indeed boycotts in the early years, they nonetheless indicate the reemergence of a "national political field" that had all but disintegrated during the civil war period.[29] This reconstituted "national political field" has been further if coercively supported and regulated by the Syrians—both by the presence of in excess of 40,000 troops and by the co-opting power of their expanding political networks. Indeed, the Syrian presence is in many ways the key to understanding the relative stability of Lebanon's postwar period.

However, while Lebanon's political center has been reconstituted, it has certainly not moved in the direction outlined in the Ta'if Accord toward the elimination of confessionalism; there is more continuity than contrast between Lebanon's prewar, war, and postwar worlds. First, it is clear that consociationalism, based as it is on the existence of "segmented autonomy" and of "distinct lines of cleavage" between different religious confessions,[30] continues to institutionalize and entrench factional bases of power in Lebanon; it not only reflects the fragmented political reality, it also reinforces it. For example, despite the existence of parliaments and constitutions, real decision making power in postwar Lebanon lies with a "troika" of sectarian political leaders that emerged at the end of the war and who represent—at least nominally if not always faithfully—the interests of the three largest religious communities in the country. Politics, therefore, is more the result of informal confessional bargaining processes—mediated by an outside and occupying power (Syria)—than it is of formal democratic practice. Moreover, as has traditionally been the case in Lebanon, this confessional logic flows right through the political system with entire branches of the state being effectively handed over and clientelistically used by a variety of different factional leaders. This includes some of the key institutions associated with Lebanon's postwar reconstruction process such the Council for Development and Reconstruction (CDR)—the preserve of Lebanon's Sunni prime minister throughout much of the 1990s, Rafik Hariri—and the Ministry of the Displaced—the preserve of the Druze leader, Walid Jumblatt.

This fragmented and colonized nature of the Lebanese state has been reinforced by the manner in which wartime militia leaders have been reintegrated into the political system. Certainly, with the exception of Hizballah, militia leaders have had little choice but to give up their right to monopolize the means of violence within their own terri- tory. That role has been transferred to the Syrian army and a reconstituted Lebanese army. Military hardware has either been returned to the Lebanese state or sold on the black market to other conflict zones—notably in the Balkans.[31] In exchange, however, militia leaders have been granted an amnesty from all wartime atrocities, providing them with an opportunity to maintain and rechannel their influence into the political arena.

Lebanon's "national political field," therefore, is very fragile and weak, full of contra- dictory social and political interests that now include former warlords.[32] The precari- ousness of this unity is symbolized by the inability of the system to confront an array of urgent but difficult problems, be it wartime injustices and "the disappeared," the endemic and systematic postwar spread of high-level corruption, let alone the future of Lebanon's 350,000-strong community of Palestinian refugees. Hence, while militias have moved toward reintegration back into the Lebanese postwar political system and have given up their right to have formal control over pieces of territory and the means of violence, the nature of the reintegration process has essentially been favorable to the preservation of these entities in a transformed politicized form.

Whether or not former militia entities have been able to take advantage of these opportunities, however, has largely depended upon the degree to which they can suc- cessfully maintain and develop the wartime economic and social aspects of their power; in other words, how the assets, "infrastructural power" and economic interests behind Lebanon's wartime states-within-states have adjusted to the postwar period. Like the Syrian-sponsored Ta'if Accord in the political realm, Lebanon's postwar program of reconstruction has provided a powerful force for the reintegration of wartime militia economies. The program is the brainchild of Lebanon's second postwar prime minister, Rafik Hariri. Dubbed Horizon 2000, it has been designed to reestablish Lebanon as a financial and commercial center in the Middle East region. On the ground, the program has accomplished much from an infrastructural point of view: roads have been rebuilt including the highway from Tripoli to Sidon, electrical generation has improved sub- stantially, and telephone services have been significantly upgraded, facilitated by the emergence of a cell phone network. The centerpiece of the reconstruction program, the holding company responsible for reconstructing the downtown core of Beirut called Solidere, has also made enormous strides. Moreover, the strategic approach with its emphasis on infrastructural development and its commitment to the maintenance of an "ultra liberal economic environment" has successfully attracted the mutual interest of Lebanon's otherwise fractious political elite. The opportunity to reinvest accumulated wartime capital into a more legitimate reconstruction program has proved especially attractive to former militia leaders—eager to compensate for the loss of the more illicit wartime methods of accumulation. Indeed, as Picard has written, it all seemed to pro- vide "a perfect opportunity for the state to rein in the militia economy by facilitating their integration into the leading sectors of Lebanon's re-emerging postwar national economy."[33]

Hence, Lebanon has witnessed a successful dismantling of the overt infrastructure of the various wartime economies. First, it appears that the fiscal infrastructure of most of the wartime states-within-states has largely disappeared and/or been handed back to the Lebanese state. The Lebanese state, for example, has regained control of the various ports in the country. Second, there has been an erosion of the economic power of militia leaders—especially with respect to the LF. Property and assets once in their hands has now been privatized and dispersed to a variety of powerful civilian economic actors. Picard goes further and argues that this erosion of the economic power of militia leaders has also resulted in a relative decline in the "patrimonial nature of politics." In other words, the accumulation of capital is less likely to be used toward the consolidation of a state-like political project.[34] Third, it is also clear that the regional and global economic context out of which emerged the initial attempts at constructing states-within-states has dramatically changed. On the one hand, the globalization of finance and the adverse consequences for Lebanon's goal of being able to recapture its past glory as a regional financial center has lessened the long-term commitment of investors to keeping their capital within the country. This has been paralleled by the increased attractiveness of greater economic integration with transnational economic networks—criminal and legitimate. Mittelman has called this a process of "de-territorialization" whereby local economic networks, criminal or otherwise, no longer exclusively base their accumulative potential upon control of territorialized environments; rather, they become "dis-embedded from their socio-cultural context."[35] Although different in scope than the prewar external linkages of the Lebanese economy, this trend only reinforces the ultraliberal and outward-oriented characteristics of this economy—a trend that was initially conceived as a way of compensating for Lebanon's lack of natural resources and industrial capacity but which also accounted in part for the country's vulnerability to developments outside its borders. Perhaps more than anything else, it is this globalization-induced decline in the economic logic behind the cultivation of territorially based political projects that has dealt a death blow to the possibility of the return of states-within-states in Lebanon.

One might expect this to lead to the kind of "durable disorder" in Lebanon that Duffield has written about in the context of West Africa—characterized by the increasing irrelevance of the state in the context of the rise of supranational, transnational, and local actors.[36] This has not happened for a couple of important reasons. First, it is clear that Lebanese economic and political elites recognize the benefits of maintaining a broader framework for economic accumulation than was provided during the war. As has been argued earlier, it was in part the near total breakdown of the Lebanese political economy in the latter 1980s that was a major contributing factor in the exhaustion of the conflict.[37] Not only does a united political framework provide a more efficient method of regulating the competition between elites for scarce resources, it also provides a mechanism for maximizing the size of the pool—both by ensuring as open and unregulated an economic arena as possible and by using the coercive instruments of the state to limit the redistributive pressures from below that seek to broaden the clientelistic bargain and limit the opportunities for "extractive" corruption. As evidenced by the successful and coercive implementation of austerity measures in the face of significant social opposition from below and by the mounting evidence of endemic corruption—what Malik has called "the politics of tycoonism"[38]—political elites have worked this minimal political cooperation to great advantage.

Moreover, in order to have access to the state, political elites in Lebanon still need some kind of localized and personalized base of influence. From rural areas like the Zghorta in the north where the Franjieh clan continues to compete for predominant political influence[39] to urban areas in Beirut where the battle for political preeminence within both the Sunni and the Shi`a community remains intense,[40] Lebanon remains a country characterized by clientelistic battles for control over local areas. However, the wartime political logic for controlling local areas has now been reversed. Political elites in Lebanon are returning to the prewar pattern of using local bases of power to enhance their leverage at the national level all the while using the resources of the state to quell challenges to their dominance at the local level. To put it another way, after a prolonged but unsuccessful wartime experiment aimed at the creation of states-within-states, political elites in postwar Lebanon have returned to their historical preference for the more diffuse option of "shadow states."[41]

This symbiotic rather than zero-sum relationship between the local and the national is also in evidence when examining postwar Lebanese politics in the sphere of social welfare—perhaps the most institutionally developed component of the various sectarian communities in Lebanon. Indeed, as we have seen, the war resulted in the accelerated development of sectarian-based social welfare institutions, particularly with respect to the previously underserviced Shi`a community. Yet, the social arms of the various states-within-states remained clearly subordinate to their broader strategic and economic activities. As the war drew to a close, many of these institutions, despite their association with militia-based cantons, experienced a dramatic decline in their access to finance and, hence, in the quality of the services they were able to offer. They too, therefore, saw advantage in the reconstitution of the Lebanese state at the end of the war that would free them from the clutches of their militia leaders while providing a more stable basis of funding. As in the case of Hizballah, they saw advantages in being included for the first time into the Lebanese state's system of confessional resource distribution.

However, an examination of the politics surrounding the rebuilding of Lebanon's confessionally based social welfare institutions reveals much about both the nature of the "national political field" that was evolving in postwar Lebanon and of its component "shadow state" parts. Consistent with the traditional dynamics of Lebanon's confessional system, those seeking to rejuvenate and modernize institutions neglected and damaged during the war were interested in the reemergence of the Lebanese state only in so much as it could provide them with finance and, with that, leave them alone. It was autonomy they sought more than anything else, both from their aspiring confessional representatives during the war as well as from the Lebanese state and from civic forces seeking to bolster the presence and penetration of more rationalized and universal state regulations in the postwar world. The emergence of NGOs, networks, and groups within Lebanese civil society, for example, that called for a more progressive and universal system of social service funding were looked upon by the established and confessionally based social welfare institutions as a direct threat to their guarded status within the country[42]—and they fought back both vigorously and successfully, calling in, when need arose, the array of other confessional institutional power bases for support.[43]

Confessionalism, therefore, is a resource to preserve and protect the autonomy of the factional. The irony of Lebanese politics, however, is that it is not a durable resource, riven as it is by factions within and intertwined with interests outside. By itself, the experience of the Lebanese war proves that it, and the cantons that emerged from its logic, cannot stand alone. The experience of Lebanon in peacetime also suggests, however, that it is a resource too entrenched and too useful for confessional elites to discard. In that sense, confessionalism is not the basis of the political system in Lebanon; the real component parts are the numerous and diffuse factional interests in the country. Rather, confessionalism as institutionalized at the national level is the mediating principle that allows the various factional interests in Lebanon to coexist within some kind of unified, albeit loose and unstable national framework.

Notes

1. The title refers to Kamal Salibi's *A House of Many Mansions* (London: I.B. Taurus, 1988).
2. Michael Hudson, "The Problem of Authoritative Power in Lebanese Politics: Why Consociationalism Failed," in Nadim Shehadi and Dana Haffar Mills, eds., *Lebanon: A History of Conflict and Consensus* (London: The Centre for Lebanese Studies, I.B. Tauris, 1998), p. 223.
3. Robert Jackson, *Quasi-States: Sovereignty, International Relations, and the Third World* (New York: Cambridge University Press, 1990).
4. Ussama Makdisi, *The Culture of Sectarianism: Community, History and Violence in Nineteenth-Century Ottoman Lebanon* (Berkeley: University of California Press, 2000), p. 65.
5. Ibid., p. 94.
6. Ibid., p.163.
7. Michael Johnson, *All Honourable Men: The Social Origins of War in Lebanon* (London: I.B. Taurus, 2001).
8. Farid Khazen, "Lebanon's Communal Elite-Mass Politics: The Institutionalization of Disintegration," in *The Beirut Review*, No. 3 (Spring 1992).
9. Michael Johnson, *Class and Client in Beirut: The Sunni Muslim Community and the Lebanese State, 1840–1985* (New York: Ithaca Press, 1985). See also Guilain Denoeux, *Urban Unrest in the Middle East: A Comparative Study of Informal Networks in Egypt, Iran, and Lebanon* (Albany: SUNY Press, 1993) and Samir Khalaf, *Lebanon's Predicament* (New York: Columbia University Press, 1987).
10. Ibid.
11. Charles Tilly, "War Making and State Making as Organized Crime," in Peter Evans, Dietrich Rueschemeyer, and Theda Skocpol, eds., *Bringing the State Back in* (Cambridge, Mass.: Cambridge University Press, 1985), pp. 169–191.
12. Robert Bates, *Prosperity and Violence: The Political Economy of Development* (New York: W.W. Norton, 2001).
13. Cf. Jeffrey Herbst, *State and Power in Africa: Comparative Lessons in Authority and Control* (Princeton: Princeton University Press, 2000).
14. Elizabeth Picard, "The Political Economy of Civil War in Lebanon," in Steven Hydeman, ed., *War, Institutions and Social Change in the Middle East* (Berkeley: University of California Press, 2000), pp. 312–317.
15. Ibid., p. 313.
16. Ibid., p. 314.
17. Ibid., p. 316.
18. Marie-Christine Aulas, "The Socio-Ideological Development of the Maronite Community: The Emergence of the Phalanges and the Lebanese Forces," *Arab Studies Quarterly*, Vol. 7, No. 4 (1997), pp. 1–27; see also Elaine Hagopian, "Maronite Hegemony to Maronite Militancy: The Creation and Disintegration of Lebanon," *Third World Quarterly*, Vol. 11, No. 4 (1989), pp. 101–117 and "Redrawing the Map in the Middle East: Phalangist Lebanon and Zionist Israel," *Arab Studies Quarterly*, Vol. 5 (Fall 1983), pp. 324–330.
19. Cf. William Harris, *Faces of Lebanon: Sects, Wars and Global Extensions* (Princeton: Markus Wiener Publishers, 1996).

20. Karim Pakradouni, *As-Salaam al-Mafqud: `Ahd Iliyas Sarkis, 1976–1982* [The Lost Peace: The Mandate of Iliyas Sarkis, 1976–1982] (Beirut: `Abr al-Sharq lil-Manshurat, 1984); Jonathan Randal, *La guerre de mille ans*, Beatrice Vierne, translator (Paris: Grasset, 1985).

21. Paul Snider "The Lebanese Forces: Wartime Origins and Political Significance," in Edward Azar et al., eds., *The Emergence of a New Lebanon: Fantasy or Reality?* (New York: Praeger, 1984).

22. Annie Laurent, "A War between Brothers: The Army-Lebanese Forces Showdown in East Beirut," *The Beirut Review*, Vol. 1, No. 1(Spring 1991).

23. Marie-Joëlle Zahar, *Fanatics, Mercenaries, Brigands . . . and Politicians: Militia Decision-Making and Civil Conflict Resolution*, unpublished dissertation, McGill University, Montreal, 2000.

24. Judith Harik, *The Public and Social Services of the Lebanese Militias*, papers on Lebanon, No. 14 (London: Centre for Lebanese Studies, 1995).

25. Marie-Joëlle Zahar, "Protégés, Clients, Cannon Fodder: Civilians in the Calculus of Militias," *Managing Armed Conflicts in the Twenty-first Century*, special issue of *International Peacekeeping*, Vol. 7, No. 4 (hiver 2001), pp. 107–128.

26. Elizabeth Picard, *Lebanon, A Shattered Country: Myths and Realities of Wars in Lebanon* (New York: Holmes and Meier, 2002); and Georges Corm, "The War System and Reestablishment of the State," in Dierdre Collings, ed., *Peace for Lebanon: From War to Reconstruction* (Boulder: Lynne Rienner, 1994).

27. Note the similar effect of dependence on outside revenue on relations between incipient state and society in Colombia. See chapter six.

28. Harris, *Faces of Lebanon.*

29. Cf. Sami Zubaida, *Islam, The People and the State* (London: I.B. Taurus, 1988).

30. Michael Hudson, "The Problem of Authoritative Power," p. 225.

31. Marie-Joelle Zahar, "Fanatics, Mercenaries, Brigand."

32. Hassan Krayem, "The Lebanese Civil War and the Taif Accord," in Paul Salem, ed., *Conflict Resolution in the Arab World: Selected Essays* (Beirut: American University of Beirut Press, 1997), p. 428.

33. Elizabeth Picard, "The Political Economy of Civil War." It is important to note, however, that the program does not conflict with external rent seeking such as Iranian assistance to Hizballah or Amal's African revenues. It does however clash with the nature of the wartime economy of the Lebanese Forces. The CDR and Solidere have monopolized economic activities associated with reconstruction and much as Prime Minister Rafik Hariri used these activities as a way of buying loyalty and weakening political opponents. This in many ways mirrors the structure of wartime economic relations in the Christian canton and the political uses to which these economic relations were put. In other terms, the two systems are based on a similar logic and would have been unable to coexist in the postwar era as each would be a direct competitor to the other. That the reasons why this competition never actualized lay in another realm does not in any way belie the importance of the observation.

34. Ibid., p. 318.

35. Ibid., p. 208.

36. Mark Duffield, "Globalization, Transborder Trade and War Economies," in Mats Berdal and David Malone, eds., *Greed and Grievance* (London: Lynne Rienner, 2000).

37. Cf. Clement Henry, "Prisoners' Financial Dilemmas: A Consociational Future for Lebanon?" *American Political Science Review*, Vol. 81 (March 1987), pp. 201–218.

38. Habib Malik, *Between Damascus and Jerusalem: Lebanon and Middle East Peace* (Washington: Washington Institute for Near East Policy, 1997), pp. 47–64. See also G. Denoeux and Robert Springborg, "Hariri's Lebanon," in *Middle East Policy* (October 1998).

39. Cf. Paul Kingston, "Patrons, Clients and Civil Society: Environmental Politics in Postwar Lebanon," in *Arab Studies Quarterly*, Vol. 43, No. 1 (Winter 2001), pp. 55–72. See also Michael Johnson, *All Honourable Men*.

40. Michael Johnson, *Class and Client in Beirut*. See also Mona Harb el-Kak, *Politiques Urbaines et Communale* (Beyrouth: Les Cahiers du CERMOC, 1996).

41. Cf. William Reno, "Shadow States and the Political Economy of War," in Mats Berdal and David Malone, eds., *Greed and Grievance* (Boulder: Lynne Rienner, 2000).

42. Cf. Paul Kingston, "The Hidden World of Governance: NGOs and Politics in the Disability Field of Postwar Lebanon," paper delivered to the Annual Meeting of the Middle East Studies Association of North America, November 2002.

43. Nawaf Salam, *la condition libanaise: des communautes, du citoyen et de l'etat* (Beyrouth: Editions Dar an-Nahar, 1998).

Chapter Six

Colombia: The Partial Collapse of the State and the Emergence of Aspiring State-Makers

Ana Maria Bejarano and Eduardo Pizarro[1]

Despite some opinions to the contrary,[2] Colombia is not a failing, failed, or collapsed state. Neither is it a "quasi-state," nor a "shadow state."[3] Colombia does, however, display many worrisome indicators of state decay and erosion: its 6,000 km of land boundaries are very porous, allowing for an unfettered flux of drugs and arms. Two million people have been internally displaced in the last decade, and another 1.2 million have left the country in the past five years.[4] With one of the highest homicide rates in the world the Colombian state is far from performing its most basic duty: guaranteeing the right to personal security.[5] Neither is it able to provide justice: in the last two decades, "the capacity of the penal system to investigate the homicides was reduced to one fifth of its original capacity."[6] Some key state institutions, such as the police and the judiciary, are too weak to confront the immense tide of criminality brought by the drug trade. The military has also become increasingly involved in the fight against drug-trafficking, which not only involves them further in domestic politics but also diverts them from their constitutional function: external defense. Many regions in the country are beyond the reach of the central state.

Historians have frequently pointed to the fact that the Colombian state, since its creation in the early nineteenth century, has traditionally been small, weak, and poor. While this is true, we want to argue that its traditional weakness took a downward turn in the last two decades of the twentieth century, reaching a point of "partial collapse" in the late 1980s and beginning of the 1990s. This turning point came as the result of two main factors: a divided elite and the emergence of powerful competitors, to the Left and to the Right, both of them financed by the rents accruing from the drug trade. Elite divisions contributed to the erosion of the state "from within," while the expansion and consolidation of its competitors meant a gradual erosion "from outside." Both trends, contributed to a spiral of state decay that led to a major contraction of the state's capacity to "broadcast its power" throughout the national territory and society.[7]

This steep erosion and contraction of the state has had many consequences, among them the consolidation of armed movements, on the Left and on the Right, which openly question the Colombian state's monopoly over the legitimate use of force. In this chapter, we will focus on the emergence and expansion of the two main rivals of the state: the *Fuerzas Armadas Revolucionarias de Colombia* (FARC), and the *Autodefensas Unidas de Colombia* (United Self-Defense Forces of Colombia, AUC), and will evaluate the extent to which we can classify them as states-within-states following the framework proposed by Ian Spears in chapter one around which this volume is organized. Our main argument is that, while the category put forth by Spears seems useful to frame and understand some of the political structures that emerge on the wake of state failure and collapse, particularly those that have a clear territorial base and a constituency demarcated by ethnic, linguistic, religious and/or national divisions, it does not seem to fit the types of entities that have emerged out of the increased weakness and even "partial collapse" of the Colombian state.

The consequences of this process of state erosion and partial collapse will be the main focus of this chapter. However, before we go into that discussion, we want to spend some time on the causes of the Colombian state's weakness and severe erosion in the last two decades. The contrast with other cases in the developing world seems at once stark and illuminating.

Alternative Sources of State Weakness: Colombia in Comparative Perspective

In his suggestive chapter entitled "States-Within-States: An Introduction to Their Empirical Attributes," Ian Spears seems to attribute the weakness and eventual failure of the state in the developing world to two main factors: first, to the fact that many of these states are "new," having recently emerged from decolonization, and second, to the fact that they are somehow "arbitrary," that is, incongruent with the societies formally under their jurisdiction. As happens with much of the recent literature on state failure, which is based mostly on African cases, Spears seems to overlook the peculiarities of one region in the developing world that does not seem to conform to this generalization—namely, Latin America. Indeed, the contrast between Africa and Latin America can be quite revealing. The states in Latin American are not new, and most of them are not perceived as "arbitrary" state units. And yet, many states in Latin America—not only Colombia, but also much of the Andean region (with the possible exception of Venezuela), as well as most of Central America—are considered weak, some even on the verge of breakdown.

Most Latin American states emerged in the early nineteenth century as a result of the wars of independence from the crumbling Spanish empire.[8] Modern state-formation in Latin America took place after the formation of the pioneer states of the modern Western world (France, England), but well before the wave of state-making in the second half of the twentieth century in Africa and Asia. Some Latin American states are even older than some states in Europe. Latin America should therefore be considered as an intermediate phenomenon, a "second wave" of state formation.

On the other hand, the states in Latin America are not "arbitrary state units," except in the obvious sense that every state is, in some sense, an arbitrary construct. In Latin America boundaries between nation-states were drawn in a much less arbitrary way than in Africa and parts of Asia, a fact that may be attributable to three factors. First, the entire region (with the sole exception of Brazil) was colonized by the same European power—Spain. Second, the administrative colonial units and borders were drawn mainly following geographical accidents (mountain ranges, rivers, and the like), which also affected the patterns of human occupation of the territory. Finally, the dual process of nation building and state formation has been taking place in Latin America for almost two centuries now. Even if it were solely for this time factor, these states have become much less arbitrary and much more congruent with their nations, so to speak, than most states in the rest of the developing world.

Additionally, the Latin American states have not confronted deeply dividing social cleavages such as those marked by competing national, ethnic, religious, or linguistic identities. Despite an increased mobilization on the part of the indigenous populations in the region in the last two decades of the twentieth century, there is not a single secessionist movement or challenge to national unity based on ethnic or national origin in the whole region.

Despite these crucial differences, the states of Latin America share some predicaments with most of the states of the developing world. Having been born in the periphery of the world system, they have followed a state-making path that differs significantly from its predecessors in Western Europe. For one, they have suffered little in the way of interstate wars.[9] Both Herbst and Centeno have made the case that this lack of interstate wars is central to explaining state weakness in Africa and Latin America, respectively. Both regions have lacked the driving force (war-making) that, according to Tilly, is behind modern state-formation, and also behind the democratic bargain between states and their populations.[10]

Very much like in Africa and some parts of Asia, there has also been plenty of internal warfare in Latin America.[11] This fact bears witness to the evident reality that the main challenges for most states in Latin America and elsewhere in the developing world are not necessarily related to defending their borders from outside challengers, but rather lie in establishing centralized control of the territory and population *inside* those same borders.

In summation, the states of Latin America share three key sources of weakness with the states in Africa and Asia—namely, their location in the periphery of the world system of states, their lack of interstate wars as an engine for state-making, and the abundance of internal conflict. By contrast with the rest of the developing world, however, they are not new nor arbitrary, nor do they face extremely divided societies. As a consequence, they cannot accurately be described with terms such as "quasi-states," "shadow states," or hollow "juridical shells."[12] Their weaknesses and shortcomings cannot be attributed to their "newness" or their "arbitrary" character. The sources of their weakness must be sought elsewhere. Based on the Colombian case and given the recent process of "partial collapse" of the state in that country—which is by far the most dramatic case of state weakness in Latin America today—we now proceed to explore some alternative sources of state weakness and failure.

Colombia: Erosion and Partial Collapse of the State[13]

Comparatively speaking the Colombian state has always been small, poor, and weak. The historical causes of the weakness of the Colombian state can be summarized as follows: a vast territory crossed by a very difficult geography; a weak economy, outwardly directed, with a very small domestic market; and finally, a nation with a very precarious common identity, crossed by regional and party cleavages.

By the mid-twentieth century, the intra-party warfare known as "*La Violencia*" (1948–1958) brought about a serious decay and crisis of the state's authority and capacity, which Paul Oquist labeled as the first "partial collapse" of the Colombian state.[14] The National Front period (1958–1974) gave way to a process of selective reconstruction and strengthening of the state.[15] However, in the 1980s, severe erosion was again caused by more contemporary factors, among them divisions within the country's elites, the protracted armed conflict with the guerrillas, and the challenges posed by drug-trafficking. The impact of this "double war," the debilitating combination of the counterinsurgency war, and the war against drugs, imposed on a state that has traditionally been weak, explains the second "partial collapse" of the Colombian state in the late 1980s.

This partial collapse of the state can be observed in two dimensions: geographically and functionally. In geographical terms, the adjective "partial" refers to the fact that the central state is unable to extend its reach throughout the territory, particularly the peripheral zones beyond the agricultural frontier. The Colombian state has never been able to broadcast its power throughout the entire territory. This is a fact widely recognized and documented by geographers, historians, and sociologists, particularly those who have devoted their studies to the "*zonas de colonización*" or regions of recent settlement.[16] But it is also a fact that such capacity has shrunk in the last two decades, as a result of the capacity of rival armed organizations (the guerrillas and the paramilitaries) to occupy and control ever increasing portions of the national territory. This geographic contraction of the Colombian state has happened *in tandem* with the growth and expansion of the state's organized rivals, who have been successful at challenging the state's control over an increasing portion of the territory under its formal control and jurisdiction. In a functional sense, the collapse of the Colombian state is also "partial" in that while some state apparatuses (i.e. the bureaucracy, the technocracy, the administration, the representative bodies) retain certain coherence and capacity for action, other crucial state apparatuses have become increasingly unable to fulfill their functions and deliver the services that are expected from them (most notably security and justice) or have become totally disfigured with reference to their constitutional functions (i.e. the armed forces).

By making an argument about the "partial collapse" of the state in Colombia we want to differentiate this case from those instances where there has been a total collapse of the state as has been the case for example in Somalia, and other cases treated in the contemporary literature on "failed states."[17]

Proximate Causes of State Erosion and Contraction

Guerrilla warfare started in Colombia a decade before the Cuban revolution.[18] In contrast with the rest of Latin America, the Colombian guerrillas avoided their extermination in the 1960s and managed to consolidate in the 1970s. This consolidation is, in fact, evidence of the secular weakness of the Colombian state. What counts however, beyond the emergence and eventual consolidation of the guerrillas, in terms of explaining the recent erosion of state authority in Colombia, is the exhaustion caused by more than three decades of internal armed conflict. The amount of resources spent for counterinsurgency purposes, added to the organizational and budget distortions implied by the need to maintain an army fighting an internal war for more than 30 years, partially explains the current configuration of the Colombian state, the enlargement of its armed forces, and the weakness of other crucial state apparatuses such as the justice system.

In addition to the protracted conflict with the guerrillas, a second cause of state weakness points to the lack of consensus among elites (political, economic, and military) on the appropriate strategy to confront this armed opposition. As suggested by Mauceri, the absence of a coherent political project shared by the elites is perhaps one of the most important causes of the weakness of the Colombian state.[19] Starting with the Betancur government (1982–1986), and because of the negotiation policy advocated by the president, a deep division among the elites has become even more evident. While some sectors have insisted on a negotiated settlement of the armed conflict, others have preferred to privatize and decentralize the counterinsurgency effort by supporting paramilitary groups and bypassing the role of the state in keeping order within its boundaries.[20] Even within the state itself, while some sectors have insisted in a political exit to the armed *impasse*, others (particularly in the armed forces) have offered these private justice groups (paramilitaries, self-defense groups, death squads, etc.) the legal coverage and logistical support needed in order to carry out their counterinsurgency strategy unfettered. Clearly, the so-called paramilitary armies in Colombia and the abdication of power by some sectors within the Colombian state, are the consequence of a political split among the elites.

The 1980s also witnessed the expansion of a market for illegal drugs in the United States and the increasing role of Colombian entrepreneurs in these transnational drug circuits. Drug-trafficking certainly occupies an important place in any explanation of the Colombian crisis, not in and of itself, as a phenomenon exogenous to politics, but instead precisely on account of its multiple economic, social, and political ramifications, particularly its impact on the process of state erosion and decay. The criminal organizations linked to the drug business have had immense and devastating consequences for society and politics in Colombia.[21] On the one hand, the drug dealers have sought to translate their enormous fortunes into political influence and have gained access to political decision-making processes via multiple paths, including the creation of personal electoral vehicles, their open participation in the traditional political parties, their financing of electoral campaigns,[22] and the enormous power they have in local politics. On the other hand, in order to combat the U.S.-backed anti-narcotic policies implemented by the state, the narcotraffickers have resorted to all kinds of means ranging from bribery and corruption, all the way to death threats, assassination of all types of officials (prison guards, policemen, judges, magistrates, military officers, and politicians) and the use of large-scale terrorism.

Besides its direct impact on the state, the rents produced by the drug trade have fed all armed actors in Colombia. From the private militias guarding the drug dealers, to the paramilitary groups, and even the guerrillas—all have based their expansion on the resources extracted from the drug business. The 1980s and 1990s boom in the drug trade changed the magnitude of the armed conflict in Colombia. Thanks to the impact of drug-trafficking, the state has seen its capacity diminish not only in absolute terms—as a result of corruption, the threat and the use of force—but also in relative terms: the rents accruing from drugs have allowed its rivals to expand their reach and their operational capacities at the same time that the state is losing its own.

In his article "War Making and State Making as Organized Crime," Charles Tilly draws a bold picture of the state-making process. According to Tilly, states perform four basic tasks, derived from their monopoly over the means of coercion: (1) "war-making," that is, eliminate or neutralize their foreign enemies; (2) "state-making," that is eliminate or neutralize their rivals within the territory; (3) "protection," that is eliminate or neutralize the enemies of their clients; and (4) "extraction," that is, acquiring the resources needed to fulfill the first three tasks. All four activities depend on the capacity of the state to monopolize the concentrated means of coercion. They may overlap and cross each other, but most importantly, success in fulfilling one of them generally reinforces the rest. In Tilly's own words "a state that successfully eradicates its internal rivals strengthens its ability to extract resources, to wage war, and to protect its chief supporters."[23] Inversely, we would argue, the incapacity to fulfill any one of them tends to weaken all the rest. A state like the Colombian one, incapable of eliminating or neutralizing its rivals within the territory, is neither able to eliminate or neutralize the enemies of its potential clients (the citizens), nor to extract the resources needed in order to perform its basic functions. Therefore, the inability of the state to monopolize the means of coercion gives rise to a vicious circle, which keeps on debilitating it, while its rivals find a fertile terrain in which to grow and thrive. As a result, Colombia has experienced, in the last two decades, the emergence and expansion of a panoply of groups with diverse ideological signs, apparently rival proto-states that accumulate power given their capacity to provide the basic goods that the state, by definition, should be able to provide: protection and justice. Whether we should consider any of these as a state-within-a-state is the question to which we now turn our attention.

The Consequences of State Decay: The Emergence of Aspiring State-Makers

The "partial collapse" of the Colombian state, plus the strategic location of Colombia in the international narcotics market, have cleared the way for the emergence and expansion of many different entities, some of which on the surface satisfy Spears's definition of states-within-states:

> States-within-states have imposed effective control over a territory within a larger state and may have an impressive array of institutional structures which, among other things, allow taxes to be collected, services to be provided, and business with other international actors to be conducted. Yet they lack the very thing that quasi-states do possess: juridical status.

Within Colombia's political landscape two groups would seem to illustrate the realities comprised under the concept of a state-within-a-state: the oldest guerrilla group in the country, the FARC[24] and the recently formed umbrella organization that groups many of the right-wing paramilitary groups, the AUC.[25] However, and despite appearances to the contrary, we will claim that neither the FARC nor the paramilitaries (especially the centralized AUC) form part of the universe of entities that should be included under Spears's concept of states-within-states. After a careful analysis of the available information on these two organizations organized according to Spears's proposed list of key elements of statehood, we have come to the conclusion that other labels, such as the more commonly used of "warlords," "coercive entrepreneurs," "aspiring state-makers," or "proto-states" are more adequate to portray the political realities of Colombia today, in the aftermath of a partial collapse of the central state. As our treatment of the Colombian case will show, it seems that Spears's proposed key elements of statehood are much more likely to be present in those cases in which there is a secessionist movement based on national, ethnic, linguistic, or religious identities—than in those cases of armed movements based on ideological, class-based appeals.

The Question of Territory

Colombia is a case where there is clearly "a disjuncture between the territory which is ostensibly under a state's jurisdiction and that which is effectively controlled by the state."[26] However, in the Colombian case, this disjuncture is not caused by any discrepancy between the actual boundaries of the state and the ones that have been recognized internationally, but by the sheer incapacity of the Colombian state to "broadcast power" throughout a large and geographically daunting terrain.[27] What's at stake in the Colombian case is not the size or the shape of the territory under the state's jurisdiction. There are no competing interpretations, neither among Colombians nor among its neighbors, about the geographic entity that should be called Colombia. The problem is rather that the central state in Colombia, due to factors that we have previously mentioned, has been unable to project its control and extend its authority, evenly, throughout the territory and the population that formally fall under its jurisdiction.[28] In parallel fashion to Herbst's findings about the African continent, in Colombia a daunting geography, ecological diversity, and underpopulation (at least in some areas) have also constituted great obstacles to state formation and consolidation.

The problem, however, is not only that the Colombian state has historically failed to control the territory under its jurisdiction, but also that its capacity to do so has increasingly "contracted" in the last two decades. In some regions, the state has delegated the fulfillment of basic functions to right-wing organizations such as the AUC, thus clearly abdicating its power in their favor. This is the case in various regions within the mid-Magdalena Valley (particularly the municipality of Puerto Boyacá) and wider regions in the north of Antioquia (most particularly the banana exporting region of Urabá) and the department of Córdoba (in the areas surrounding the municipality of Valencia).

In other areas, the state's control is seriously challenged by rival armed organizations (the guerrillas), as in the zones where coca-growing has expanded during the last two decades (the lowlands east of the Andean range, including the Orinoco and the Amazon basins). Additionally, in 1998, and as the result of a fledgling negotiation process between the government and the FARC, the former ceded its control over five municipalities in the departments of Meta and Caquetá (the so-called *zona de despeje* or demilitarized zone) to the FARC's central command. Together, these five municipalities comprised a territory the size of Switzerland (42,000 sq. km). However, this only represents 3.6 percent of the total territory under the Colombian states' jurisdiction (which is 1,147,148 sq. km).[29] In addition, the territory covering these five municipalities is populated only by 100,000 inhabitants who represent a mere 0.24 percent of Colombia's total population estimated at 41,564,000 people.[30]

This demilitarized zone only lasted until February 20, 2002, when the peace negotiations broke down between the government and the FARC. President Pastrana declared an end to the negotiation process in a televised speech and the armed forces took control of the five municipalities immediately thereafter—which goes to show how little control the FARC had gained on this piece of territory. Throughout the period when they were granted absolute control of this territory, the rebels were not able to increase their grip on it, neither were they able to resist the army's military takeover of the region once the peace process broke down.

In terms of the territorial presence on the part of the paramilitaries, estimates are that they have acted militarily in at least 400 municipalities (of a total of 1,092 in the country). But they only exert unfettered control over a few municipalities mainly located in the mid-Magdalena Valley, Antioquia, Cordoba, and the Eastern Plains. Together, this handful of municipalities is even smaller (territorially speaking) than the ones controlled by the FARC but they may include a slightly bigger population.

Contrary to most apocalyptic accounts of the Colombian situation, we would therefore argue that the central government still controls more than half of the total territory, including the bigger and medium-sized cities, where over 70 percent of the Colombian population lives. While it is true that a big portion of the territory, sparsely populated and beyond the agricultural frontier (starting in the lowlands of the Eastern-most mountain range and extending all the way to the borders of Venezuela, Brazil, Peru, and Ecuador), is not fully controlled by the central government, neither is it under the grip of either the guerrillas or the paramilitaries. In this part of the country, some strategic economic enclaves (such as Arauca and Putumayo where there is both petroleum and coca) are the object of sharp competition for control between the state, the guerrillas, and the paramilitaries. The rest of it, however, is very sparsely populated and inhospitable territory.

It must be noted, however, that the political influence of both the FARC and the AUC goes beyond their territorial strongholds and extends throughout the national territory by way of capturing or otherwise influencing the structures and relations of power at the local level. Out of a total of Colombia's 1,092 municipalities, at least 600 (more than half) are being targeted "politically" by one group or the other,[31] causing much of the current violence. In these municipalities, the guerrillas and/or the paramilitaries give open or tacit approval to candidates, forcing some to withdraw and assassinating others. During the campaign preceding local elections in the year 2000, 36 candidates for mayor, council, or other offices were killed and another 50 were kidnapped. Twenty-four mayoral candidates and 64 candidates for town councils withdrew after meddling by armed groups. And 29 towns have registered only one candidate for mayor, "a sign that the tampering has frightened away other candidates."[32]

There are at least three degrees of local control indicated by the capacity of either armed actor to sabotage or otherwise influence the electoral process: Elections are routinely sabotaged in approximately 10 percent of municipalities every election round; control of candidates and influence over elections happens in another 10–20 percent of the territory; and violence spreads out over a much wider portion of the territory, making evident the existence of a fierce competition between the state and its armed rivals (as well as between them) for the control of local political power.[33] Neither of them amounts, however, to the kind of total control of territory and population that we would ascribe to a state-within-a-state.

We thus agree with Spears in the sense that these two regions (one under control of the AUC and the other under the control of the FARC) constitute proof of a "disjuncture between the territory which is ostensibly under a state *jurisdiction* and that which is effectively *controlled* by the state." This lack of capacity of the Colombian state to control the entire territory under its jurisdiction does not translate automatically, however, into the fact that its rivals do. The areas under control of the FARC or the AUC are neither larger nor more permanent than those controlled by the central state. On the contrary, territorial control on the part of the state's rivals is very tenuous in the best of all cases, and also very fluid, constantly shifting from one region to the next. If one of the criteria for using the category of state-within-a-state is that "the area they contain is often more permanent and larger than the territory under the effective control of the central government," then clearly there are no states-within-states in Colombia. We argue instead that their seeming control of territory and the population within it is an indication of their aspiration to statehood, and in that sense, we would rather classify them as "proto-states," "states-in-the-making," or "aspiring state-makers" rather than as "states-within-states."

Extension of Force

As the central state looses its monopoly of coercion and becomes, as a consequence, less able to offer protection to the citizenry, alternative suppliers of protection come into the scene. Not all of them, however, become "proto-states" or alternative states-within-states. Some of these "security providers" remain within the boundaries of the legal, with the state formally delegating power to them. This is the case of many state-sanctioned firms that have long existed in Colombia and provide "private security," mainly in the urban areas.[34] These have existed for a long time in Colombia as a way to supplement the functions of a police force, which by all ratings is far too small regarding both the number of inhabitants and also the challenges posed by organized crime.[35]

By contrast, the protection business in the rural areas is increasingly dominated by a wide array of illegal groups ranging from local bandits, to mafias and their private armies, all the way up to the left-wing guerrillas. The difference between these groups and the private security companies is not only their illegal (non-state-sanctioned) character or the fact that many of them (at least the guerrillas and the more organized paramilitaries) claim to have a political objective that justifies their use of violence. It is also that the protection they provide is first and foremost protection from their own capacity to wield force, and as such, they behave as veritable organized criminals.

It is obviously very difficult to calculate the extension of the forces operating within each one of these groups and the figures tend to be very fuzzy, but at least for the most organized and centralized guerrillas and paramilitary groups, the estimates for their current size is as follows (see table 6.1).

Table 6.1 Extension of the forces—state *versus* rivals in Colombia

Organization	Number of men in arms (late 1990s)
Central state[a]	143,761
FARC[b]	15,000–18,000
ELN[c]	3,500–4,200
AUC[d]	5,915
Other paramilitary groups[e]	2,000

[a] Includes Army, Navy, and Air Force but excludes the Police and other armed security forces. Davila (2001: 3). According to Llorente (1999: 470), the Police had 95,188 members circa 1998.

[b] In its "Survey of Colombia," *The Economist* refers to a force of perhaps 18,000 of whom 6,000 are lightly armed urban militia. They are divided into some 70 "fronts" each averaging about 250 combatants. Cf. *The Economist*, April 21, 2001, p. 11

[c] *The Economist*'s figure is 3,500. Cf. "A Survey of Colombia," April 21, 2001, p. 13.

[d] Dirección de Inteligencia EJC (Folleto Evolución y Composición Grupos Terroristas), Junio 2000.

[e] *The Economist* calculates the size of the paramilitaries at 8,000 troops ("A Survey of Colombia," April 21, 2001, p. 12). Not all of them, however, are organized under the leadership of Carlos Castaño in the AUC.

As the capacity of the state to monopolize power dwindled in the late 1980s, the size of these illegal forces expanded. Both the guerrillas and the paramilitaries have expanded enormously since the early 1980s, but the latter seem to be growing at a greater pace. According to Molano, "[b]etween 1970 and 1982, the FARC grew from a movement of only about 500 people to a small army of 3,000, with a centralized hierarchical structure, a general staff, military code, training school and political program."[36] Between 1982 and 2000 the FARC has grown to a force that today is calculated between 15,000 and 18,000 men. As for the paramilitaries, the force has grown from an estimated 650 men in 1987,[37] to a force that is today estimated between 6,000 and 8,000.[38] Not all of them are organized in one single group but apparently the AUC, which encompasses at least 18 different regionally based groups,[39] has managed to centralize 75 percent of all paramilitary forces. As will become clear in the following section, the growth and expansion of these two groups throughout the 1980s and 1990s is also associated with their access to the rents accruing from the drug trade.

Again, despite their growth, even summing them all up, these forces do not come close to equaling the size of the forces under the command of the central state. While it is true that "the government in Bogotá does not exercise full sovereignty over all of its territory," we still argue that this fact does not automatically grant its challengers the status of states-within-states.

Revenue Generation

Alfredo Rangel, an economist studying the Colombian guerrillas, estimates that the annual income accruing to the FARC must be in the order of $300–375 million per year.[40] Both the FARC and the ELN, but most particularly the FARC, have progressively multiplied the sources of their revenue. According to Rangel, their resources come from at least seven sources.[41] First is from business related to the production and export of drugs (cocaine and heroine),[42] which include taxing coca farmers and traffickers and running processing laboratories and airstrips. Second is kidnapping for ransom. In the third place come "forcible contributions" or extortions to any productive enterprise in the zones under their control or wherever they can pose a credible threat (racketeering). Fourth is cattle robbery. Fifth is bank robbery, whose main target is the government's development bank for the rural sector (*Caja Agraria*), which has a branch in each and every single municipality (or county) in the country. Sixth is the forcible extraction and use of the fiscal resources belonging to municipal-level administration. And finally, gains accrued from investing the money obtained from the previous six sources.

Trafficking in drugs and kidnapping for ransom—among other varieties of extortion—have become the main sources of revenue for both guerrillas. While the ELN still derives most of its revenue from extortion and kidnapping (common crime), revenues from drugs are the main source for the FARC.[43] Rangel calculates that the FARC is capable of taxing 80 percent of the activities related to the production and export of cocaine and that it obtains approximately $140 million dollars from such taxation. In a startling report from the FARC-dominated *zona de despeje*, Juan Forero describes how the economy is built on coca production and coca paste has become a main currency. "Paper money is in short supply, since conventional business are few. Instead, everything revolves around coca [. . .]. It is not unusual for people to be paid for their work in coca. They, in turn pay for necessities with the paste, which is soft and powdery like flour."[44] A second major source of income for the guerrillas is kidnapping for ransom.[45] According to one source, the FARC and the ELN collected about $250 million in ransom payments in the year 2000.[46] This would amount to almost 42 percent of their total revenue.

By contrast with other insurgent experiences then, the Colombian guerrillas do not rely on external sources of aid (they had very little in the way of external support even before the end of the Cold War) as much as on domestic extraction via two criminal activities: one which taxes the illegal commerce on drugs, and the other that taxes individual wealth and income (kidnapping and extortion in various forms). In Rangel's own words,

> the underground economy of the guerrilla has acquired the characteristics of a complex war economy system in which there is a combination of various forms of resource extraction from the formal economy as well as from the underground economy, which guarantee that the insurgents will have a permanent and predictable flow of resources. This enables them to plan its availability and destination in predictable ways, both for the operational expenses of the war against the state, as well as for their investments which ensure and increase their resources.[47]

The paramilitaries, on the other hand, are not short of money. "They pay their gunmen comparatively handsome wages of $300–400 a month, and arm them with mini-Uzi machine guns."[48] If we take this figure as a credible base from which to calculate their income, and multiply it by 6,000 men per 12 months, then the ACU spends close to 30 million dollars per year just in wages. According to another source, "an American investigator in the United States Embassy who has tracked paramilitary financing schemes for years, speaking on condition of anonymity, says the group has anywhere from $200 million to $1 billion in bank and investment accounts in Switzerland, Italy, Luxembourg and other countries. Untold sums are also in Colombia [. . .] and the group most likely hid assets in the form of hotels, shopping centers and other property under its control."[49]

The paramilitaries extract revenue from the local population, through forcible extortions (racket payments) or voluntary donations, the latter most notably from the landowners and cattle ranchers who willingly support these groups in exchange for security from armed robbers and common criminals, but also and most importantly, from the predatory activities of guerrilla groups. An investigation by the attorney general has shown how landowners and businessmen in Cordoba and its neighboring provinces "donated heavily to transform a small group of outlaws into an 8,000 man militia,"[50] the AUC. The most important source of their revenue, however, is the capture of rents derived from the illegal traffic in drugs. Even more so than the guerrillas, the paramilitaries—particularly the AUC—finance their organization via the extraction of rents from the illicit drugs trade. In a televised interview in 2000 Carlos Castaño, leader of the AUC, conceded that 70 percent of his group's financing comes from drug-trafficking.[51]

Nazih Richani has aptly summarized the sources of funding for the paramilitaries by stating that they "have three ways of getting money and resources. They tax small businesses and multinational corporations whose operations fall within their territorial control. They collect contributions from large landowners and cattle ranchers. And they traffic in illegal drugs."[52]

In a way then, both of these proto-states behave like "rentier states,"[53] capturing rents from the international market in illicit drugs. That explains their autonomy vis-à-vis both the international actors who try to exert some leverage upon them but also, and most importantly, vis-à-vis the population that they pretend to control. This relative autonomy afforded by the rents extracted from the drug trade, also explains why the conflict has become so degraded in the last decade or so, since neither one of these two groups really needs the support of the peasantry or the population at large in order to continue waging its war. Except perhaps for the small coca-growing peasants, the drug connection will not create the strong links between these "proto-states" and their taxpayers, which are expected to come as a result of fighting wars.[54]

Again, if we compare the resources that these groups are able to collect with the central state's revenue, their extractive capacity becomes very relative (see table 6.2).

Contrast $300 million in the hands of the FARC with $10.27 billion in the hands of the central government. The revenues accrued to the FARC amount to 2.9 percent of the extraction capacity of the Colombian state, and to 10.7 percent of Colombia's defense budget (including army and police pensions), which amounts to $2.8 billion dollars.[55] While this is not an insignificant quantity, it is however very far from approaching the levels of funding available to the central state.

More generally, regarding the sources of revenue generation, Colombia contradicts the generalized assumption that domestic armed conflicts should have changed fundamentally as a result of the end of the Cold War in 1990–1991. For one, the Colombian guerrillas never derived a significant proportion of their resources from external sources (such as Cuba, Nicaragua, the Soviet Union, or other Communist countries). Long before the Berlin Wall fell, the Colombian guerrillas had already developed an efficient kidnapping and extortion industry, and were already involved in taxing and profiting from the drug trade. Most probably then, the end of the Cold War caused them to intensify these practices as they became their main and only ways of collecting resources. On the other hand, the Colombian state has continued receiving aid from the United States, in quantities that contradict the general prediction that after the Cold War client-states would be deprived from the resources accruing from the bipolar hegemons. In the Colombian case, because of the central role the country plays in the drug trade, and since the United States declared the war on drugs a national security priority, the state has been benefiting from a steady and increasing flow of aid from Washington.

Table 6.2   Central state—revenue sources, 1999 (in billions of dollars)

Source	Total value[a]	As a percentage of total revenues	As a percentage of GDP[b]
Taxation of economic activities	6.57	63.97	10.29
Taxation of external trade	1.96	19.08	3.07
Not based on taxes and others	1.74	16.94	2.72
Total revenues	10.27	100	16.09

[a] Values were calculated from the data in Restrepo Moreno (2000, table 27, p. 226). We used an average exchange rate of 2,000 pesos per dollar.
[b] GDP was calculated from IDB (2000) by using data on GDP per capita in 1990 U.S. dollars (table 3, p. 142) and multiplying it by the population data shown in table 2 (p. 141). That calculation yields an estimated total GDP of $63.8 billion dollars for 1999.

In 2000, after the approval of $1.3 billion in emergency aid, Colombia became the biggest recipient of American aid anywhere outside the Middle East.

In closing this section, we can safely say two things regarding the political economy of the war in Colombia. First, not much has changed since the end of the Cold War. Rather, there has been an intensification of previous practices on the part of both the central government and its rivals. Second, and perhaps more importantly, despite an increasing availability of funds for waging this war derived from the illegal trade in narcotics, the extractive capacity of the emerging state rivals is still very far from matching that of the Colombian central state. This is especially true in the post–September 11 era, as the country becomes the test case for the U.S. war against the "evil" marriage of drugs and terrorism in its own Latin American backyard.

"National" Identity and Internal Legitimacy

What about the social identification with these aspiring state-makers? One must realize that a major difference between Colombia and most of the cases explored in Spears's chapter is the absence of national, ethnic, religious, or linguistic cleavages that could account for the emergence of these armed actors or eventually become a source of allegiance on the part of their constituencies. Rather, in the Colombian case, it is regional and class-based cleavages that help to explain the emergence and consolidation of the guerrillas.[56]

Traditionally an agrarian guerrilla group, whose origins lie in peasant self-defense groups organized by the Colombian Communist Party in the 1950s,[57] FARC's members (rank-and-file) are of peasant origin. Sociologically, the FARC can be seen as representing two groups from the Colombian peasantry: the "*colonos*," property-less peasants who have been expelled beyond the agricultural frontier into the inter-Andean valleys and the Llanos,[58] as well as the peasants and day-laborers in the coca-growing regions. Note, however, that more than 75 percent of the Colombian population is now urban, with most of it concentrating in a complex web of major and medium-sized cities. At best, one can consider the hypothesis that the FARC represents a segment of the Colombian peasantry, but nothing much more beyond that. While it may be true that in some regions the FARC "act as the state in the areas they control, organizing such services as education, courts, health, road construction, and loans to farmers and small businessmen," the fact that they also terrorize the population under their control and that many in the *zona de despeje* saw their domination as the result of an arbitrary decision, must not be overlooked.[59] On the other hand, urban rejection of FARC's ideologies, activities, and practices is widespread as shown by various opinion polls. The overall national approval figure for the guerrillas is around 3 percent.[60]

Support for the paramilitaries is socially more diversified. It ranges from sectors within the state armed forces to encompass diverse groups throughout society, such as traditional landowners and cattle ranchers, narcotraffickers just-turned-into-landowners, local and regional politicians from the traditional (Liberal and Conservative parties) all the way down to rich and middle-class peasants. This is the revenue-raising basis of support. Beyond that, public opinion support for the paramilitaries, especially in the cities has been increasing, most noticeably after two televised interviews of the leader of the AUC, Carlos Castaño, in the year 2000. Opinion polls show that 10–15 percent of the population approve of Mr. Castaño and the AUC.[61] In the zones they dominate they may act, just like the guerrillas, as veritable proto-states: "they regulate the morality of the people (in Tierralta, Córdoba, the paramilitary commander of the zone gave men a month's warning to decide if they stay with their wives or with their lovers), they promote local development projects [. . .] and they administer the death sentence, without trial, to robbers, prostitutes, homosexuals and drug-addicts."[62]

However, they accomplish most of this through the use of terror, not on the basis of the "active consent" of the population that they dominate. Their preferred tactic, short of combating the guerrillas, is to massacre the civilian population that is perceived by them as aiding the guerrillas—"the water in which the fish thrives." According to the Ministry of Defense, in year 2000, the paramilitaries murdered 988 civilians not involved in combat. Between 1991 and 1999 there were 1,837 massacres in Colombia;[63] the paramilitary groups were responsible for 75 percent of them. They have also penetrated the cities where they mainly carry out selective assassinations of human rights workers, trade union leaders, political activists, journalists, teachers, and academics. Death sentences, threats, massacres, selective assassinations, and forcible displacement are the preferred tactics of the paramilitaries to take and keep control over their territories. Except for those who pay for and command their operation, there is all reason to doubt that the people who live under the control of the paramilitaries do so under some sense of consented acquiescence.

As a result of the ongoing warfare between these organizations (the guerrillas and the paramilitaries) and the state, there are approximately 1.8–2 million internally displaced people in Colombia, people who have been forced out of their homes or who have fled under the threat of being killed by either one of the armies in combat. The fact that neither the guerrillas nor the paramilitaries try to gain the active consent of the populations under their control, once again speaks about the autonomy that has been gained by these two organizations vis-à-vis their respective social bases or constituencies, thanks to the revenues accrued from the cocaine trade. Just as any "rentier" state, these groups can afford to lose the support of their local or nationwide potential supporters and survive despite a nationwide rejection of their political projects, strategies, and tactics.

The war in Colombia has not led to the emergence of common identities or strong solidarities between the population and these state-like entities. This is both because they continue to use terror against the population itself, and because they do not necessarily link their action to one specific region or geographical area but instead move from one region to the next in typical guerrilla fashion. Lastly, in Colombia there is no such thing as a crisis of our common identity as Colombians. Even if people have grown accustomed to expect little from the Colombian state, their identity as Colombian nationals is not in question. Neither of the contending groups purport to embody a different national identity and there is no question that, regardless of who wins this war, the Colombian state, its territory, and the national identity that accompanies them both will remain unchanged.

Conclusion

The states-within-states category proposed by Spears seems to fit a specific type of intrastate conflict—namely, that pitting a clearly defined, territorially based, minority group (based on either ethnic, religious, linguistic, or national criteria) against a central state that is either extremely weak, failing, or has already collapsed. While Colombia fits the second part of the equation, with an extremely eroded state, it doesn't fit the first. The armed confrontation that has ravaged Colombia in the last four decades is not a conflict about ethnic, racial, linguistic, national, or religious cleavages that become translated into political terms. Rather it is a conflict whose main origin is a politico-ideological animosity between the armed protagonists, who perceive each other as irreconcilable enemies. The parties in conflict in Colombia do not want to secede or create a new and different entity; rather, they would like to take control of the existing state, with its present boundaries and accompanying national identity, and use it as an instrument for social transformation (of one kind or another). Additionally, in terms of the territory, the population and the resources under the control of both the central state and these groups, the asymmetries tend to be so great that it is difficult to grant these state's rivals the label of states-within-the-state.

Therefore, while we agree with Spears in the sense that Colombia is an example of those cases in which there is a "disjuncture between the territory which is ostensibly under a state *jurisdiction* and that which is effectively *controlled* by the state," we did not find enough evidence to support the idea that the rivals of the Colombian state measure up to the expectations entailed in Spears's proposed category of "states-within-states." We argue instead that their seeming control of territory and the population within it is an indication of their aspiration to statehood, and in that sense, we would rather classify them as "proto-states," "states-in-the-making," or "aspiring state-makers" rather than as states-within-states.

With regard to the specific case of the demilitarized zone granted by the central state to the FARC, Spears argues that this is a potential example of a confidence-building measure. However, in the Colombian case, the FARC failed to live up to this more benevolent appraisal. Not only did the FARC fail to enter serious negotiations during the time in which the *zona de despeje* was in effect (1998–2002), but it actually turned it into a stronghold to pursue its own strengthening as a military force. It is telling, however, that the FARC did not use the ceded territory and the three-year tenure they had over it, to prepare and organize for future statehood. They did not invest in developing the region, did not build new roads or communications systems, did not have their own currency or bank. They did provide security in the region in terms of police and protection from paramilitary attacks in the towns.[64] They did provide "revolutionary justice" in the same way they do in the localities that fall under their control. However, the available evidence also shows that the FARC used the demilitarized zone for recruiting and training purposes, as a safe haven for kidnapped and kidnappers alike, as a base for its cocaine-related business and as a receiving end for the arms trade. Instead of a "confidence-building measure" then, the *zona de despeje* provided the FARC with a golden opportunity for carrying out warfare against the central government.[65] Despite the generous concession on the part of the government, the FARC were unable to show either their fellow Colombians nor the outside world that they were capable of governing competently. If anything, the FARC came out of this three-year experiment more discredited than ever, in the eyes of both nationals and foreigners.

In the case of the AUC, it is important to note that their explicit purpose is not to create an alternative state, but to defend the status-quo, and as such, they do not even behave as "aspiring state-makers" but as a kind of "surrogate state" (*estado sustituto*). At worst, and this is true for most paramilitary groups that are also heavily involved in drug-dealing, these groups are just "coercive and self-seeking entrepreneurs,"[66] exercising a "coercive exploitation" in the regions under their control. In a situation where the central state has severely contracted, there are unparalleled opportunities for accumulation of group and personal power and wealth. Each one of these groups conceived as "coercive enterprises," invests heavily in controlling or overcoming their competitors in order to enjoy the advantages of power within a secure and expanding territory.

In closing, we would like to propose a word of caution about the prospective scenarios following from a collapse, even partial, of the state. Despite Spears's optimism regarding the prospects of state breakdown and collapse, we do not see, at least in the Colombian case, the emergence of political entities that are more logical or congruent, neither more coherent, viable or effective than the central state. Instead, by describing the types of effects and consequences of the partial collapse of the state in Colombia we have painted a much grimmer picture of what it looks like when the state loses its coercive and normative capacities and a multiplicity of infra-state groups take over the tasks of controlling power and regulating society via the unfettered use of force.

Notes

1. We would like to thank Erica Cosgrove, Elisabeth Hilbink, Catherine Legrand, and Sarah Pralle for comments on previous drafts. Ana Maria Bejarano would also like to thank her students in the seminar on "State Building and Failure in the Developing World" at Princeton University for their generous input.

2. See e.g., Ann Mason, "Exclusividad, Autoridad y Estado," in *Análisis Político*, Instituto de Estudios Políticos y Relaciones Internacionales, Universidad Nacional de Colombia, No. 47 (September/November 2002); Susan E. Rice, "The New National Security Strategy: Focus on Failed States," *The Brookings Insitution Policy Brief # 116* (Washington D.C.: Brookings Institution, 2003) and Robert I. Rotberg, ed., *When States Fail: Causes and Consequences* (Princeton: Princeton University Press, 2003).

3. Robert H. Jackson, *Quasi-States: Sovereignty, International Relations and the Third World* (New York: Cambridge University Press, 1990); William Reno, "Shadow States and the Political Economy of Civil Wars," in Mats Berdal and David M. Malone, eds., *Greed and Grievance: Economic Agendas in Civil Wars* (Boulder and Ottawa: Lynne Rienner and International Development Research Council, 2000).

4. According to data from the International Organization for Migration (IOM), at www.iom.int.

5. Since the mid-1980s the homicide rate in Colombia has suffered a dramatic increase, reaching a new peak close to 80 homicides per 100,000 inhabitants in 1991. Colombia's levels of violence are unusually high, even when compared with other Latin American cases. El Salvador is the only country surpassing Colombia in terms of homicide rates in the 1990s. See Steven Levitt and Mauricio Rubio, "Understanding Crime in Colombia and What Can Be Done About It." Fedesarrollo, Working Paper Series—Documentos de Trabajo, Agosto, No. 20 (2000), pp. 3–4.

6. Mauricio Rubio, "La justicia en una sociedad violenta," en Malcolm Deas y Maria Victoria Llorente, eds., *Reconocer la Guerra para construir la paz* (Bogotá: Ediciones Uniandes—CEREC—Grupo Editorial Norma, 1999).

7. Jeffrey Herbst, *States and Power in Africa. Comparative Lessons in Authority and Control* (Princeton: Princeton University Press, 2000).

8. For an interesting comparative appraisal of the process of state formation in Latin America, see Fernando Lopez-Alves, *State Formation and Democracy in Latin America: 1810–1900* (Durham and London, Duke University Press, 2000), and more recently Miguel Angel Centeno, *Blood and Debt: War and the Nation-State in Latin America* (University Park: Pennsylvania State University Press, 2002).

9. Ibid., p. 44 counts 28 instances of international war in Latin America between 1825 and 1995.

10. Charles Tilly, "War Making and State Making as Organized Crime," in Peter Evans, Dietrich Rueschemeyer, and Theda Skocpol, eds., *Bringing the State Back in* (Cambridge: Cambridge University Press, 1985), pp. 169–191; and *Coercion, Capital and European States, AD. 990–1990* (Cambridge, MA: Blackwell, 1990).

11. See Centeno, *Blood and Debt*.

12. Except perhaps for some of the Central American states and even in those cases, we would doubt the accuracy of such a description.

13. This section draws heavily from our paper "From 'Restricted' to 'Besieged': The Changing Nature of the Limits to Democracy in Colombia," working paper # 296, The Helen Kellogg Institute for International Studies, University of Notre Dame, April 2002.

14. Paul Oquist, *Violence, Conflict and Politics in Colombia* (New York: Academic Press, 1980).

15. Ana María Berjarano and Renata Segura, "El fortalecimiento selectivo del Estado durante el Frente Nacional," *Controversia*, No. 169, Segunda Etapa, noviembre de 1996.

16. See the work of historian Catherine Legrand, *Frontier Expansion and Peasant Protest in Colombia 1850–1936* (Albuquerque: University of New Mexico Press, 1986) and sociologist Alfredo Molano, *Selva adentro: Una historia oral de la colonizacion del Guaviare* (Bogota: El Ancora Editores, 1987).

17. See I. William Zartman, ed., *Collapsed States: The Disintegration and Restoration of Legitimate Authority* (Boulder: Lynne Rienner, 1995); and Robert I. Rotberg, "Failed States in a World of Terror," in *Foreign Affairs* (July/August 2002), pp. 127–140; and Rotberg, *When States Fail*.

18. Eduardo Pizarro, *Las Farc 1949–1966: De la autodefensa a la combinación de todas las formas de lucha* (Bogotá: IEPRI—Tercer Mundo Editores, 1991), and *Insurgencia sin revolución. La guerrilla colombiana en perspectiva comparada* (Bogotá: IEPRI—Tercer Mundo Editores, 1996).

19. Philip Mauceri, "State, Elites and Counter-Insurgency: Some Preliminary Comparisons Between Colombia and Perú," unpublished manuscript (2001).

20. Here we run into a slight disagreement with Mauceri's argument. While Mauceri states that the Colombian elite as a whole opted for a privatized counterinsurgency strategy, we insist on the need to understand the complexity of the Colombian elites and the existence of at least two different responses to the challenges posed by the guerrilla. See Mauceri, "States, Elites and Counter-Insurgency," pp. 1–2 and 11–14.

21. Andrés Lopez, "Narcotráfico y elecciones: delincuencia y corrupción en la reciente vida política colombiana," in Ana María Bejarano y Andrés Dávila (compiladores), *Elecciones y Democracia en Colombia, 1997–1998* (Bogotá: Universidad de los Andes—Departamento de Ciencia Política—Fundación Social—Veeduría Ciudadana a la Elección Presidencial, 1998).

22. The most renowned case but by no means the only one was the presidential campaign of Ernesto Samper in 1994 that was partially funded by the Cali Cartel.

23. Tilly, "War Making and State Making," p. 181.

24. For a history of the FARC, see Pizarro, *Las Farc 1949–1966*.

25. To understand the emerging AUC see Fernano Cubides, "Los paramilitares y su estrategia," in Malcolm Deas y Maria Victoria Llorente, eds., *Reconocer la Guerra para construir la paz* (Bogotá: Ediciones Uniandes—CEREC—Grupo Editorial Norma, 1999); and Nazih Richani, "The Paramilitary Connection," *NACLA. Report on the Americas*, Vol. XXXIV, No. 2 (September/October 2000), pp. 38–41.

26. Spears, chapter one in this volume, p. 19. Spears attributes this disjuncture to the reluctance to create a more rational basis of statehood on the part of regional organizations and the international community at large. Again, we would like to argue that while this may be the case in Africa, it is certainly not the case in Latin America.

27. Herbst, *States and Power in Africa*.

28. A telling indicator of this incapacity is the fact that in more than half of the territory the state is either completely absent or just minimally felt. According to the Minister of Defense, today, 15% of all municipalities in Colombia do not count on the presence of one single member of the police force. Moreover, another 44% of all municipalities only count on a minimal presence by the state's security forces. "Discurso de la Señora Ministra de Defensa, Marta Lucía Ramírez de Rincón, en la Reunión Annual de Comandantes de Policía." Bogotá, September 2002. Source: http://www.mindefensa.gov.co/.

29. To give the reader a comparative point of view, Colombia is twice the size of France and 50 times as that of El Salvador.

30. This is the estimate of the Inter-American Development Bank, in its 1999 Annual Report (2000), p. 141.

31. Marc Chernick, "Elusive Peace," in *NACLA. Report on the Americas*, Vol. XXXIV, No. 2 (September/October 2000), p. 33. The figure of 600 municipalities where some form of electoral tampering by the FARC or some other armed group including the right-wing paramilitaries takes place comes from organizations like the Confederation of Municipalities, which groups all the country's mayors. Juan Forero, "Behind Colombia's Election Hoopla, Rebels Wield Power," *The New York Times*, October 29, 2000.

32. Juan Forero, "Behind Colombia's Election Hoopla."

33. For information on local elections and the multiple ways the armed actors interfere with or attempt to influence them see Bejarano and Davila, *Eleciones y Democracia*.

34. According to the Ministry of National Defense, "the number of [legal] security companies has increased to more than 600 from 380 in the past six years, and the number of watch-men and security guards has risen to about 140,000 from 93,500. And the population of legal bodyguards has leaped sevenfold, to nearly 21,800." See Kirk Semple, "The Kidnapping Economy," in *The New York Times Magazine*, June 3, 2001, p. 48.

35. The size of the police force is close to 100,000 men. With a population of 41,500,000 inhabitants, this means a ratio of 1 policeman to 415 inhabitants.

36. Alfredo Molano, "The Evolution of the FARC," *NACLA. Report on the Americas*, Vol. XXXIV, No. 2 (September/October 2000), p. 27.

37. The government denounced the existence of 138 self-defense groups with a total of 650 men for the first time in 1987. Since then, until 1999 they multiplied ten-fold and by 1999 their size was estimated at 5,915. See Dirección de Inteligencia, E.J.C., "Evolución y Composición Grupos Terroristas," Junio 2000.

38. According to Castaño, 30% of those come from the guerrillas, more than 1,000 are ex-military and ex-policemen, included ex-officers and NCOs. According to the Ministry of Defense, "between 1998 and 2000 their growth was 81 percent, five times that of the guerrillas for the same period." See "La Guerra de los Paras," Semana.com (April 5, 2001), p. 3.

39. See Dirección de Inteligencia, E.J.C., "Evolución y Composición."

40. His estimates are based on the information gathered by an official committee, "Comité Interinstitucional de Lucha contra las finanzas de la guerrilla," *Informe 1998*, Bogotá, Marzo de 1999. *The Economist's* estimates are closer but lower "the best estimate of their [FARC] income from drugs, extortion and kidnapping is perhaps $250–$300 million a year." See *The Economist*, "A Survey of Colombia," April 21, 2001, p. 9.

41. Alfred Rangel, *Guerra insurgente: Conflictos en Malasia, Peru, Filipinas, El Salvador y Colombia* (Bogotá: Intermedio Editores, 2001), p. 391.

42. For the past two decades, Colombia has been the world's main supplier of cocaine. Whereas in the 1970s and 1980s Colombia would import the coca paste from Bolivia and Peru, in the 1990s coca growing became concentrated in Colombia. According to *The Economist*, Colombia produced 266 tonnes of cocaine and 88 tonnes of opium (for heroin production) in 2000. Colombia produces four-fifths of the total trade

in cocaine in the world but is only a small heroin producer. Cf. *The Economist*, July 28–August 3, 2001, pp. 6–7. Estimates of the money repatriated by the drug industry range from $2.5 billion to $5 billion a year, according to *The Economist*, "A Survey of Colombia," p. 9.

43. Rangel, *Guerra insurgente,* p. 391.

44. Juan Forero, "Where a Little Coca is as Good as Gold," *New York Times*, Sunday, July 8, 2001, p. 12.

45. Almost half of the kidnappings in the world take place in Colombia. There were a record 3,706 kidnappings reported to the government 2000. A little more than half of those are done by the guerrillas (52.3%), with most of the rest (40%) being done by organized but nonpolitical criminal gangs. Only 7.7% of the total number of kidnappings are actually attributed to the right-wing paramilitary groups (percentages are from Rangel, *Guerra insurgente*, who in turns draws from data provided by the National Police). The Colombian guerrillas are, by far, the organizations that realize the highest number of kidnappings in the world. See Semple, "The Kidnapping Economy," pp. 46–50.

46. The source is Colonel Jesus Antonio Bohórquez, national director of the Colombian armed forces' antikidnapping squads, but the author who quotes him clarifies that this figure is only an estimate, actually "a guess." See Semple, "The Kidnapping Economy," p. 48.

47. Rangel, *Guerra insurgente*, p. 391.

48. *The Economist*, "A Survey of Colombia," p. 12.

49. Juan Forero, "Ranchers in Colombia Bankroll Their Own Militia," *New York Times*, August 8, 2001, p. A6.

50. See Forero, "Where a Little Coca is as Good as Gold."

51. The paramilitaries earn perhaps $200 million from activities related to drugs is the estimated figure presented in *The Economist*, "A Survey of Colombia," p. 9.

52. Richani, "The Paramilitary Connection," p. 40.

53. For a definition of the rentier state see Hazem Beblawi and Giacomo Luciani, eds., *The Rentier State* [Vol. 2 of Nation, State and Integration in the Arab World] (London and New York: Croom Helm, 1987).

54. To paraphrase Herbst's assertion that "fighting wars may be the only way whereby it is possible to have people pay more taxes and at the same time feel more closely associated with the state," quoted in Spears, chapter one in this volume, p. 24.

55. This figure comes from *The Economist*, "A Survey of Colombia," p. 9.

56. On this issue see Pizarro, *Insurgencia sin revolución*, especially chapter 5 on the issue of the relationship between peasants and guerrillas in Colombia.

57. The history of the FARC can be found in Pizarro, *Las Farc 1949–1966*.

58. For an account of the relationship between the FARC and the *colonos* see the work of Molano, synthesized in his recent article (2000).

59. Chernick, "Elusive Peace," p. 37.

60. *The Economist*, "A Survey of Colombia," p. 12.

61. Ibid.

62. "La guerra de los paras," in Semana.com, Abril 5, 2001, p. 3.

63. In some cases the massacres involve massive acts of torture such as burning the victims alive, throwing acid on them, or cutting their bodies with chainsaws. On the number of massacres, see Jaime Zuluaga, "El proceso de paz: hacia un acuerdo nacional?" in Luis Alberto Restrepo, ed., *Síntesis 2000. Anuario Social, Político y Económico de Colombia* (Bogotá: IEPRI— Fundación Social—TM Editores, 2000), p. 44.

64. The government initially agreed to withdraw its military and police presence from the zone, leaving it under control of the guerrillas except for a few civilian state agencies (judges and prosecutors) that the guerrillas were quick to expel. The only remaining authorities from the official state were the elected mayors of the five municipalities and a

small, poorly trained and equipped "civic" police, composed of civilians, half selected by the guerrillas and half by each county mayors. See "La policía del Caguán es un decir," in http://eltiempo.terra.com.co/15-10-2001/poli116892.html.

65. Spears, chapter one in this volume, p. 29.
66. Tilly, "War Making and State Making," p.169.

Chapter Seven

Providing Humanitarian Assistance Behind Rebel Lines: UNICEF's Eastern Zaïre Operation 1996–1998

Lauchlan T. Munro[1]

This chapter is a case study of one UN agency's efforts to provide humanitarian assistance to local and refugee populations living in territory under the de facto control of a rebel group, while continuing to work in government-held territory as well. The chapter also outlines what took place after the rebel alliance became the de jure government and then fell apart to such an extent that a rebel state-within-a-state was in effect reestablished in the heartland of the previous rebellion even before armed conflict broke out again. The case study is the United Nations Children's Fund's (UNICEF) Eastern Zaïre Operation from 1996 to 1998. The purpose of this chapter is to give readers an idea of how a multilateral agency responds to a situation where it must work with a state-within-a-state, and to illustrate some of the legal, ethical, and practical issues that may arise in such situations and how they may be dealt with. Implications for theory and policy are derived.

This chapter does not claim to be a purely objective piece of social science research. It is rather a set of reflections from someone who was there, and deeply involved in many of the events and processes described here. Though this chapter is not a memoir, it has many of the strengths and weaknesses of that genre. Nor does the chapter pretend to be comprehensive either in the sense of telling the whole story of the UN's work in the Democratic Republic of the Congo (ex-Zaïre, DR Congo)[2] in recent years, or in the sense of covering all the issues facing multilateral agencies in dealing with states-within-states. To write a comprehensive essay in the first sense would be an immense task, and inappropriate for this forum. And no case study can be comprehensive in the second sense; that is simply the nature of a case study. What I hope readers will get from this chapter, though, is a sense of what it was like to be there, how issues arose, how they got worked through, what the consequences were, and what lessons there are for the United Nations and others in dealing with other states-within-states.

Historical Background

The conflicts that have beset the eastern provinces of the DR Congo in the past decade have deep historical roots. The social formations that lie at the origins of much of the current conflict date back at least 300 years.[3] These conflicts are also closely linked with recent conflicts in neighboring states, especially Rwanda, but also Uganda and Burundi, with the ways colonialism interacted with precolonial social formations, and with the failed politics of the postindependence era.[4]

The immediate trigger to the conflicts that have afflicted the eastern provinces of the DR Congo since 1994 is usually taken to be the Rwandan genocide of April–June 1994. In fact, however, the fires of ethnic hatred and ethnic cleansing were burning in North and South Kivu provinces of Zaïre for over a year before that, as members of other ethnic groups attempted to clear the Tutsi ethnic group out of the Masisi and Mulenge mountains.[5] This ethnic cleansing was encouraged by the Zaïrois government of President Mobutu Sese Seko, which had just reversed an earlier decision granting Zaïrois citizenship to the Tutsis, and had since 1990 been alarmed by the Tutsi-led rebellion against the then friendly government of neighboring Rwanda. After the genocide of the Rwandan Tutsis, around a million Rwandan Hutus poured over the border into Zaïre and were settled in refugee camps near the border. Included in their number were some members of the *Interahamwe* militia and the ex-*Forces Armées Rwandaises* (ex-FAR) who had been responsible for the genocide in Rwanda. The Mobutu government, which was probably complicit in the genocide itself and certainly complicit in protecting the perpetrators afterward, showed no desire to disarm the *Interahamwe* and ex-FAR and separate them out from the genuine refugees. In the absence of any such desire by Mobutu's government, the international community made no serious effort to force the separation of the militias from the refugees. The *génocidaires* of the *Interahamwe* and the ex-FAR, for their part, were happy to use the civilian members of the refugee population as human shields and as bait to attract food and other aid from the international community.

The presence of these large refugee camps in North and South Kivu provinces had a profound impact on the host communities. Initially, there was a wave of epidemic diseases affecting both the refugees and the local populations, when the sudden arrival of around a million poor and unhealthy people overwhelmed the already fragile public health infrastructure of the Kivus. In addition, land had to be set aside for the refugees, which displaced some locals. The refugees needed to eat and to cook, and so the local biomass was rapidly degraded as refugees felled trees and took food from nearby natural and domestic sources, including the farms of local Zaïrois. The *Interahamwe* and the ex-FAR soon set themselves up as the de facto government of the refugees camps and as an organized crime syndicate who committed crimes against their fellow countrymen in the refugee camps, local Zaïrois, and occasionally, the aid workers sent to assist the refugees. The *Interahamwe* and the ex-FAR also participated in attacks against Zaïrois Tutsi and in cross-border raids against the new government that was installed in Rwanda in June 1994. All this was condoned by the Zaïrois authorities, who were already unpopular due to decades of misrule on a colossal scale. The amount of aid flowing into the refugee camps, estimated at around US$1 million per day in 1994–1996, caused further resentment amongst the locals; the economic, nutritional, and epidemiological situation of the Zaïrois populations living next to the refugee camps was broadly similar to the situation of those in the camps, but the locals got far less assistance than the refugees.

The spark that lit the powder keg was an attempted ethnic cleansing of the Tutsis living in and around the town of Uvira in South Kivu in August–September 1996. The Tutsis struck back and quickly formed alliances with other groups who were disaffected with Mobutu's regime and/or hostile to the refugees. The Rwandan and Ugandan governments saw an opportunity to settle old scores against Mobutu's government and quickly provided military and political assistance. A political party was soon cobbled together under the name of the *Alliance des Forces Démocratiques pour la Libération du Congo* (AFDL). The AFDL united behind a platform called the Lemera Declaration, named after the town in South Kivu where the AFDL's founding conference was held. The Lemera Declaration called for the overthrow of Mobutu's corrupt regime and the removal of the Rwandan and Burundian refugees from Congolese soil.[6] Though members of the Tutsi ethnic group quickly took on leadership positions in the AFDL, the new opposition movement needed a leader from a different ethnic group to give it broader legitimacy, both inside and outside the Kivus. It is widely believed that, around October 1996, Ugandan President Yoweri Museveni introduced the Rwandan Vice President and Minister of Defence Paul Kagame, the *éminence grise* behind the AFDL, to a Congolese radical and failed revolutionary whom Museveni had known in exile in Tanzania years before; that man was Laurent Kabila, and he was installed as the president of the AFDL.[7]

Events moved quickly between late September and early November 1996. The AFDL troops, aided by the Rwandan army and returning Congolese exiles from throughout east Africa, quickly captured most of South Kivu. Rebellion soon erupted in North Kivu in sympathy with the South Kivu rebels, and the two branches of the AFDL joined up by early November. Mobutu's troops, ill-disciplined, unpaid for months, and demoralized, put up only token resistance, preferring instead to pillage local communities, then flee, or desert.

The AFDL made no secret of its hostility toward the Hutu refugees from Burundi and—especially—Rwanda living in Zaïre, and attacked the refugee camps. The camps, each of which contained tens or hundreds of thousands of refugees, quickly disbanded, usually in a matter of hours. Most of the refugees returned to Rwanda and Burundi, but around a fifth or a quarter—no one knows for sure—fled west into the dense rain forests of the central Congo basin, a thinly populated and virtually infrastructure-free zone. Lost under the dense canopy of trees, over a 100,000 refugees disappeared from the world's radar screens; many never came back. It was not long before reports began to emerge concerning massacres of refugees in the forests by AFDL and Rwandan troops. The AFDL denied these reports, or dismissed them as isolated incidents, and certainly not the policy of the AFDL. The Rwandan government, for its part, at the time denied that it had any troops in Zaïre.[8] I have seen and interviewed enough refugees, and spoken to enough aid workers who were on the spot, to convince myself that the massacres of refugees were deliberate policy. The UN Joint Mission charged with investigating allegations of massacres and other human rights violations in Zaïre came to a similar conclusion.[9]

The situation in eastern Zaïre in late 1996 and the first half of 1997 can only be described as dire. The local population had been deeply impoverished by over three decades of socioeconomic decay and gross misrule,[10] compounded by the refugee crisis and associated armed conflict. Public infrastructure was degraded to the point where, in the 1990s, Zaïre was the only country in the world with fewer kilometres of road than it had had a quarter century earlier.[11] Many schools and health centers, already poorly staffed and equipped before the crisis, had been looted and/or occupied by one military group or another; health and education staff were often dead or internally displaced. Commercial activity had been severely disrupted, especially outside the major towns. Tens of thousands of refugees and internally displaced people were out in the jungle, out of reach of any kind of assistance. Tens of thousands of internally displaced people were scattered in different parts of the country, on both sides of the front line between the AFDL–Rwandan army and Mobutu's *Forces Armées Zaïroises* (FAZ). There was a crying need for international humanitarian relief for both refugee and local populations.

By the end of November 1996, the AFDL was the de facto authority governing a territory covering most of North and South Kivu, an area roughly the size of Uganda and containing perhaps six million people or more. President Mobutu was forced to ask for negotiations and a truce. By the time the United Nations, which had evacuated its international staff from the Kivus in late October and early November, returned to the Kivus almost a month later, they found they had to deal with the AFDL as the de facto government of that territory.

The AFDL and the UN Agencies, November 1996–May 1997

Having liberated large parts of the Kivus from the corrupt rule of Mobutu's government, the AFDL declared itself to be the responsible authority (*autorité responsable*) for the governance of the territory behind its front line.[12] As such, it assumed responsibility for law and order and for relations between eastern Zaïre and foreign states and international organizations. The AFDL also claimed the power to regulate all economic, social, political, and developmental activity, including the affairs of the UN agencies and both local and international NGOs.

The main UN emergency agencies, namely the UNHCR, the World Food Programme (WFP), and the UNICEF,[13] quickly returned to the AFDL-controlled territory in November 1996. The UNHCR had to return, since its core business, the protection of refugees under the 1951 *Convention on Refugees*,[14] continued to be a burning issue. The WFP returned because food insecurity was a major concern for refugee and local populations alike, and its mandate required it to act to help restore food security. UNICEF, for its part, had in the 1980s and 1990s pioneered three seperate humanitarian concepts: humanitarian corridors, days of tranquility for children, and children themselves as zones of peace. UNICEF had for over a decade provided protection and basic services to children on both sides of the front line in several civil wars. Like the UNHCR, UNICEF's obligation to work behind rebel lines was grounded in international law. UNICEF's interpretation of the UN *Convention on the Rights of the Child* was that children on both sides of a civil war had the right to the benefits of "international co-operation,"[15] including UNICEF's assistance. The presence of the UN agencies in AFDL territory was therefore based on more than a simple humanitarian urge; it was grounded in the agencies' internationally agreed mandates and in international humanitarian and human rights law.

In pursuing their mandates in eastern Zaïre in 1996–1997, the United Nations had to work with the de facto authority controlling that area, the AFDL, on a wide variety of issues. The UN agencies were willing to work with the new de facto authorities. This willingness to cooperate was facilitated in many instances by the fact that the UN's counterparts before the AFDL takeover had hardly changed at all after the AFDL takeover. This was particularly true for the technical staff of the line ministries such as

Agriculture, Public Health, National Education, and Social Affairs, and parastatals such as Water Supply and Roads. Only the political and security staff in areas like the Governors' offices and the *Agence Nationale des Renseignements*,[16] the secret police, had changed after the AFDL takeover, and some new political structures had been created, such as the AFDL Secretariat and the *Comités Techniques* charged with AFDL–UN liaison in North Kivu and Province Orientale (formerly Haut Zaïre). But the United Nations also had to deal with this political side of the AFDL regime in the months before the AFDL took Kinshasa, especially on the refugee question, but also on other issues. In the early months, AFDL–UN relations were severely complicated by political issues, even very old ones. Some of the AFDL's leaders, not least Kabila himself, still had bitter memories of the "betrayal" of the Congo by the United Nations in the early 1960s, and spoke quite openly of their contempt for the United Nations.

More immediately, the main UN agencies in the Kivus had all been deeply involved in the Rwandan and Burundian refugee camps and were therefore viewed as suspect by the AFDL's senior leadership. We were constantly asked why we had supported the *génocidaires* and ignored the legitimate needs of the Congolese people. Of the three big UN agencies in the Kivus, the UNHCR and the WFP had come explicitly to deal with the refugee influx. The smallest of the three, UNICEF, had had an office in Bukavu, capital of South Kivu, since the 1970s and had established an office in Goma, the capital of North Kivu, a year before the refugee influx. Still, the UN's work in the Kivus in 1994–1996 had overwhelmingly to do with refugees, and even UNICEF was viewed by many in the Kivus as a part of the UNHCR or as a junior contractor doing some of UNHCR's business. When I was appointed in March 1997 to head UNICEF's new Eastern Zaïre Operation, one of my first challenges was to prove to the AFDL authorities that UNICEF was there to work with and for Congolese children, while still playing a credible role fulfilling the agency's duty toward children caught up in the refugee crisis, which was grabbing the attention of the world's media. It was not an easy task, nor one at which I succeeded particularly well. AFDL–UN relations were further complicated by an investigation by the UNHCR into the allegations of massacres of refugees by AFDL and Rwandan forces. This investigation was deeply resented by the AFDL—and Rwanda—who wanted to know why the investigation of these alleged massacres was so much more important than the horror of the Rwandan genocide, which had not been so investigated. The UN investigation of the massacres colored the AFDL's views of all UN agencies, even those that had been working and continued to work with and for the Congolese population.

The UN's programs and projects in eastern Zaïre showed both continuity and change in the wake of the AFDL's takeover. The activities of the UNHCR, the biggest UN agency, changed dramatically from a focus on camp management to emergency assistance to Rwandan and Burundian refugees who were on the run in the jungle. The WFP's work also changed significantly to address the plight of the now mobile refugees, though the WFP retained some of its earlier activities supporting the food security of local populations. UNICEF supported UNHCR and WFP in the refugee rescue operation, but still put most of its resources into assisting local populations with immunization, essential drugs, water and sanitation, and child protection services. The large international NGOs present in eastern Zaïre at the time (e.g. Action internationale contre la faim, CARE, Médecins sans frontières, OXFAM, Save the Children) adjusted their program activities in a manner similar to the WFP and UNICEF, that is with a dual focus on both the refugee emergency and assistance to local populations.

The International Committee of the Red Cross did tremendous work in favor of the internally displaced Zaïrois. Unfortunately for the humanitarian relief organizations, the international media's intense interest in the humanitarian aspects of the Zaïre crisis in 1996–1997 centered almost entirely on the assistance to the Rwandan refugees, while the work with and in favor of local Zaïrois went unreported. This media slant, though understandable given the dramatic nature of the refugee crisis, had unfortunate ramifications for humanitarian operations in eastern Zaïre/DR Congo in later months, as it reinforced the AFDL's impression that the United Nations and the international NGOs cared more about Rwandan refugees than about Congolese citizens.

The AFDL was an ideologically disparate alliance, bringing together groups whose only common goal was the removal of Mobutu. Two of the dominant—and interconnected—ideological tendencies in the AFDL in 1997 were, however, an unreconstructed 1960s Afro-Marxism and a strong Congolese nationalism.[17] Both reacted strongly against Mobutu's chaotic rule and his reliance on Western powers for money and military support, as well as against the proliferation of NGOs in Zaïre.[18] Both these tendencies within the AFDL viewed the United Nations with great suspicion and sought detailed state regulation of economic and developmental activity, including UN operations. In their desire to regulate the UN agencies' operations in AFDL territory, the AFDL authorities often asked, or even ordered, the UN agencies in their territory to do things that fell outside of, or even violated, their mandates. The United Nations naturally refused. UNICEF was asked, for example, to provide tents and water facilities for a military cantonment, and to finance construction of a road in a militarily sensitive area. The UN agencies' refusals to comply with such requests were in turn interpreted as a lack of willingness to cooperate with the AFDL.

AFDL officials also routinely referred to UN agencies as "NGOs" and tried at times to register and regulate them as NGOs. This effort was stiffly resisted by the UN agencies, who were understandably protective of their status as international organizations. All the UN agencies had signed basic cooperation agreements with the government of Zaïre or its predecessors and, in both Zaïrois and international law, these were the relevant legal instruments, along with the *Convention of the Privileges and Immunities of the United Nations*,[19] which Zaïre and Rwanda, Uganda and Burundi had ratified. The AFDL authorities either simply did not understand these facts due to inexperience and lack of training,[20] or chose to ignore them because it suited their purposes to do so. At times, AFDL officials denied that such agreements existed or that they were binding on a "revolutionary government." Some AFDL officials in the eastern provinces continued to make such denials and evasions even after the AFDL became the internationally recognized government in Kinshasa.

In practical terms, the AFDL forbade direct contacts between UN offices in its territory—or "zone" as the United Nations called it—and UN offices in the rest of the country. The reason given was that the AFDL was afraid that spies could send military intelligence information to the AFDL's enemies in Kinshasa. UN offices were therefore strict in observing radio silence between the two zones, since high frequency radio signals are easily monitored by third parties.[21] Cellular telephone contact between Kinshasa and the east was cut off by the AFDL through the simple expedient of disconnecting the cell phone hubs in the four cities that had them, namely Bukavu, Goma, Kisangani, and Lubumbashi.[22] UN offices did have satellite telephones that could connect the two zones, but access was strictly controlled and interzonal calls were made only in extraordinary circumstances. Faxes could also be sent by satellite phone, but were sent only in unusual circumstances, since they created a paper trail and the news of a fax arriving from the other side of the front line could start rumors spreading, even if the contents of the fax were totally innocuous. The main form of contact between the two zones was e-mail sent by satellite phone through each agency's headquarters server. Access to e-mail and the small number of computers on which e-mail software was installed had to be strictly controlled, and was usually limited to the head of office, his deputy and the IT or security officer. E-mail traffic was not printed out, but was saved electronically.

Adherence to these strict rules on how (not) to communicate with the other side of the same country paid off for the United Nations in terms of minimizing the number of incidents that might have arisen if communications protocols had been more sloppy, but they did make life more difficult for UN staff. Many issues still had to be discussed between the UN's Kinshasa offices and UN offices in the rebel east, not least the fate of UN local staff displaced onto the other side of the front line, and important questions of management structures and budgets (see later). One way of addressing these questions without arousing suspicions was for senior UN management from both sides of the front line to meet face-to-face. Since both Mobutu's government and the AFDL refused to admit into their respective territories people having visas or stamps in their passports from the other zone, such meetings had to take place in third countries. I attended such meetings in Nairobi and Brazzaville.

Even so, the AFDL showed great interest in the UN's communications hardware, software, and procedures and tried on a number of occasions to interfere with them, regulate them, and monitor them. The fact that such interference, regulation and monitoring are illegal made the UN agencies resist such intrusions vigorously.[23] This resistance was interpreted on the AFDL side as a lack of willingness to cooperate at best, and as proof that the United Nations was on the side of the AFDL's enemies at worst. After reports began to appear concerning the massacres of refugees in the forests, those agencies and the NGOs most involved in assisting refugees in Zaïre had all the more reason to protect their information and communications.

Finally, the UN agencies had to engage in a delicate balancing act from the time they resumed operations in AFDL-held territory in November 1996 until the fall of Kinshasa to the AFDL in May 1997. Mobutu's government in Kinshasa was still the internationally recognized government of the whole of Zaïre, and indeed Zaïre was still the internationally recognized name of the country, the AFDL's assertions notwithstanding. All the UN agencies continued to maintain offices in Kinshasa and in other cities still under the control of Mobutu's forces, and UN-supported projects and programs continued to operate in territory controlled by the Government of Zaïre. The Kinshasa government jealously guarded its role as the internationally recognized government even as the last shreds of its de facto authority were disappearing before the advancing AFDL troops. The Mobutu government constantly reminded the UN agencies to behave "correctly" toward it; since UN offices in Kinshasa had already been looted twice by the FAZ in the 1990s, these reminders were interpreted as thinly veiled threats. By March 1997 the situation became even more complicated as it became increasingly clear that the Mobutu government's days were numbered and that, sooner or later, the AFDL would capture Kinshasa and become the officially recognized government. Not only did the United Nations have to deal with a de jure state and a de facto state within that state but it had to deal with the fact that the latter would soon replace the former, and with the fact that both could do considerable damage to UN staff, property, and project beneficiaries if the United Nations did not play its cards right.

UNICEF's Internal Administration and the Two-Zone System in Zaïre

In addition to the interzone communication issues mentioned earlier, the UN agencies had to address important policy issues in the divided territory of Zaïre in 1996–1997. These policy issues were particularly important for UNICEF as an agency that was present in country before, during, and after the refugee crisis and the ensuing civil war.

In late 1996, UNICEF appointed a temporary "program coordinator" to supervise the UNICEF offices in AFDL-held territory. The donor funds arriving for UNICEF programs in eastern Zaïre were deposited into the budget of UNICEF's Rwanda country office, though the program coordinator reported to the UNICEF regional office in Nairobi. This situation was less than satisfactory, and a new solution was devised in February–April 1997.

A new "Chief of Operations"—the author—was appointed in March 1997 to run the UNICEF operation behind AFDL lines.[24] This operation was called the "Eastern Zaïre Operation" (EZO) and it was given its own budget and a full complement of established posts. UNICEF decided, however, that the EZO, though autonomous in its day-to-day operations, should be linked to the main Zaïre country program run out of UNICEF's Kinshasa office. The EZO Chief of Operations reported to the head of the Kinshasa office and had to consult him on all strategic issues and on all issues that could potentially cross the front line between the AFDL army and the FAZ. The territory under the responsibility of the EZO Chief of Operations was to be the territory behind the AFDL front line. As various cities with UNICEF sub-offices—Lubumbashi, Mbuji Mayi, and Kananga—fell to the AFDL forces, those sub-offices would come under the authority of the head of EZO. This management system was modelled loosely on UNICEF's *modus operandi* in another country divided by civil war, namely the Sudan.

UNICEF's main office in Kinshasa continued to fund those staff posts, administrative costs, and routine program activities—such as immunization—in AFDL territory that had existed before the outbreak of the rebellion in the east. Supplies for such activities were ordered by Kinshasa office from third countries and delivered to EZO territory via the airports in Entebbe (Uganda) and Kigali (Rwanda) and the ports of Mombasa (Kenya) and Dar es Salaam (Tanzania).

Most importantly, it was decided that UNICEF would uphold national—Zaïrois—policies and standards in education, health care, and child protection in all programs and projects in AFDL-held territory. Maintaining the integrity of national standards was easy since the AFDL was never a secessionist organization, and never placed the territorial integrity of the Zaïrois/Congolese state in question. In short, everyone accepted that Zaïre/DR Congo would one day be reunited under one government, so there was never any question of developing separate standards and policies for the east.

This flexible approach to managing UNICEF operations in a country divided by civil war made a lot of sense,[25] but it was designed for a long civil war like Sudan's. In fact, the AFDL's military victory came much more quickly than anyone expected, after only seven-and-a-half months of fighting. UNICEF was then faced with the problem of having a unified country with two country programs, one for the east and one for the whole country! All new funding received for eastern DR Congo—as the country was renamed in May 1997—was placed in the main budget managed by UNICEF–Kinshasa from December 1997 onward. UNICEF spent the second half of 1997 and 1998 using up the funds in the EZO budget and reconciling and winding up the EZO accounts. A new management structure integrating the former EZO offices back into the main UNICEF country program for DR Congo was implemented from January 1998.

UNICEF's own internal organization under the EZO period was deeply influenced by that agency's system of country-based programming. Under this system, a locally based office negotiates a program of cooperation with the host government. This system is ideally suited to countries in "normal"—nonemergency—programming situations, and in situations where any emergency does not spill over international borders. This system is in contrast to that of the UNHCR, whose mandate calls upon it to deal with problems that, by definition, have cross-border dimensions, that is refugees. The UNHCR is much more likely to organize itself regionally, rather than in a country-based fashion.

The State-Within-a-State Reemerges: "The Democratic Republic of North Kivu"

Laurent Kabila's honeymoon with the Congolese people, his neighbors, and the international community did not last long. Most of the civil service—and even large parts of the security apparatus—remained unchanged since Mobutu's time, and, despite some positive changes in public sector performance brought in by the new government, the old habits of inefficiency, corruption, and brutality soon reemerged.[26] For the ordinary Congolese, the *nouveau regime* came quickly to resemble the *ancien regime* in its day-to-day workings. At the policy level, the new AFDL government, once installed in Kinshasa, struggled to define a coherent political strategy, economic policy, and attitude toward the donors and the international financial institutions, on whose debt Mobutu had already defaulted. There were several ideological and other fault lines. The Afro-Marxist and nationalist tendencies in the AFDL government struggled against the more technocratic elements who argued the need for international assistance and, hence, some accommodation with the United Nations, the international financial institutions, and the Western donors. Divisions within the new government based on ethnic and regional origins were also evident. Much was made of the differences between the "Katangan faction," including President Kabila, "the Kasaïan faction" including Economy Minister Pierre-Victor Mpoyo, and the "Rwandan" or "Tutsi faction," which included Foreign Minister Bizima Karaha, AFDL Secretary-General Déogratias Bugera, and army chief Moïse Nyarugabo.[27]

Congolese Tutsis, and their Rwandan and Ugandan allies, became prominent members of the new army, the *Forces Armées Congolaises* (FAC). Tutsi elements of the FAC and the Rwandan army used their military power to extract economic resources from rich and poor Congolese alike, and occasionally from expatriates as well. Such predations usually went unpunished,[28] and were particularly frequent when the army's pay day came and went without anyone being paid, a common event in the middle months of 1997, as the new government struggled to get a handle on the looted treasury of the nation. Stories of the Tutsis' newfound wealth, power, and arrogance began to circulate throughout the country. Rightly or wrongly, many Congolese who had months before welcomed the Tutsi-led armies of the AFDL and Rwanda as liberators came to view the Tutsis as interlopers, thieves, and oppressors.

Within a few months of Kabila's installation as president, it became obvious that the alliance that had brought him to power was crumbling. In particular, frictions arose between Kabila and the Tutsi/Rwandan faction, and between Kabila's government and his supporters in the governments of Rwanda, Burundi, and Uganda. First of all, Kabila no longer needed their military support since the war with Mobutu was over and, given his nationalist leanings, he probably did not want the DR Congo to continue to be under their influence. Second, the Tutsi alliance was becoming a political liability for Kabila as anti-Tutsi feeling rose and as his government's nationalist tendencies became more apparent. Finally, and most importantly, Kabila's new government proved unable and—at least in the Tutsis' eyes—unwilling to control the remnants of the *Interahamwe* and the ex-FAR who still roamed the forests and hills of the eastern provinces, harassing local Tutsi populations and occasionally crossing the border to attack Rwanda itself. Similarly, rebel groups fighting the governments of Burundi and Uganda also were able to use Congolese territory as bases from which to attack those countries. The rising level of mistrust between Tutsis and other ethnic groups was also both the cause and the effect of a dual system of administration, which took root in the eastern provinces of the DR Congo in the months after the AFDL takeover.[29]

Throughout North and South Kivu, Maniema, Province Orientale, and the northern parts of Katanga, Tutsis were placed in key positions in Governors' offices, district, and zonal offices and in the security forces, especially the FAC, and the *Agence Nationale des Renseignements* (ANR), the secret police. Where a Tutsi was not officially in the top post, one was frequently found in the deputy's post. To a lesser extent, the same was true in parts of the Kinshasa bureaucracy. In the eastern provinces, where a non-Tutsi was in charge of the civil administration, the local military chief was often Tutsi, and relations between the military authorities and their nominal civilian masters were testy, or nonexistent.

Over time, it became evident that this ethnically based arrangement of powers and posts amounted to a system of dual control, since the allegiance of most of these Tutsi officers lay elsewhere.[30] Many of the Tutsis were rumored to be Rwandan, and some Ugandan or Burundian. Many whom I met spoke with had Ugandan accents;[31] some freely confessed to origins in Rwanda, Uganda, or Burundi. It became common both in Kinshasa and in the eastern provinces to differentiate between "Congolese" and "Rwandans," the latter referring to all Tutsis, regardless of whether they originated in DR Congo, Rwanda, or elsewhere. Ethnic tensions mounted dangerously.

The system of dual control of the state structures, especially in the security forces, created high levels of uncertainty for civil servants, the general public, and for the UN agencies and NGOs. It was frequently difficult—even impossible—to tell who was in charge, since job titles meant little and the real power centers rarely dared speak their own names in public. Both sides issued conflicting instructions, or quietly—sometimes, not so quietly—blocked the other side's instructions from being carried out. Opportunists inside and outside the state structures sought to profit from the confusion for political and/or personal gain.

In other instances, two or more branches of government claimed authority over the same area or activity. In any judicial proceeding, several tribunals and quasi-judicial or administrative bodies claimed jurisdiction. Former UN staff who had been dismissed or who had not had their contracts renewed appealed for assistance from the *Parquet de Grande Instance*, the *Parquet de Petite Instance*, the *Tribunal*, the Ministry of Labor, the ANR and the *Comité Technique*. In North Kivu, the ANR, and the *Police des Frontières*, the former rumored to be allied at the time with the Governor's office and the Tutsi/Rwandan faction and the latter reportedly loyal to Kinshasa, argued over who should control immigration at Goma airport and at the border crossings with Rwanda and Uganda. Each body told the UN agencies and international NGOs in North Kivu that it had sole authority for issuing visas to foreign development workers, and each issued summonses to those who did not comply with its directives.

Of particular interest were the AFDL's two *Comités Techniques*, established during the civil war in North Kivu and Province Orientale to deal with AFDL–UN liaison. After the AFDL took power in Kinshasa and the normal public services slowly reestablished themselves, the *Comités Techniques* continued in both provinces to claim the power to coordinate the developmental and humanitarian activities of the United Nations and the international NGOs, and their relations with the Congolese line ministries. Since the Congolese state was effectively bankrupt and the United Nations and NGOs were a major source of funding for the line ministries, the nature and extent of this coordination function was of concern to the line ministries, no less than to the United Nation and the NGOs. In North Kivu, the *Comité Technique* functioned as part of the Governor's office and, hence, was closely linked to the Tutsi/Rwandan faction. The North Kivu *Comité Technique* had generally poor relations with the line ministries' offices in Goma; civil servants more or less openly challenged the legal basis for the *Comité Technique*'s claims to authority. The *Comité Technique* in turn regularly by-passed the line ministries and issued orders directly to UN agencies about what developmental projects and activities should be supported.

In September 1997, the *Comité Technique* in North Kivu sponsored an "evaluation" of UN agencies and international NGOs operating in that province, with the avowed intention of kicking out those who were not performing. The evaluation, which used NGO registration forms identical to those used by the Government of Rwanda, resulted in the expulsion from North Kivu—but not from other provinces—of a half-dozen "nonperforming" international NGOs. Reliable sources put it to me that there had been intense debates between the *Comité Technique* members of the evaluation team and some of the representatives of the line ministries. A few months later, the *Comité Technique* in North Kivu tried to regulate the qualifications of expatriate technical assistance workers in the province, thereby usurping functions of the Ministry of the Interior and the Ministry of Foreign Affairs in Kinshasa. It was around this time that people began talking about "the Democratic Republic of North Kivu," an allusion to the province's increasing de facto independence from Kinshasa.

In Province Orientale, the *Comité Technique* claimed similar powers and enjoyed similarly poor relations with the line ministries, but operated independently of the Governor's office. The *Comité Technique* in Province Orientale did, however, appear to work in close collaboration with a senior military officer of "Rwandan" origin. No *Comité Technique* was established in any other province. The Ministry of International Co-operation in Kinshasa tried on at least one occasion to exert its authority over the *Comités Techniques*, but without success.

Conflicts between the two sides in the dual control system usually simmered, but occasionally erupted into open violence, even before the outbreak of the new civil war and invasion from the east in August 1998. The Kabila government's attempts to rotate army units led to mutiny and running gun battles in the streets of Uvira in South Kivu and Kalemie in Katanga in December 1997, as Tutsi units refused to obey orders from non-Tutsi officers to relocate away from DR Congo's eastern border. The Tutsi troops apparently wished to stay close to the DR Congo's border with Burundi and Rwanda, both to guard Tutsi-inhabited areas and the borders from incursions and predations by the remnants of the *Interahamwe* and the ex-FAR. They believed, quite reasonably, that other Congolese troops would not be so zealous in defending either the Tutsi communities in DR Congo or their cousins in Burundi and Rwanda. The Tutsi troops may also have feared for their own fate if they were rotated at a time of rising ethnic tensions to other parts of the DR Congo, away from their home communities and the support of friendly neighboring states to the east. The *Police Nationale* fought running battles with the Rwandan army and elements of the FAC in Goma almost every night between May and September 1997. The *Police Nationale* and some Tutsi-dominated units of the FAC also fought in Kinshasa in early 1998 when a Tutsi officer was arrested by the Police.

For many months after the AFDL captured Kinshasa with Rwandan support, both the Rwandan and Congolese governments denied that such assistance had been provided. At the same time, however, the Rwandan army operated openly in North Kivu, South Kivu, and, to a lesser extent, in Province Orientale. The Burundian army operated in the southern parts of South Kivu province. The Burundian troops were easy to spot because they were the only army in the region to use the Belgian FN rifle; every other army used the Russian AK47. I occasionally encountered Ugandan soldiers or Ugandan members of the ANR in North Kivu and often heard rumors of the presence of Ugandan security forces in the eastern parts of Province Orientale. Members of the security forces, the North Kivu Governor's office, and prominent Tutsi residents of Goma all crossed to and from Rwanda without having to go through border formalities; they were simply waved through the border checkpoint while others waited in line.

In addition to these facts, the eastern provinces of the DR Congo in general, and North Kivu in particular, were full of rumors about the role of Rwanda and the Rwandans in the governance of that area in late 1997 and early 1998. All these rumors asserted that the Rwandans—and occasionally the Ugandans and the Burundians—were running the show behind the façade of a Congolese administration; all these rumors asserted that the Rwandans' role was entirely nefarious. Some of these rumors turned out to be false. (Rwanda did not invade and annex the Kivus in September 1997, though dozens of people assured me that it would.) Some of them turned out to be true. (I was warned in May 1998 that "the summer will be hot.") Some others may be true or false; I cannot say anything for sure except that they have some plausibility in the light of subsequent events. (I was told in March 1998 that all tax revenue in South Kivu went to the Rwandese capital of Kigali, not to Kinshasa, and that a Rwandan army unit was to be found at the top of the mineshaft of every gold mine in the Kivus. The United Nations has documented extensive stripping of Congolese assets by all foreign warring parties in DR Congo since the invasion of August 1998 and the ensuing civil war.[32])

Whether these rumors were true or false is possibly of less importance than the fact that they circulated widely and were repeated and believed by so many and with such vehemence. If nothing else, they were evidence of a shocking growth of the ethnic and international tensions that exploded a few months later, and which still fuel the flames of war in the DR Congo as I write this essay four years later. These rumors were also reflections of what ordinary Congolese in the Kivus intuitively felt about their governance in 1997–1998, namely that they were living in a state-within-a-state, and that the most important parts of the governance and security structures in eastern DR Congo were responsive—and responsible—to governments other than the legal government of the DR Congo in Kinshasa.

Needless to say, it was extremely difficult to run humanitarian or development projects in such an atmosphere. Humanitarian organizations were criticized by the civilian authorities for not addressing the crying needs of the Congolese people, while the military authorities were preventing those same agencies from going to the field, citing "insecurity" outside of the major cities as a reason. Frequently, the military requisitioned humanitarian vehicles, communications, and supplies. Appeals from the humanitarian agencies to the civilian provincial authorities for help in recovering these items were fruitless, as were appeals to the national authorities in Kinshasa. The situation was made more complicated by the fact that the politics of the dual control system were different in every province and district, and changes in civilian and military personnel—and, consequently, changes in alliances and systems of control—were the only constant. To give just one example of how complicated things had become, in November 1997, an outbreak of polio in Walikale District of North Kivu required immediate action by the Regional Health Director's staff and UNICEF. Since Walikale was a militarily sensitive area rumored to hold lots of *Interahamwe* and ex-FAR, the Regional Health Director sought the permission of the governor, a Tutsi, and the permission of the local military commander, a Katangan. But the area in question was populated largely by Hutus and was the home area of the Vice governor, who was Hutu. The relief flight of vaccines required complicated negotiations over several days before it could take off. In the meantime, of course, the outbreak spread, and hundreds of children were affected.

Conclusions

Three conclusions emerge about states-within-states; two deal with the UN's relations with such entities, and the third is a more general conclusion about the phenomenon of states-within-states. The first is that the UN's humanitarian agencies must inevitably find themselves working from time to time behind rebel lines; their mandates and indeed international humanitarian and human rights law require it. The fact that UN agencies are accustomed to—or even designed to—work primarily with de jure national governments does not preclude them from working within—and with—states-within-states. It does mean, however, that UN agencies are at the same time required to deal with the de jure authorities as well as the de facto authorities, and that the United Nations must often tread carefully between the two, for both practical and diplomatic reasons.

The second is that, when the United Nations works in and with such states-within-states, history is important. Even the apparently long distant past of UN involvement in a country can have important repercussions on cooperation today. This is especially true in the DR Congo, but is also true, for example, in Somalia.[33] The more immediate origins of large-scale UN involvement in a country may also have important implications for how the United Nations is perceived and handled by local authorities. It is impossible, for example, to understand the complex relationships between the AFDL—before and after it became the internationally recognized government of the DR Congo—and the United Nations without looking at the UN's huge refugee programs in eastern Zaïre in the mid-1990s. The circumstances that bring a rebel movement and the United Nations into contact with each other will shape much of the future evolution of their relationship.

The third conclusion, and perhaps most important from a theoretical point of view, is that what constitutes a state-within-a-state may sometimes be hard to tell. The state-within-a-state may come in some respects to resemble what other branches of political science call the "penetrated state," that is, the situation where a state's independence is compromised from within by the agents of another state capturing key parts of the administrative apparatus. Even normal categories like "government" and "rebels" or "bandits" may be of little use. What happened in the eastern provinces of DR Congo after the AFDL took power in Kinshasa is illustrative. At what point did North Kivu become a state-within-a-state? My own experience on the ground tells me that North

Kivu and, perhaps to a lesser extent, South Kivu were out of the control of Kinshasa long before the invasion and outbreak of the new civil war in August 1998. Yet from the time the AFDL took Kinshasa in May 1997 to the outbreak of the new war in the east 15 months later, North and South Kivu looked legally just like any other Congolese province. What lay underneath was a much more complex reality, and one that was much more difficult for the United Nations to deal with.

Notes

1. The views expressed here are entirely personal, and do not reflect the official policy of any organization. I would like to thank the editors for their advice and encouragement.
2. From 1971 until May 1997, the country was called the Republic of Zaïre. Since May 1997, the country has been called the Democratic Republic of the Congo. I will use the terms Zaïre and Zaïrois to describe the country in the period up to May 1997, and the terms DR Congo and Congolese to describe the country since then.
3. Archie Mafeje, *The Theory and Ethnography of African Social Formations: The Case of the Interlacrustine Kingdoms* (Dakar and London: CODESRIA Book Series, 1991).
4. Kisangani N.F. Emizet, "Congo (Zaïre): Corruption, Disintegration and State Failure," in E. Wayne Nafziger, Frances Stewart, and Raimo Väyrynen, eds., *Weak States and Vulnerable Economies: Humanitarian Emergencies in the Third World* (New York and Oxford: Oxford University Press, 2000). See also Mahmood Mamdani, "From Conquest to Consent as the Basis of State Formation: Reflections on Rwanda," *New Left Review*, Vol. 216 (1996); Kakwenda Mbaya, ed., *Zaïre: What Destiny?* (Dakar: CODESRIA, 1993); and William Senteza-Kajubi, "Background to War and Violence in Uganda," in Cole P. Dodge and Magne Raundalen, eds., *War, Violence and Children in Uganda* (Oslo: Norwegian University Press, 1987).
5. Emizet, "Congo (Zaire)." Thomas Turner, "The Kabilas' Congo," *Current History*, Vol. 100 (2001), pp. 213–218.
6. From the very beginning, the AFDL rejected the name "Zaïre," one of Mobutu's innovations, and insisted that the country return to its original name of "Congo."
7. A note on the ethnic politics of the region is in order here. Kagame is a Tutsi who grew up in exile in Uganda. Though his official title at the time of these events was vice president and Minister of Defense he—rather than the president—was the real power in Rwanda. During the Ugandan civil wars of the 1980s, Kagame was a close ally of Yoweri Museveni, who became president of Uganda in 1986 and is himself half-Tutsi. The president of Burundi since a July 1996 coup was Pierre Buyoya, also a Tutsi. Though all three share the same ethnicity, one should not assume that they have always seen eye-to-eye; indeed, since 1998, Ugandan and Rwandan troops have fought each other in DR Congo. Kabila was from much further south, in Katanga; in the 1960s, Kabila's rebel forces allied themselves with the Babembe people in their dispute with the Banyamulenge, a branch of the Tutsi in South Kivu. Many people were thus surprised to find Kabila in the late 1990s at the head of an alliance containing so many Tutsis.
8. The Rwandan vice president, Paul Kagame, admitted after the war was over that the Rwandan army had indeed helped Kabila to power. No one in eastern Zaïre at the time doubted for a moment that Rwandan army troops were in Zaïre; they operated openly, making no attempt to hide themselves or their identity. I have encountered Rwandan, Ugandan, and Burundian armed forces inside Zaïre/DR Congo in both 1997 and 1998.
9. UN, *Report of the Joint Mission Charged with Investigating Allegations of Massacres and Other Human Rights Violations Occurring in Eastern Zaire (Now Democratic Republic of the Congo) Since September 1996* (New York: United Nations, General Assembly, Document A/51/942. July 2, 1997), para. 42–49.

10. République du Zaïre, *Enquête Nationale sur la Situation des Enfants et des Femmes au Zaïre en 1995: Rapport Final* (Kinshasa: Ministère du Plan et Reconstruction Nationale, UNICEF, PNUD and OMS, 1996), pp. 6–9.

11. World Bank, *World Development Report* (New York and Oxford: Oxford University Press, 1994), p. 224.

12. Yet the AFDL did not declare itself to be the legitimate government of Zaïre/Congo until it captured the capital city of Kinshasa on May 17, 1997. Kabila was then sworn in as president of the Republic and the AFDL was established as the only political movement allowed to operate.

13. The UNDP and the WHO also had offices and small numbers of staff in the eastern provinces, but their staff, budgets, and operations were very limited in scope at the time.

14. UN, *Convention Relating to the Status of Refugees* (Geneva and New York: United Nations, 1951).

15. UN, *Convention on the Rights of the Child* (Geneva and New York: United Nations, 1989), Article 4.

16. This agency had been called the *Service National d'Intelligence et de Protection*.

17. Turner, "The Kabilas' Congo."

18. The proliferation of NGOs in Zaïre was as much a reflection of the collapse of the state under Mobutu as it was a tribute to the vibrancy of civil society. Many of these NGOs undertook functions that are often associated with the state—e.g. health care, education, water supply, agricultural development—and many were foreign funded.

19. UN, *Convention on the Privileges and Immunities of the United Nations* (Geneva and New York: United Nations, 1946).

20. The AFDL's Commissaire for Foreign Relations, Bizima Karaha, was a medical doctor by training, with no previous experience in diplomacy or international cooperation. The head and deputy head of the *Comité Technique* of the AFDL charged with UN liaison had before the AFDL's "revolution" been respectively a clerk in a rural health center and the head waiter in a Goma tourist hotel.

21. The AFDL had access to the same types of radio equipment as the United Nations, having looted dozens of radio-equipped UN vehicles and at least six UN office base stations. When I first arrived in Goma, my AFDL counterparts were openly using UNICEF stationery looted from UNICEF office.

22. The landline-based telephone system had long since disappeared from Goma due to looting of the wires. Though rudimentary landline systems continued to exist in Kisangani and Bukavu, the AFDL disconnected them from the inter-urban network so that no one could call out or in.

23. The *Convention on the Privileges and Immunities of the United Nations* of 1946 states that UN communications shall be inviolate and that the host country will provide and allow the United Nations such communications as its operations require. The Congolese government ratified that Convention over 30 years before the events in question. The basic agreements between individual UN agencies endorsed the Convention as well.

24. The title was later changed to "Senior Project Officer (Emergency)."

25. I can say this in all modesty, since the system was largely designed by my predecessor, and I contributed only small refinements to the basic design.

26. Associated Press, "Euphoria is Ebbing in Zaïrian Rebel Territory" (May 6, 1997). UN, *Report of the Special Rapporteur on the Situation of Human Rights in Zaire (Now Democratic Republic of the Congo)* (New York: United Nations General Assembly, Document A/52/496, October 17, 1997). U.S. Department of State, *Democratic Republic of the Congo Country Report on Human Rights Practices for 1997* (Washington DC: Bureau of Democracy, Human Rights and Labor, January 30, 1998).

27. None of these ethnic-based factions was entirely homogeneous, however, and members of an ethnic faction were frequently separated by ideological differences. Much has been

made of the strength and unity of the Tutsi faction, but it too was never entirely cohesive. In particular, there were important tensions between the Congolese Tutsis and their Rwandan allies, and between Rwanda, Burundi, and Uganda.

28. UN, *Report of the Special Rapporteur on the Situation of Human Rights in Zaire (Now Democratic Republic of the Congo)* (New York: United Nations General Assembly, Document A/52/496, October 17, 1997).

29. Turner, "The Kabilas' Congo."

30. Department of Humanitarian Affairs, *South Kivu, Uvira-Fizi Zone: Overview of the Humanitarian Situation* (Goma: Office of the UN Field Coordinator for Eastern Congo, DHA, 1997). *Libération* (Paris). "Au nouveau Congo" (August 28, 1997).

31. Many Tutsi members of the government that took control of Rwanda in 1994 after the genocide had grown up in exile in Uganda and spoke English with a Ugandan accent. Some of them spoke little or no French, which is the official language of Rwanda and Zaïre/DR Congo, and the medium of instruction in the schools there.

32. *Financial Times* (London). "Plundering of Congo Goes On" (October 22, 2002). Turner, "The Kabilas' Congo."

33. The former Italian Somaliland was a UN mandate territory until it was amalgamated with the former British Somaliland and granted independence as Somalia in 1960.

Chapter Eight

Why Not to State-Build New Sudan

Kenn Crossley

> We have come to the unanimous conviction that the situation of war in Sudan at the present stage has become immoral and a tragic farce. It is not any longer a struggle for freedom of the Sudanese people and for the defence of human rights. The war has become a struggle for power, business and greed. Many heartless people are taking advantage of it and enrich themselves at the expense of the poor.
>
> —Statement of the Comboni Missionaries in southern Sudan, January, 2001

International forces have recently prosecuted two wars, one in Afghanistan and one in Iraq, with an explicit intention to ensure "regime change." These forays have announced, with punctuation, that it is hip again to try a hand at state-building. A melee of prospective candidates alternatively hoping to maintain, reconfigure, or topple the existing Sudanese regime will no doubt be monitoring these international developments with varied measures of anxiety or exhilaration.

A more subtle upheaval is potentially brewing on another front as intrepid scholars, spurred on by an opening sally from Ian Spears in chapter one, debate whether or not the state-within-a-state is a helpful analytic category. On this front, academia and world politics are not out of synch. From a policy perspective, Spears's invitation to appreciate states-within-states is, in effect, an invitation to consider the merits and mechanisms of state-building. Granting for the sake of argument that states-within-states can be usefully and functionally identified, a corollary question must also be faced: should policy makers engage states-within-states as salient tools for state-building?

In Sudan, at least, the answer to this narrow question must be "no." The New Sudan of the SPLM/A[1] does seem to satisfy Ian Spears's conception of a state-within-a-state. Furthermore, given the history of Sudan, international observers might be tempted to use this state-within-a-state as a foundation for accelerated state-building in the South of Sudan. However, New Sudan teems with "post–Cold War combatants"—influential individuals who gain much from perpetuating war to the detriment of the people they claim to represent—while a further cadre of well-intentioned individuals lack the tools and resources to actually serve their constituents. Therefore we would do better by the southern Sudanese at large if we explicitly reject overt and accelerated state-building efforts in New Sudan.

Though negotiation with the SPLM/A is necessary to achieve peace and deliver humanitarian aid, these benefits should not be conflated with a rationale for setting up the SPLM/A as the foundation on which to build New Sudan as an independent southern State—that is "state-building." To politically recognize and nurture the fledgling administrative structures of New Sudan would be to prematurely foster an unrepresentative and ill-equipped political elite in southern Sudan at the expense of the broader interests of southerners at large.

More than a southern State, southern Sudanese need a broad-based, better-informed, and politically empowered *civil* society. Rather than nurturing the SPLM/A, international attentions could promote civil empowerment and related social and economic enhancement initiatives that would indirectly enable more Sudanese to participate in the process of taking informed decisions about the nature and direction of their State.

The New Sudan: A State-Within-a-State

Candidates for viable statehood typically control territory, monopolize force, mobilize shared identity within a populace, generate revenue, develop administrative structures, and exhibit political *raisons d'etre*. The New Sudan ballyhooed by the SPLM/A scores well on most counts.

Though the GoS asserts sovereignty over all of Sudan, significant southern chunks of the country are clearly outside of government control. Governors and civil administrators in most districts throughout the South mutually acknowledge each others' jurisdictions and represent and answer to armed opposition factions. Borders are imprecise, but de facto control is seldom difficult for international actors to verify. In negotiating terms of humanitarian access, for example, all parties to the conflict concede unofficial maps depicting conflict zones, transition zones, and "corridors of tranquility."[2] These negotiations imply and even chart at least temporary SPLM/A control over the regions in question. Humanitarian agencies still apply to the GoS for legal rights to fly into southern airspace and airstrips, yet it is well known that in most spots where planes might land and at most borders entered by road, the greeting party will be SPLM/A, not government, authorities. These crude but effective yardsticks repeatedly show that GoS towns and garrisons are well distinguished and isolated and that SPLM/A territorial control is broadly established at least in Western Equatoria, Lakes, and Bahr el Ghazal regions.[3]

The extent to which the SPLM/A monopolizes the use of force is only slightly more ambiguous. Many southern Sudanese carry and use light weapons. In the low-intensity conflict conditions prevalent in much of the region, armed citizenry drift back and forth between civilian life and participation in military affairs. However when citizens use force against each other outside of the parameters of warfare, they can be brought before an SPLM-convened court to answer for their crimes. Further, where police do exist they typically report to a Movement-affiliated Governor.[4] There are also roving bands of cattle raiders, armed marauders, and irregular militias, but to maintain supplies of ammunition and weapons these warlords often operate as well in affiliation with the SPLM/A. Thus, to the extent that any use of force is organized, it is fair to say that the SPLA exercises monopoly on the use of force in the areas under SPLM/A control.

A potential impediment to state-within-statehood, Sudan totes a long history of internecine animosity. There are 19 major language groups in Sudan, comprised in turn of nearly 600 subgroups. Many of the subgroups see themselves as tribally distinct from the next. So in addition to violent tribal conflicts between Dinka, Nuer, Murle, and Jikaney, among others, grievances could also flare up between, for example, Bor Dinka,

Ngok Dinka, Agar Dinka, and so on. One result of this fractious environment is a constant flux of political allegiances and factional realignments. There is little sense of deeply shared southern identity—until it comes to "the Arabs."

Though few people living in rural Sudan share a sense of what the SPLM/A is fighting for, many share a sense of what the SPLM/A is fighting against. From childhood, southerners endure annual seasons of government-sponsored warfare, population displacement, aerial bombardment, looting, cattle-raiding, and abduction of women and children. In response, despite significant inter- and intratribal divisions, the SPLM/A galvanizes a common resistance against, ostensibly, Islamicization and, more directly, the GoS. This shared anti-identity deftly incorporates otherwise competing tribal groups into the SPLM/A. The sentiment is sufficiently strong that wherever SPLA troops move, they will usually be fed and tended by supportive-ish populations[5] living in the areas under SPLA control.

In addition to subsistence support from the populace for the rank and file, the SPLM/A is adept at generating revenue for the Movement. Though accounting records are not easily come by, signs of SPLM/A wealth are clear. Soldiers are usually armed and often uniformed. Ranking officials maintain expensive lifestyles and work from well-equipped offices in Nairobi and Kampala. A rampart between Islamic Africa and the rest of the continent, the SPLM/A has at various times enjoyed significant financial support from governments of Eritrea, Ethiopia, Kenya, and Uganda. International governments, overseas sympathizers, and the southern Sudanese diaspora wine and dine SPLM/A big shots in capital cities throughout the developed world. Subsequent funds help keep the war effort rolling.

Inside Sudan, SPLM/A administrative structures proliferate. At airstrips and international border crossings, innumerable SPLM bureaucrats monitor travel and restrict the passage of expatriates to those with standardized SPLM/A-issued travel papers. Answerable to the SPLA Commander in Chief and Chairman of the SPLM, John Garang, there are governors, county secretaries, and town mayors, all assisted by endless deputies. There is a National Liberation Council of New Sudan that essentially functions as an advisory Parliament, and there are Commissions and Commissioners for everything from Finance and International Affairs through Agriculture to Health and Education. The SPLM/A sports a Criminal Code and non-martial judges to administer it. There is an SPLM Tax Code, an SPLM curriculum for education, even an SPLM policy on HIV/AIDS. And to top it off, senior SPLM/A officials are trying to introduce new currency. Throughout the region under SPLM/A control, the basic institutions of bureaucratic government do exist.

There is, further, some ethos of government. John Garang's wife is often referred to as "the First Lady." Adolescent villagers are taught to speak of SPLM/A policies as "decisions of our national government." SPLM/A programs refer to themselves as "national" programs. In workshops conducted by international humanitarian agencies, regardless of the subject matter, always at least one participant will rise and request that the facilitator use the terminology of New Sudan.

Finally, SPLM/A public statements, released by a Commission for Information, are rife with grievances against the Khartoum government and lists of SPLM/A political *raisons d'etre*. The litany includes: to resist the enforced Islamization of southern peoples, to ensure that southerners benefit from the exploitation of southern resources, and to shape and maintain a New Sudan in which southerners control and influence the political processes that affect the South.

Thus, though denied juridical status and any international recognition, key Weberian elements are clearly present throughout much of the SPLM/A-controlled south. The New Sudan can stake a credible prima facie claim that it constitutes an internationally unrecognized state-within-a-state. From this point of view, the elements are in place for accelerated state-building in New Sudan.

Interpreting New Sudan to Invite State-Building

Mark Duffield identifies two broad interpretive schemes that might apply to analysis of Sudanese conflicts.[6] On the one hand, conflict can be construed as a consequence of poverty and underdevelopment in conditions of scarcity and fractured social systems. By this conception, states and peoples make war to address specific political grievances or to create systems that are responsive to their particular material and social needs. To achieve peace, it is necessary to reconstruct civil society, build local capacity, and focus not only on emergency relief but on long-term political and economic development.

On the other hand, Duffield identifies a form of deadly violence rooted in natural adaptations of opportunistic leaders to post–Cold War security adjustments. By this account, a peaceful state will not be built through political and economic development because conflict is not intended to achieve long-term growth or social stability. Violent conflict is itself the intended economic and political development. The goal is not the long-term benefits of successful warring for society; the goal is fruitful perpetuation of war for the enrichment or empowerment of the warriors.

The following account of "the Sudan conflict" best fits the first of Duffield's interpretive schemes. It is against such an interpretation that sympathetic international engagement with New Sudan makes the most sense.

In 1898, Anglo-Egyptian forces decisively captured Khartoum from the government of the Mahdis. Over the ensuing 50 years an Anglo-Egyptian Condominium government subdued and ruled the territory now encompassed by Sudan. Thriving along important trade routes between the Nile and the Red Sea, northern Sudanese populations included wealthy, Islamic elites experienced in forms of politics familiar to outsiders. In contrast, the largely agro-pastoralist South featured diverse traditional tribal groups characteristic of non-Arab non-Islamic East Africa. Partly due to economic and social bemusement or indifference, and partly to preserve a buffer between Islam and colonial holdings to the south, the Condominium Government ruled northern and southern Sudan differently. The Southern Policy included indirect rule that formalized the leadership of traditional chiefs and separate tracks for social and economic development in north and south.

Through the mid-1940s, Condominium rule preserved strident social and religious distinctions, entrenched regional economic disparities, and fostered significantly divergent political cultures and institutions. Britain nevertheless granted in 1947 that the South ought to be included with the North in an independent Sudan. In 1953, Egypt settled with the Khartoum political establishment on terms of self-government. Britain seconded the plan while southerners were excluded from the negotiations. A group of southern soldiers in the government army mutinied in Torit in 1955. The following year, already engaged in a low-intensity civil war—the "first war"—Sudan declared to the world its independence.

Early Khartoum governments made few serious efforts to address the concerns of southerners but instead pursued aggressive policies of Arabicization. Southern political institutions were staffed by northern politicians and civil servants. Higher education was conducted in Arabic and aimed at "Islamizing" southerners. Many of the wealthiest merchants and traders commercializing the south were northerners exploiting southern teak, agriculture, and cattle. For the first few years, the outside world paid little heed.

Then in 1969, Jaafar Nimeiri seized power in Khartoum in a military coup d'etat. In his early going, Nimeiri expressed pan-Arabist pro-Soviet sympathies. U.S. ire was piqued, Sudan was blacklisted, and southern rebels garnered international support. Before long Nimeiri felt pressured into negotiating the Addis Ababa peace deal of 1972. Among other details, the Addis agreement defined North–South borders, made provisions for a modicum of southern regional autonomy within a united Sudan, and allotted profits from southern resources to the South.

Within months, some of Khartoum's Communist element narrowly failed to remove Nimeiri from power, dampening his Soviet zeal. America's ally in the Horn of Africa, Ethiopia's Emperor Hailie Selassie, was toppled in 1974 by factions sympathetic to the Soviets. And in 1978, significant reserves of oil were proven in southern regions of Sudan. True to Cold War form, the United States and the USSR flip-flopped in the Horn. Ethiopia cozied up to Moscow and the United States began pumping millions of dollars in military aid and hardware into Khartoum.

Buoyed by U.S. support, Khartoum soon felt ready to continue Islamizing the South, as well as to make a bid for southern resources. In the early 1980s, the GoS restaffed key southern posts with northerners, floated the idea of refining southern oil in a northern city, and tried to redefine regional boundaries to include key oil-producing regions that had previously fallen outside Khartoum's direct sphere. Nimeiri's flagrant disregard of the Addis agreement sparked a mutiny by southern soldiers in Bor in May 1983. In July, the SPLM/A formed in Ethiopia under the leadership of mutineer John Garang with massive technical, political, financial, and military backing from Soviet-friendly Mengistu. In September, Nimeiri declared *sharia* law in all of Sudan. *Jihad* and a second civil war were underway.

In the early 1990s, much changed. Citing humanitarian reasons, the United Nations intervened militarily in the Balkans and, more worryingly to Khartoum, in neighboring Somalia. Mengistu's government fell and Soviet sympathies became anachronistic in the Horn. In the Gulf War, an international coalition spectacularly tested conservative conceptions of international respect for sovereignty, and President Bush declared a New World Order. Khartoum sympathized with Iraq, opting for the U.S. doghouse and convincingly cutting itself off from military and development aid. With the fall of Mengistu the SPLM/A had meanwhile lost its major backer and was scrambling for alternative support.

Bereft of guidance from Cold War normative schemes, the international community had little clue what "the New World Order" could mean in terms of an Africa policy. The most desirable option seemed to be an African Renaissance of market-oriented, democratically inclined, human rights–talking leaders of politically self-defining African nations.

Worried that apparently burgeoning international interventionist appetites could seek space in Sudan, a fretful Khartoum reluctantly opened doors for UN humanitarian presence in the South. The SPLM/A rushed to rid itself of the spectre of Mengistu and, instead, to learn to speak like Renaissance men. In 1994, in Chukudum, the SPLM/A trumpeted a U.S. Congress position supporting the right to self-determination of marginalized peoples and declared itself the founding father of New Sudan.

For humanitarians, the New Sudan had apparently emerged from a purportedly typical pattern of conflict in Africa. Colonial policies had developed elitist political establishments at the expense of ethnically, economically, and regionally alienated nonelites. The groups were next lumped together in a single sovereign state. Fluctuating with the regional and global balance, Cold War policies alternatively rewarded and punished strong central governments and tenacious armed resistance.

On this interpretation, the socially, economically, and politically impoverished South harbored legitimate grievances that required humanitarian and political redress. Since the SPLM/A were the best mobilized southerners, the international community might have permitted itself a certain flexibility in dealings with the New Sudan.

Humanitarian Engagement with the New Sudan

Humanitarian engagement with southerners could not have been de-linked from international engagement with the SPLM/A for at least two reasons. Pragmatically, engaging the Army facilitated humanitarian action. Politically, despite the inherent risks, engaging the Movement encouraged internal reform and political evolution of the south.

In 1986, the United Nations estimated that almost 700,000 people were at risk of famine in the Bahr el Ghazal region of southern Sudan. An interagency humanitarian assessment team estimated that at least 38,250 metric tons (MT) of food aid would be required in the first six months of 1987 to preempt widespread starvation. Aid agencies managed to provide 4,000 MT of food aid in 1987 and only 1,300 MT to Bahr el Ghazal the following year. In 1988, war-related famine lead to the deaths of an estimated 250,000 people.[7]

Numerous humanitarian agencies had been willing to provide emergency relief, but the people in deepest need were beyond international reach. All parties to the conflict hampered efforts to deliver humanitarian aid by targeting relief personnel, diverting supplies, or legally or physically barring access to areas and populations in need. International failure to mitigate the humanitarian catastrophe of 1988 prompted the United Nations to explore innovative mechanisms for delivery of aid.

In 1989, the UN Secretary General charged UNICEF Executive Director James Grant with the task of securing humanitarian access to Sudanese populations. In a series of ad hoc agreements launching the OLS, Grant persuaded both the GoS and the SPLM/A to respect temporary cease-fires in clearly delimited and carefully negotiated "corridors of tranquillity." For a few months in 1989 and then a few more in 1990, relief operations went ahead by negotiated air, land, and water routes.

Building on these early successes, the United Nations negotiated the OLS Tripartite Agreements of 1994 and the OLS Ground Rules of 1995. Like the earlier OLS deals, the Tripartite Agreements and the Ground Rules affirmed the principle of unimpeded humanitarian access to war-affected civilian populations and defined mechanisms by which the world could safely access those in need.

The OLS Ground Rules thereby enabled humanitarian results that would have been extremely difficult to achieve by other means. Foremost among these victories was the fundamental principle of negotiated access to guarantee the relative security of humanitarian personnel and operations in the course of ongoing conflict. Rather than relying on peacekeeping troops or military convoys of any sort, parties to conflict pledged to respect humanitarian personnel and property and, in cases where the humanitarian enterprise was nevertheless threatened, to provide security advice such that evacuations could be undertaken on short notice.

There is little doubt that humanitarians have won, pragmatically, by engaging the movements. Thanks in large part to the OLS agreements, more than 50 international and national agencies and NGOs deliver millions of dollars in humanitarian assistance to war-affected civilian populations in need throughout southern Sudan.

The pragmatic humanitarian victories gained by directly engaging the SPLM/A are not without corresponding political benefits. In the mid-1990s, humanitarians were keen on local capacity-building and the development of civil administration in southern Sudan. As Paul Murphy notes, OLS agencies specifically sought to establish meaningful engagement with warring parties with a view to improving the quality of humanitarian interventions and boosting self-reliance among Sudanese communities.[8] To be self-reliant, Sudanese needed to have assistance in policy development, assistance in institutional development, and political affirmation at the grassroots levels. Moreover, many in the humanitarian community felt, "if you meaningfully seek to protect and empower the civilian being oppressed (starved) by the tyranny of war, then you also have to engage with the person holding the gun."[9] In addition to disseminating humanitarian principles, "meaningful engagement" consciously included the formation of humanitarian units for the political organs in order to precipitate internal debate within the warring movements.[10] Reading the winds, the SPLM/A established, with international technical advice, the Sudan Relief and Rehabilitation Association (SRRA)—legally a nonprofit humanitarian organization impartial and independent on paper but still answering directly to the leadership of the SPLM/A and staffed largely by seconded or retired SPLM/A officers and officials.

An argument can be made that internal debate has been fruitful. The SPLM/A now has prohibitions against the recruitment of child soldiers and has realized a program to demobilize underaged combatants. In comparison to many armed movements engaged in civil wars in Africa, the SPLA has a credible record on the treatment of POWs. And rather than brazenly boasting of commercial self-enrichment, the SPLM/A leadership are always concerned to present themselves as cognizant of human rights and democratic thinking.

Of course these positive strides have posed some potential political risks. Humanitarian action can change the internal political dynamics and reward certain players at the others' expense. Similarly, humanitarian engagement can create an image of viability where none exists.

Both the 1989 OLS I agreement and the 1990 OLS II agreement were ad hoc attempts to deliver the loot without the good guys getting shot. Neither deal trumpeted formal signatures from any party. Both deals took pains not to overtly challenge GoS sovereignty. As the OLS review of 1996 explicitly acknowledged, any potentially political considerations had to be "couched in the non-political language of disaster prevention and alleviation."[11]

Careful language could not divert all the heat. In June 1989, Prime Minister Sadiq al-Mahdi was ousted from Khartoum in a coup d'etat just before he could settle with the SPLM/A. Before year's end, the not-entirely-independent Khartoum press was pounding the OLS as a violation of Sudanese sovereignty. Then in August 1991 a so-called Nasir Group lead by SPLM/A insider Riek Machar posed itself as a southern secessionist alternative to Garang's mainstream SPLM/A. When UN Under-Secretary General

James Jonah arrived to broker a third OLS deal in October, heated attention focused on whether or not Riek's representative, Dr. Lam Akol, could or should be represented in negotiations. Not keen to grant any special standing to the SPLM/A mainstream, the GoS insisted that since both factions were rebels both might as well be treated equally.[12] The SPLM/A mainstream insisted that they were the only real SPLM/A and that Lam Akol should be excluded. The United Nations decided not to deal on the grounds that the Nasir Group was not in demonstrable control of any territory where the United Nations was seeking a corridor of tranquility for humanitarian operations. In an ensuing series of Nairobi press releases, Riek and Akol vented their fury. The government, the SPLM/A mainstream, and numerous subsequent splinter groups suspected that by securing UN recognition an opposition movement was securing international acknowledgment of de facto administrative control.

Simply by isolating the SPLM/A as the primary interlocutor, the OLS bestowed a certain pride of place on one armed movement over the others. The United Nations further invited the SPLM/A to formally endorse, in the Ground Rules, the Geneva Conventions and Protocols and the UN Convention on the Rights of the Child. Though not in any sense legally binding (and, frankly, periodically violated) these benchmarks of international good citizenship granted the SPLM/A a beguiling schtick with which to go a-wooing.

The Ground Rules approach also accelerated the instantiation of an SPLM/A facade of legitimate civil administration. International humanitarian staff were required to carry valid travel documents issued by the SPLM/A. The Ground Rules agreed that the (southern) "Authorities" could tax Sudanese UN staff provided that taxation was not undertaken on OLS compounds. The United Nations also agreed to pay rent to these same authorities for residential and office facilities but was granted exemption by the SPLM/A from taxation on equipment, goods, or services.

Over the years, these basic arrangements mushroomed with formal cooperation agreements between UN/OLS and the SRRA. By mid-2000, for example, the United Nations not uncommonly paid for SRRA office facilities, SRRA stationery, SRRA electricity generators, SRRA vehicles and vehicle repairs and maintenance, and even a specified number of flights of SRRA personnel between southern Sudan and Nairobi. When new SPLM/A bodies were established for specific humanitarian programs in Sudan, there was also often a significant UN presence. In May 2001, for example, the SPLM/A, SRRA, UN, and OLS agencies created a Joint Taskforce on Demobilized Child Soldiers. The Child Solder Demobilization project is self-styled as a "national program owned by the SPLM." The Taskforce leadership were appointees of the SPLA, SPLM, and SRRA, but stipends for each SPLM/A official were covered by UN agencies or OLS member NGOs, as were the costs of communications equipment, residential and office compounds, administrative expenses, and transportation.

It matters that the SRRA is a showpiece of the SPLM/A capacity in service delivery. The United Nations does not support SPLM courts or SPLM political posts such as governors or regional secretaries. But the SRRA is widely recognized as the service-providing organ of the SPLM/A. It could be significant, then, that since the SRRA is the prime evidence that the SPLM/A is sincere about having a nonmilitary service-implementing presence on the ground in Sudan, the OLS has effectively fostered the SPLM/A's main claim to social legitimacy and created the most impressive civilian trapping of New Sudan's state-within-a-state. That is, in effect, international humanitarian action might have already laid a possible foundation for state-building.

I do not wish to argue that such arrangements are unjustified from the point of view of humanitarian aid. It is precisely because of the humanitarian gains that this gradual, indirect, and low-key form of state-building seems most warranted.

We must, though, be careful with how we interpret the humanitarian politics. The question at hand is whether the humanitarian benefits of engagement with New Sudan's state-within-a-state are such that the international world might consider overtly and directly fostering the SPLM/A's New Sudan as a formal political unit—that is, consider accelerated state-building. The answer must still be no.

Post–Cold War New Sudan—Why Not to Build the State

"But surely," an argument might run, "by proliferating SPLM bureaucratic structures on a separate track from the SRRA and without support from the international human-itarian community, the SPLM/A shows commitment to nation building and only requires some technical help. The New Sudan is a fait accompli. Ours is but to recognize and develop that which nature hath already wrought."

Unfortunately, such reasoning is shaky on several counts. The Chukudum declara-tion was just that—a declaration with no civil apparatus on which to draw for support and without a plan or hope of creating one. A growing SPLM bureaucratic structure indicates little about the viability of an SPLM civil administration. Further, there is a significant difference between military occupation of a territory and instantiating a potentially viable state. Far from being a fait accompli, a state of New Sudan is, and should remain for some years to come, a rhetorical idée fixe.

We noted earlier that the SPLM/A has established a Taskforce on Demobilized Child Soldiers. We noted as well that to the extent that it is programmatically viable, the Taskforce is an SPLM/A organ in name and a product of international humanitarianism in practice. Sadly, such is the case throughout much of the SPLM bureaucratic structure—it exists largely in name only.

The SPLM does have a bare bones penal code and a handful of nonmilitary judges to administer it. These judges are highly intelligent, highly dedicated men usually trained in Khartoum or Egypt in the between-wars period. Yet they receive little more than moral support from the SPLM/A. Judges and lawyers hear cases and pronounce judge-ments largely on a volunteer basis. They have negligible nonmilitary apparatus for main-taining functioning courts, collecting fees or fines, or meting out justice. Further, rather than being overworked, they are often avoided altogether. Many southern Sudanese cultures have long histories of traditional courts administered by chiefs and elders rather than by government or para-government authorities. When citizens are prompted to take a case to a court, they often choose first to go through the traditional court system. For cases that do end up before the SPLM courts, the judges often (wisely) bring traditional law to bear and moderate the relevance of the SPLM/A legal code.

The Commission of Education is equally frail. There is a smattering of nominally-SPLM administered schools where teachers trained in Old Sudan[13] teach on a volunteer or community-supported basis without books, supplies, or basic materials. With virtually no financial or material support from the Movement for a school system, the Commission of Education is a well-intentioned administration with nothing to administer. The few teachers' training programs and schools that do actually function in southern Sudan are almost always funded by the United Nations or by interna-tional NGOs.

The Commission of Health manifests similar symptoms. In all of New Sudan, there are a few primary health care units and maybe a half dozen hospitals administered by the SPLM. These health facilities typically rely on funding from outside the Movement. What few drugs, supplies, and equipment there are in the health facilities are usually provided by international donors. Sudanese medical staff almost invariably received their training internationally or in Old Sudan. Wherever possible, citizens tend to seek assistance from international medical agencies.

Southern Sudan in general is in tough shape. There are few roads left from Old Sudan and fewer still new roads. Those that do exist are typically built and maintained for military purposes or else by the United Nations, international NGOs, or private transport companies from Uganda and Kenya. There is no communications infrastructure. There are no functioning sources of power other than small petrol-operated generators usually belonging to or provided by international humanitarian agencies. Commerce, other than some teak and cattle trade (and a putative slave trade) largely controlled by SPLM/A insiders, tends to be limited to household-level cattle auctions and basic subsistence products in local markets. Southern Sudan is still very much a chronically underdeveloped, rural, traditional society.

Against this backdrop, it is important that the SPLM/A in many ways goes unrecognized by the people themselves. Much of the populace does in some sense support a war effort. Families and communities send people to fill the ranks while soldiers are fed and watered and given places to rest.[14] But when there is no actual combat in a given area, the SPLA, the SPLM, and the SRRA play little part in most people's lives. If trouble arises within a family, the oldest males take decisions and offer guidance. If disputes arise between families or clans or tribes, chiefs and elders broker resolutions or offer rulings. When a community is displaced by war and looting, chiefs and elders typically guide people on where best to run. Where families are expected to be self-sufficient, where trade and commerce are barely existent, where subsistence depends on seasonal rains, civil administration is a quaint notion. The day-to-day struggles important to most southern Sudanese—water and grazing for cattle, land and irrigation issues governing cultivation, rites of marriage, inheritance, and family succession—are not governed by authorities at all but by centuries-old norms and traditions or by the weather. In all such matters, the SPLM/A is not simply underdeveloped but irrelevant.

In New Sudan there is a defined populace in a defined territory, a monopoly on the use of force, a shared anti-identity, and a revenue-raising bureaucratic structure that is flirting with international recognition. But, though perhaps impressive on paper, the SPLM/A on the ground has a bureaucracy that implements few to no relevant programs or services. Officials formulate policies and demand recognition but, for all intents and purposes, govern nothing and have nothing with which to govern. The SPLM/A simply is not a tool with which to build a viable state.

Some might argue that it is precisely because there is so little civil administration in New Sudan and so little to be civilly administered that the SPLM ought to be internationally recognized and developed. However the gap between expansive paper bureaucracy and diminutive administrative capacity should come as no surprise to SPLM/A-watchers. Throughout the course of the second war, the SPLM/A has at times intimated that it is uninterested in creating a viable civil administration for southern Sudanese. Instead, cynics might contest, the SPLM/A leadership has to date been intent on furthering the interests of the SPLM/A leadership.[15]

To articulate such a discouraging claim is to invoke the second of Mark Duffield's frameworks for conflict analysis outlined earlier. To warrant such a claim is to level allegations that are at best contentious and at worst dangerous. Yet to ignore such a claim is to premise future Sudan policy on a doctrine devoid of relevant nefarious context.

Recall that Duffield's post–Cold War framework of conflict analysis considers political violence that is not so much a means to a wider social end as a means to achieve narrow personal goals. One characteristic of such war is that the populace is not treated as a beneficiary of conflict waged on their behalf but is, rather, a resource to be controlled. In a related vein, the tools of civil life are likewise potential aids to the enemy and therefore treated as military targets in their own right.

These symptoms of post–Cold War conflict are certainly manifest even now in areas such as Western Upper Nile. Conflict in this tragic region repeatedly features rampant and indiscriminate killing of noncombatants, widespread and manipulated population displacements, looting and cattle raiding, abductions of women and children, burning of towns, villages, and crops, and ransacking of humanitarian operations. It is disingenuous to argue that such warfare is waged on behalf of the populace. And much of such conflict pits southern commanders against southern commanders in tangled webs of government, opposition, and mercenary alliances.

The SPLM/A might claim that only southern turncoats, warlords, and forces aligned with other political movements, not the SPLM/A, wage war against the people. Or, the SPLM/A might claim that such warfare is a response to GoS tactics and is not SPLM/A doctrine. However one of the most notorious commanders in Upper Nile has been Peter Gadet. Gadet was armed and mobilized by the SPLA in the late 1990s and early 2000s to strike at the oilfields that sustain GoS coffers. In practice, Gadet's troops instead waged scorched earth warfare against the villages occupied by other southern commanders. His exploits included the looting and burning of several humanitarian compounds in Nyal. These tactics were not the stuff of campaigns to defend populations against GoS-sponsored aggression. These were campaigns against civilian populations by an SPLM/A-aligned commander.[16]

Other instances of antipopulation behavior abound. In Eastern Equatoria, the largely Dinka SPLA occupies the traditional territory of the Toposa and Didinga peoples. Since the SPLA took control there have been countless complaints of SPLA harassment, SPLA plundering of local produce, SPLA soldiers raping local women, SPLA conscription of local youths, and so on.

Lest we generalize too hastily, let us look back as well to the Bahr el Ghazal famine of 1998. Hundreds of thousands of Dinkas died of starvation in the home areas of many SPLM/A officials. Nevertheless, Human Rights Watch carefully documented widespread and massive diversion of humanitarian food aid from the populace by the SPLM/A.[17] These diversions do suggest that the SPLM/A has not always been on the side of its people and, if it is so now, has been reformed only in the last couple years.

Some in the SPLM/A camp might remark that it was not really the SPLM/A but renegade commanders like Kerubino Kuanyin Bol, for example, who engaged in activities clearly contrary to the public good. Such a claim simply draws attention to a third aspect of Duffield's account of post–Cold War conflict—the frequent sacrifice of ideological coherence and allegiances for the purposes of personal gain. Unpopular within the Movement or not, Kerubino was periodically a leading SPLA commander and it suited SPLM/A leadership not to move against him or his antipopulace activities for the longest time. Indeed, since its inception in 1983, the SPLM/A has been rife with splintering and unsplintering factions, defecting and undefecting commanders, and narrowly escaped (and severely suppressed) palace coups.[18] And none of this is to mention the dramatic and, if it is taken at face value, ideologically bizarre about-face from Mengistu's sponsorship to human rights–talking Renaissance men in the space of a few short years spent with meagre international patronage.

It could well be that the muckraking of the last few paragraphs is unwarranted. Perhaps the past is the past and important corrective measures are being taken. Nevertheless, it is relevant that the SPLM/A has historically attracted its fair share of opportunists and unsavory elements who have gained personally at the expense of the populace. For the sake of southern Sudanese, the SPLM/A should be encouraged in ongoing efforts to reform itself as a disciplined military force and to redeem itself of its ribald past. But to encourage institutional reform within one political faction is a far cry from encouraging this military–political movement with a sketchy record for harming the people to become a civil administration in a land still unfamiliar with the concept and workings of a viable state.

One political faction is the operative key here. The SPLM/A is certainly the leading military–political organization in de facto control of southern Sudan. The SPLM/A is not *the* representation of the views of southerners or of the South.

The concept "the South" is conveniently fuzzy, even among armed opposition movements and within the SPLM/A. As noted earlier, the early days of the SPLM/A featured numerous divisions and undivisions including periodic spats between John Garang and Riek Machar. Their 1991 split was ostensibly over competing visions of the South. Garang claimed to be for southern self-determination but not necessarily secession while Riek pushed for full secession. In the following years, other voices for self-determination-but-not-necessarily-secession emerged. Garang, unofficially, slagged these self-determinists as being too soft on secession. Twenty years into the war, the SPLM/A has yet to substantiate its own concept of or position on secession and/or self-determination let alone manage to represent the views of southerners.

Some might object that in fact draft discussion papers on southern self-determination have been circulating informally in the lead-up and postlude to recent Machakos meetings between the SPLM/A and the GoS in Kenya. These papers do begin charting viable options for including a process of self-determination into any final comprehensive peace agreement. While certainly welcome additions to the peace dialogues, it is relevant to this chapter that many of these ideas originated not within the SPLM/A nor within the GoS but with third-party advisors to the process. Supporters of the peace process who are cautious of overemphasizing the merits of the SPLM/A might well note that if indeed the perpetuation of the war was ideologically motivated, a position on self-determination would have been among the first policies that the SPLM/A could have been expected to articulate rather than one of the last. Moreover, it is again relevant that the processes being explored in the discussion papers risk paving the paper way to a paper peace that ensures the centrality of the negotiators in defining the direction of life after a peace deal. Developments on the legal front do not necessarily translate into capacity on the ground to build the structures that the paperwork might one day stipulate. All of which is to say that the current positive efforts to define self-determination might not so much exhibit a political *raison d'etre* for the SPLM/A to further the interests of Southerners as much as a belated addition to the rhetoric that serves the personal interests of those at the table very well.

Ambiguity over a notion as difficult as self-determination of the South is pardonable. For the SPLM/A leadership, it is also politically expedient. To adopt outright secession could be to alienate influential and wealthy members of the Sudanese diaspora and many in the international community who support a pluralistic, democratic, unified Sudan. To reject secession out of hand could be to alienate and provoke the messy resistance of hard-line southern military commanders.

Intra-south bickering compounds the ideological and strategic problems with southern self-determination. It is handy for academics and politicians to deal at the level of North vs. South. An equally accurate unit of analysis is perhaps the tribe. The SPLM/A typically mobilizes support among Dinkas and among Equatorian tribes such as the Xande. The SRRA humanitarian counterparts are likewise typically Dinkas and Equatorians. With the notable exception of Peter Gadet, most Nuer Commanders have until recently sided against (Dinka) Garang's SPLA with the Sudan People's Democratic Front (SPDF) of (Nuer) Riek Machar or even with the GoS. Riek's band of humanitarian counterparts in the now-fizzled Relief Association for South Sudan are likewise predominantly Nuer. A third major tribal group, the Shilluk, feature their own entirely different armed movement and humanitarian counterpart.

All alliances are malleable. After a stint in the SPLM/A, a stint with the Nasir Group, a short stint with the GoS, and a stint as head of the non-SPLA non-GoS SPDF, Riek Machar is now back again in an uneasy alliance with Garang's SPLM/A. The Shilluk have acquiesced to a delicate truce with the GoS and are in inactive opposition to the SPLM/A and to any of Riek's former forces. Meanwhile, Southern Blue Nile boasts Islamized non-Nuer non-Dinka who side with the SPLM/A against the GoS. In Abyei in Southern Kordofan, there is a large group of influential Dinka who live officially in the North but who fight with their kinsmen from the South against their Islamized non-Arab neighbors, the (erroneously lumped) Bagarra tribes.

Outside the jockeying of the movements, the tribal scene is just as muddled. In conversation, the well-known Sudanese scholar Dr. Ushari Mahmood estimates up to 35 intertribal squabbles that feature low-intensity deadly violence. Intertribal fighting is not ideological but concerns access to water or pasture lands, tribal-border disputes, cattle raiding, and abductions of women and children.

Although the international world speaks of "the peace process" in Sudan between North and South, southern Sudanese are party to numerous peace processes between southern tribes. Dinka and Nuer subgroups, for example, have marked a peace accord at Wunlit with the ceremonial sacrifice of a white bull. Groups of Murle and Jikaney and others likewise sealed terms of peace in direct discussions at Lilir between chiefs, elders, spiritual leaders, and various community members. These are the showpieces of the so-called people to people peace processes.

While the SPLM/A sanctioned the meeting and provided security at Wunlit, recent people to people peace efforts have not been so well received by the SPLM/A. A people to people peace conference facilitated in 2001 by the New Sudan Council of Churches in Kisumu, Kenya was boycotted by the SPLM/A. Though never formally articulating reasons for the boycott, ranking SPLM/A members explained off the record that the people to people peace processes challenge SPLM/A primacy of place. As deals progress on the ground and intertribal fighting is seen to abate, chiefs and elders, community leaders, and civic groups increase in stature as a potential set of parallel authorities[19] who are active in the communities and who do not necessarily share the jargon of an SPLM/A New Sudan.

Parochial SPLM/A frostiness toward the people to people peace meeting was not completely out of character. Throughout the course of IGAD-brokered peace talks with the GoS, the SPLM/A has made no effort to include the views of "the people." With the exception of the highest cadres of Movement leadership and the best-informed politicians and academics in the diaspora, people in and from southern Sudan do not speak of self-determination, redefinition of the Sudanese federation, wealth-sharing arrangements, regional hydro-politics, or blurred jurisdictions of religion and state. The SPLM/A popular support is not mobilized around coherent ideology and policy but around a cult of personality and shared dislike of "the Arabs." Schoolboys sing anthems to John Garang but their volunteer teachers have no idea where he stands on interim arrangements for power succession nor that he should even take a stand. Village elders sadly watch their youth trudge off to fight the SPLA's war but have no idea if the SPLM/A can or will or even wish to provide their children with an infrastructure for education.

The imaginers of New Sudan, meanwhile, prolong negotiations in comfortable secrecy in foreign capitals that "the people" have never heard of, discussing at length issues for which "the people" have no idea they're taking up arms. In this context, a carelessly negotiated peace could be a personal disaster for the senior ranks of the SPLM/A. Peace would require that they abandon the fast pace, luxury, and prestige that they find in Europe, Nairobi, and Kampala to actually try and govern in the darkness, disease, and anonymity of chronically dysfunctional southern Sudan.

At best, the SPLM/A is incapable of delivering a New Sudan. At worst, they are uninterested. At the very least, the SPLM/A's New Sudan is not representative of, not inclusive of, and not engaging with the very people who need a new Sudan. The international community has very good reason not to expect or to help the SPLM/A to build a viable state that promotes the human security of southerners.

What Then?

Having advocated against state-building while raising the very real grievances of southern Sudanese, it is necessary to at least briefly extend a promissory note of alternatives that might stem from accepting the arguments mentioned earlier.

Essentially, this chapter has suggested that to address the bona fide and overwhelming human security needs of southerners, international parties ought not directly or officially promote the state-within-a-state that is New Sudan—that is, there should be no direct and explicit attempts at state-building using the SPLM/A as the building blocks. Holding off on using the SPLM/A for state-building does not discount, and indeed highlights, a crucial need to continuously refine conceptions of southern self-determination. This chapter has simply suggested that we can and should do so even while advocating against overly zealous political dealings with New Sudan at this time. Were we to recognize the SPLM/A as government by default, we would be nurturing a self-appointed civil administration that is at best incapable and at worst pernicious.

Instead, we should engage in building a civicus without building a state. Some might worry that the strategy is conceptually incoherent.[20] It is not. Conventional wisdom holds that states are the most enduring mechanism known for promoting the human security of a populace. Such is the case, however, where those who direct the apparatus of power do so in a fashion that is at least not knowingly contrary to the interests of the populace and, preferably, that promotes the interests of the people being governed. It is crucial at least that governors respond to their constituents' interests, that capacity exists on the ground to respond, and ideally that the populace can periodically and broadly articulate the interests to which the governors ought to respond. Section IV earlier demonstrates that these conditions are not and would not be met by an SPLM/A New Sudan that is built by the current cast of characters in the current socioeconomic and political circumstances in Sudan. In order for a state to work for the Sudanese, the capacity and readiness of southerners at large needs to be developed. To address their enduring human security needs, Sudanese do require assistance in state-building. That's why we should not build New Sudan as an SPLM/A state.

Not state-building does not mean ignoring the SPLM/A. A concerned world did win humanitarian access to populations in need by working with the SPLM/A's state-within-a-state. Further, to maintain and enhance humanitarian development, we should continue to constructively engage the Movement. To engage the Movement is not, though, to set the SPLM/A up as a government unless the difficulties outlined here should be overcome. The needs of southern Sudanese greatly outstrip the limitations of the SPLM/A. An apparatus of state, politically defined but bereft of capacity and intent to deliver services, will not provide the desired human security.

Rather than relying on New Sudan, new Sudanese will often have to rely on themselves. Instead of national services, the most effective level of response to people's basic needs will best operate for now at decentralized local levels and best draw upon community leaders, burgeoning civil society groups, and traditional chiefs and elders. As and when local expertise emerges from the communities, the necessary human resources will be increasingly mobilized to extend services to broader and broader levels. As the number and scope and responsiveness of the private sector and service-delivery civic groups grows, more and more southerners will be increasingly adept at formulating and articulating broader social and political objectives. And as the capacity and initiative of civil society increases, governors will have more incentive, and more capacity to draw upon, to meet the social and political aspects of the human security needs of the people. To encourage and develop administrative, governance, commercial, and human resource capacity during a decade (perhaps) of explicit nondecisions on the eventual political shape of a new Sudan would be to build the state without state-building. By not immediately constructing the political apparatus for a New Sudanese state, but by first trying to mobilize the resources, social capital, and technical expertise necessary to underpin the development of a viable state, we do move toward the sort of political unit that can provide human security for a needy population.

We should, then, do our deals with de facto military controllers. We should carry on peace talks, broker cease-fires, and open all avenues of developmental engagement. But we should do so in order that we can work directly with all populations and build governance capacity that draws on all constituencies at community and regional levels. In supporting communities and regions without seeking to construct nations, we expedite the evolution of viable and legitimate and lasting states.

Thus we are faced with daunting political and socioeconomic problems, but not a conceptual one. The political task is to engage and distract the guns and the politics to seal and sustain a comprehensive cease-fire and subsequent peace deal until such time as the people of Sudan declare themselves ready to make informed decisions for themselves regarding the preferred shape of future. We do not build the state-within-a-state that is New Sudan into an internationally recognized state.

Conclusion

What then do we make of the broader question posed by this volume? Simply that policy responses to states-within-states should vary with the specific contexts. In New Sudan, the best tactic is to exploit the state-within-a-state for humanitarian ends without trying to sidestep necessary social evolution toward a political unit capable of providing human security to its citizens. We may be content with an incomplete political definition for the current political unit, provided that progress is taking place on the ground. There is no need to rush the juridical status of the empirically inept such that leadership capacity and good governance are targeted after the fact at self-appointed nominal leaders. In the long run, it is more promising to slowly develop the capacity of the empirically viable such that juridical status is imparted (or not) to capable leaders who emerge from the ranks of good local and regional governance.

Notes

1. The formal distinction between the Sudan People's Liberation Army (SPLA) and the Sudan People's Liberation Movement (SPLM) is that between the military and political wings of the same umbrella organization. For the purposes of this chapter, little hangs on making a distinction—it would be impossible to promote "state-building" using the Movement as agent without at one and the same stroke promoting the Army since the individuals involved—the leadership of the Army and the leadership of the Movement—are the same people ranked in the same hierarchy. Unless referring to a discrete act or condition of one arm or the other, this chapter shall follow the stylistic convention of the SPLM/A itself and refer to the umbrella structure.
2. These maps are of course unpublished, for publication would risk institutionalizing government concession of control.
3. With the political remarriage of John Garang's SPLA with Riek Machar's forces in 2000, SPLM/A control might soon be plausibly said to extend as well to much of Upper Nile.
4. The currently ranking governors are typically leading (or retired) commanders.
5. There are of course nonsupportive populations as well, often for good reason. Toposa tribes people in Eastern Equatoria are a case in point.
6. Mark Duffield, "Aid Policy and Post-Modern Conflict: A Critical Review," Occasional Paper 19 (Birmingham: The School of Public Policy, University of Birmingham, 1998).
7. David Keen, *The Benefits of Famine: A Political Economy of Famine and Relief in Southwestern Sudan, 1983–1989* (Princeton, N.J.: Princeton University Press, 1994), pp. 130–131; Ataul Karim, Mark Duffield, et al., *OLS, Operation Lifeline Sudan: A Review* (Nairobi: July 1996), p. 15.
8. Paul Murphy, "Critical Engagement for Change: Capacity Building and Humanitarian Affairs," UNICEF/OLS, 1997.
9. Ibid., p. 18.
10. I should note as well that certain individuals representing the SPLM at the time impressed UN officials as especially progressive and open to ideas of human rights, humanitarian principles, and international humanitarian law. Sadly, much of that group was effectively sidelined by a Conservative backlash within the SPLA not long after the Ground Rules were negotiated.
11. Karim, Duffield, et al., p. 22.
12. There was also speculation at the time that Riek might have been in negotiation with the GoS and, therefore, that the GoS wished to have "their" SPLA internationally recognized. This interpretation would add even more strength to the claim that UN humanitarian efforts were a vehicle for low-key state-building.

13. Old Sudan is the term applied to the early period of Sudanese Independence before Garang launched the ongoing "second war" and during which the bureaucracy established and maintained by Khartoum was still functioning. Most current teachers were southerners trained either at the University of Juba or in Khartoum before the war. Other teachers were trained by international NGOs in places like Kakuma refugee camp in northern Kenya.

14. Public maintenance of the SPLA is not always completely voluntary nor ideologically motivated. Though incomes and food are scarce, soldiers typically eat. In probing the origins of child soldiery in Sudan, international humanitarians have found that guns can be as effective as appeals to people's political sympathies for ensuring that soldiers and their families are fed and clothed. Basic household economics thus prompts some to enlist for rather nonideological reasons.

15. The nature of this chapter compels me to write in broad strokes. There are many dedicated people within the SPLM/A who are intent on advancing the well-being of southern Sudanese and whom I regard with the utmost respect. Sadly, it is not clear that the group of well-motivated and dedicated people always overlaps with the group of powerful or influential people. Thus I write this chapter not in a spirit of antagonistic cynicism but of quiet sadness.

16. More recently, rumors abound that Peter Gadet, without altering tactics, has changed allegiances and is now GoS-aligned. If such is the case, it would reinforce the next claim that the SPLA is a congregation of opportunists lacking a coherent ideological agenda.

17. Human Rights Watch, *Famine in Sudan, 1998* (New York: Human Rights Watch, 1999). Note as well that though there is no documentation, many Sudanese and some international humanitarian workers are puzzled why the quantities of food aid known to be diverted were so far in excess of that required to feed the army. This fact fuels undocumented suspicions that influential SPLA leaders sold food to famine-affected northern populations, to merchants in Uganda, and to Bor Dinka who traded cattle for grain, which they in turn sold for cash in northern Kenya. John Garang is a Bor Dinka. I have no evidence with which to either confirm or deny these reports and so have chosen to leave them in the realm of intriguing hearsay.

18. For an insightful account of the tempestuous political positionings of various movements and various players within the movements, see Peter Adwok Nyaba, *The Politics of Liberation in South Sudan: An Insider's View* (Kampala: Fountain Publishers, 1997).

19. For steering thinking down these lines, I am grateful to Ken Bush.

20. For enlightening conversation on this subject, I am grateful to Don Hubert.

Chapter Nine

Safe Havens as Political Projects: The Case of Iraqi Kurdistan

David Romano

Since 1991, a de facto state has existed in northern Iraq. It was brought about by the historically unprecedented convergence of the temporary collapse of the Iraqi state after the Gulf War in 1991 and the emergence of international support for the creation of a Kurdish safe haven. This fledgling Kurdish political entity—variably referred to as the Kurdish Autonomous Zone of Northern Iraq, Iraqi Kurdistan, or (to the greater displeasure of neighboring Turkey, Iran, and Syria) South Kurdistan—has quietly been developing many of the attributes of a "state" within the larger Iraqi state. It controls its designated areas with a fairly solid monopoly of force (although since March 2003 this monopoly has been partially compromised with the presence of American troops); it boasts some, albeit limited, capacity to generate revenue; its administrative infrastructure provides basic services to the populations within its borders; and, finally, it enjoys legitimacy in the eyes of its population bolstered by a clearly developed sense of Kurdish national identity. While this entity still faces deep internal contestation between rival factions, each of which controls parallel administrative apparati within subdivided portions of the territory under its overall control, it nonetheless represents the most significant instance of de facto statehood in modern Kurdish history.

With the fall of Saddam Hussein's regime in April 2003, Iraqi Kurds now seek to preserve the de facto statehood they have enjoyed from 1991 to 2003. At a minimum, they are hoping that the autonomy they experienced may come to receive juridical recognition in the form of a decentralized Iraqi federation. The preservation of this autonomy, however, will depend on the interplay between three factors: the degree to which the Kurds can overcome their fractious history and consolidate their identity and strength as a group; the power and composition of the emergent post-Saddam political order in Iraq; and the ability of the Iraqi Kurds to convince the American and British administration in Iraq, as well as neighboring states, to take their demands for recognition and autonomy seriously. After examining the interplay of these three factors from an historical perspective, this chapter will analyze the present viability of the Kurdish political entity with an eye to determining what its future might be in the context of an Iraqi state in the throws of being reconstructed.

The Kurdish Struggle for National Recognition—A Historical Perspective

The modern political history of the Kurds dates back to the post–First World War period when the political boundaries of the Middle East were being redrawn. Included within the proposals for the new post-Ottoman political order was that of an independent Kurdish state, subject to the acceptance of the idea by the majority of the Kurdish population. Article 64 of the Treaty of Sèvres (1920) stated,

> if within one year from the coming into force of the present Treaty the Kurdish peoples within the areas defined in Article 62 shall address themselves to the Council of the League of Nations in such a manner as to show that a majority of the population of these areas desires independence from Turkey, and if the Council then considers that these peoples are capable of such independence . . . no objection will be raised by the Principle Allied Powers to the voluntary adhesion to such an independent Kurdish State of the Kurds inhabiting that part of Kurdistan which has been hitherto included in the Mosul Vilayet.[1]

Kurdish history up until 1991, however, has been a betrayal of this original commitment. This section of the chapter seeks to outline some of the reasons for this frustration of Kurdish aspirations focusing on the three factors outlined earlier relating to a degree of internal social and political cohesion, the nature of political opportunities provided by the Iraqi state, and the consistent reticence of regional and international actors to recognize, let alone support, Kurdish political concerns for fear of opening a Pandora's box of secessions and irredentism.

The Kurds operate within a complex social and political framework. As a result of the state system created after the First World War, the Kurdish population that numbers between 23 and 28 million is dispersed throughout the four states of Turkey, Iran, Iraq, and Syria, with an additional 800,000 expatriate Kurds living abroad, mostly in Europe. They form around 20 percent of Turkey's population, 15 percent of Iran's population, 27 percent of Iraq's population, and less than 10 percent of Syria's population.[2] Because of the large numbers of Kurds in each of these countries, the governments of the region view them as a potential threat to their nation-building and modernizing policies and have either refused to acknowledge the existence of the Kurds (Turkey), or in practice sought to exclude them as a group from any substantive role in the state (Iran, Iraq, and Syria), prioritizing instead Turkish, Arab, or Persian ethnic identities. Although these four states are usually at odds with each other over many issues, their single point of common ground has been the consensus that no examples of Kurdish self-determination should be allowed in the region.

Complicating this political dispersion of the Kurdish population are the complex internal patterns of social stratification characterized by divisions along geographical, linguistic, tribal, and religious lines. The Zagros mountain ranges within which the Kurds predominantly live provides a starting point for understanding the diversity of the Kurdish population. This diversity is enhanced by the existence of two major dialects—Kurmanji and Sorani—which also roughly form the dividing line between the two major Kurdish parties in northern Iraq today.[3] Finally, Kurdish life is also characterized by a strong affiliation to tribes and clans, a legacy of its mountain pastoral–nomadic past. Despite the fact that the majority of Kurds no longer view tribal attachments as their primary identity,[4] Kurdish *peshmerga* fighters are disproportionately tribal and most people can still identify family attachments to specific tribal groups. As a result, the dynamic of tribal politics in the area has often been divisive with Kurdish nationalist factions led by one tribal grouping being played off against other less successful ones by the Iraqi government in a classic divide and rule strategy.[5] Moreover, while the Kurds have come together in the face of reaction to the intervention of external forces, these reactions have often been motivated as much by a desire to preserve local tribal autonomy as they have been by a desire to promote a broader Kurdish political agenda.

Nonetheless, despite their historical lack of unity and coordination, the Kurdish populations have a history of uprising and rebellion against the political frameworks within which they have found themselves. They rebelled against the presence of British troops in 1919, forcing the British to deploy the RAF to aerially bombard Kurdish rebels and civilian areas in rebellion, setting an enduring precedent for both the region and the world. Another major Kurdish uprising in 1943, led by Mustafa Barzani, also required British intervention to save an Iraqi army that had been overrun by Barzani's tribal forces. Retreating to Iranian Kurdistan, Barzani assisted in the Kurdish separatist efforts there in establishing the short-lived Kurdish Mahabad Republic (1945–1946). Moreover, in the decade and a half after the overthrow of the Iraqi monarchy in 1958, five major military campaigns were fought between Baghdad's often-changing government and the Kurds in the north.[6]

One of the reasons for continued Kurdish rebellions was the political opportunity provided by the weakness of the Iraqi state, at least up until the early 1970s. That the young and artificial Iraqi state, carved out three provinces of the Ottoman Empire, could not control its northern regions bore witness to its weak and quasi-state nature.[7] Without the British military support and international recognition of its juridical existence, Iraq might have gone on to become a collapsed state. Alternately, Iraq might have lost its northern region and been left with the central and southern regions, a better basis from which to build a strong, more legitimate Arab Iraqi state. Hence, as a result of divisions amongst the Kurds and a weak central Iraqi government that commanded little loyalty even from most of its Arab subjects, neither side was able to achieve victory.

A classic example of this "dynamic stalemate" revolves around the offer of autonomy for the Kurds by the Iraqi Prime Minister Abd al-Rahman Bazzaz in 1966.[8] After a battle at Hendrin in which Kurdish irregulars ambushed and killed over 3,000 Iraqi soldiers, the Iraqi government sued for peace, offering the Kurds far-reaching autonomy including a provision for parliamentary democracy in Iraq. While the offer was considered sincere by some analysts,[9] Iraqi army officers, determined to avenge their defeat, forced the resignation of Bazzaz, starting the cycle of conflict anew. In 1970, yet another autonomy agreement between Baghdad and the Kurds also failed, scuttled both by the unwillingness of Baghdad to concede sufficient territory and power to the Kurds, and by the Kurds themselves, emboldened by the emergence of support from Iranian, CIA and Mossad agents interested in countering the consolidating power of the Ba'thist state.

However, the tide turned against the Kurds in the early 1970s. Buoyed by Soviet assistance and the huge income available after the rise in oil prices in 1973 and the nationalization of the petroleum industry, the Iraqi government embarked upon a more concerted attempt to consolidate its hold over its territory. In 1974, for example, heavy fighting again broke out sparked by the decision of the Iraqi government to send 120,000 men, 700–800 tanks, 20 battalions of mobile artillery, and the entire air force with several hundred planes including modern Tupolev-22 and Mig-23 bombers against a force of roughly 50,000 Kurdish *peshmerga* guerrillas. Not surprisingly, Kurdish forces were eventually pushed back close to the Iranian, Turkish, and Syrian borders. In 1975, the Kurdish resistance was dealt a decisive blow when the Shah of Iran and

Saddam Hussein concluded the Algiers Agreement, resulting in the withdrawal of Iranian support for Kurdish rebels in Iraq. Within a day, CIA and Mossad agents also packed their bags and left the area at their Iranian ally's request. Two weeks later, Kurdish forces were compelled to concede defeat and lay down their arms. Barzani and hundreds of thousands of Kurdish refugees were forced to flee to Iran, while others surrendered in Iraq.[10]

Smaller numbers of fighters continued guerrilla warfare within Iraq, hiding by day and mounting occasional attacks at night. By June 1975, dissenters from Barzani's Kurdish Democratic Party (KDP) formed the Patriotic Union of Kurdistan (PUK), and began launching guerrilla attacks in 1976. The KDP also renewed guerrilla operations around the same time, under Barzani's sons, Masoud and Idris. Other Kurdish groups, such as the Kurdistan Socialist Party, did likewise. Unfortunately for Kurdish nationalists, personal differences, tribal feuds and ideological disagreements saw these groups fight each other as often as they attacked Baghdad's forces. The period after 1970, therefore, marked the point after which Iraq could no longer be considered a quasi-state, let alone one in danger of collapse. The influx of oil money and superpower aid allowed the government in Baghdad to maintain a large and effective state administration and enjoy a relatively solid monopoly of force over the vast majority of the country, even without enjoying legitimacy in the eyes of important segments of its population. Without greater unity and more concerted outside assistance, it was clear that the Kurds could no longer pose an existential challenge to the Iraqi state.

Up until 1991, however, international support for the plight of the Kurds in Iraq— now facing an emboldened Iraqi state—was glaringly absent. In response to Iraqi Kurdish cooperation with the Iranians during its eight-year war with Iran, for example, Baghdad initiated a campaign of vengeance against the Kurdish populations to the north, attacking a series of Kurdish villages with poison gas in order to eliminate a sizeable portion of the Kurdish minority. Code-named "Anfal," these attacks culminated in the gassing of the village of Halabja in January 1988 in which roughly 5,000 civilians were killed. A total of eight "Anfal operations" were conducted, in which roughly 180,000 Kurdish civilians were rounded up and massacred.[11] Despite very clear and certain evidence of Iraq's genocide, however, the community of states took no action other than issuing a UN Security Council Resolution (UNSCR 620) condemning the use of chemical weapons in general and calling for "proper and effective measures" when such use occurred.[12] The U.S. administration, for example, killed a Senate resolution to impose sanctions on Iraq and later approved $1 billion in credit guarantees for Baghdad;[13] Turkey delayed UN teams from going to examine Iraqi Kurdish refugees on its territory;[14] and Britain doubled its export credits to Iraq, not long after its foreign secretary had stated, "we have been at the forefront of anxiety and grave concern about these [chemical weapons] allegations." This prompted *The Guardian* to comment, "the bulldog still refuses to give even the softest bark against the most blatant use of chemical weapons for 50 years."[15]

Attitudes toward Iraq changed on August 2, 1991, however, when Saddam ordered the invasion of Kuwait and thereby threatened to control a much more substantial proportion of the world's oil supply. During the pre–Gulf War propaganda offensive, reports of how Iraq had used chemical weapons on the Iranians and the Kurds were fetched from the shelves where they had lain since 1988, and no longer questioned for their veracity. An international coalition of states mobilized troops and expelled Baghdad's forces from Kuwait in February of 1991. At the same time that the ground war against Iraq was being conducted, George Bush publicly called for the people of

Iraq to rise up and overthrow Saddam. His message was carried on virtually every television and radio station in the world, including the CIA-run Voice of Free Iraq, broadcasting out of Jedda, Saudi Arabia.[16] When the Kurds in the north and the Shiites in the south heeded George Bush's call and rose up in March, they succeeded in immediately capturing many cities throughout both regions. Both Iraqi Kurds and Shiites believed that not only was the Iraqi state weakened and vulnerable, but also that international support for their rebellion could now be counted upon.

The U.S. administration, however, suddenly worried that a mass uprising in Iraq could lead to unexpected and "difficult to control" outcomes, decided not to support the rebels.[17] As soon as it became apparent to Saddam that the Americans would do nothing to assist or protect the revolt, Baghdad initiated a swift and unrelenting counterattack. He mobilized his best Republican Guard units (which were left intact far from the front lines of Desert Storm) to first quell the Shiites in the south. Then the brutal repression moved north, precipitating a massive run of over 2 million Kurdish refugees toward the Turkish and Iranian borders. Columns of refugees were bombarded by Iraqi helicopter gun-ships, which the United States had permitted to fly. Live international television coverage of these events, along with images of panicking refugee men, women, children being denied entry at the Turkish border, deeply embarrassed the Allied coalition. An international public outcry demanded that something be done and the United States, Britain, and France began exploring options with their Turkish allies. Turkey, under significant pressure to admit the refugees, submitted the idea of a temporary, allied-protected safe haven in northern Iraq. Only when they were assured of protection from Saddam would the Kurdish refugees return to northern Iraq, and Turkey certainly did not want them to stay in its territory, where its own Kurdish population was waging an intense guerrilla war against the government.[18] With Turkish cooperation and under the juridical cover of UNSCR 688, Allied forces were put in place to dissuade Baghdad from moving against the Kurds in the north and a "no-fly" zone for Iraqi air forces was declared north of the 36th parallel. Finally, in October 1991, facing continual ambushes from Kurdish *peshmerga* and unable to employ their air force in the region, Iraqi forces and government personnel withdrew from an area roughly the size of Switzerland, minus the oil-producing areas of Kirkuk and Mosul, giving birth to Iraqi Kurdistan's safe haven.[19] What is interesting about this case study and what distinguishes it from others in this volume is the decisive role played by international actors in its creation. What we turn to now is an examination of how the Kurds in northern Iraq have taken advantage of this political opportunity afforded by the creation of this internationally sanctioned safe haven to promote their long-held dream of political autonomy and/or independence.

Iraqi Kurdistan—Political and Economic Characteristics

General Kurdish sentiment has always supported the idea of political autonomy. Indeed, it would be difficult to find a single Kurd in Iraq that did not believe in the Kurdish people's de jure right to self-determination and statehood for all Kurdish peoples, be they in Iraq, Turkey, Iran, and Syria. Moreover, from a legal point of view, the 1966 and 1970 Autonomy Agreements offered by Baghdad already provided sufficient justification for such an enterprise in Iraq and the genocidal Anfal campaign of 1988 removed what little moral right Baghdad had to rule over them in any case.[20]

Nonetheless, general national sentiment does not automatically translate into concrete institution building on the ground. In the first two years after the creation of the safe haven, for example, a power vacuum emerged in the political arena leading to a grave situation on the ground. The coalition of Kurdish representatives called the Kurdish Front was failing to care for a population left destitute under two embargos—the international one against Iraq and Baghdad's embargo of the Kurdish Zone—forcing people into the streets chanting "We want bread and butter, not Saddam and not the Kurdistan Front."[21] The situation was made worse by the decision of the Iraqi government to withdraw all administrative infrastructure from the region. Government buildings were left bare, and the region was denied access to crucial public works infrastructure such as electricity, a working phone system, water treatment facilities, and waste disposal mechanisms. While most lower-level officials (clerks, doctors, etc.) chose to remain allowing for a rudimentary civil governing system,[22] the situation was nonetheless dire with some accounts describing the central Kurdish authority as being "nearly paralyzed":

> Thieves steal food stocks and vehicles; corrupt Kurdish officials carry anything they can over the frontier to sell in Iran. Local militia commanders run their areas as personal fiefs. Each member of the Kurdish Front exercises a veto power, with the result that few decisions are made.[23]

The turning point for the Kurdish autonomous zone was the elections in 1992. Although the electoral rules set an inordinately high threshold for smaller parties (7 percent of the vote to win a seat), the London-based Electoral Reform Society pronounced the process "free and fair," with "no evidence of substantial fraud that would have significantly affected the results."[24] Perhaps the biggest indicator that the Kurds had pursued a relatively legitimate and fair exercise in electoral politics was PUK leader Talibani's remarks that "everyone ended up dissatisfied with the results."[25] The KDP and PUK respectively won 50.22 and 49.78 percent of the vote, and decided to evenly split the 50 seats in the Kurdish National Council while leaving five seats for the Christian minority. No overall leader was chosen after the final vote left Masoud Barzani and Jalal Talibani too close in standing (466,819 votes to 441,057 respectively). Although Baghdad had pronounced the election high treason, the PUK leader stated that he "personally believe[d] that the elections proved that the Kurdish people are worthy of freedom and capable of engaging in democracy and the electoral process, despite the lack of experience . . . . This people can exercise the right to self-determination within a unified democratic Iraq." Although there had been "dissent and objections," the result was one that "all Kurdish parties accepted, albeit reluctantly, in order to safeguard the unity of Kurdish ranks and to portray the Kurds as civilized people before the world."[26]

For two years the Parliament seemed to function and there was talk of merging the various structures of the KDP and the PUK. Yet, beneath the institutional facade of a functioning Parliament was the informal reality of factional power dominated by the clientelist networks of the two major parties.[27] By summer 1994, disagreements over the sharing of limited resources in the Zone, together with disputes over land between groups allied to the two different parties, ignited armed clashes between them. In a June 1994 visit to Arbil, the scene of many of these clashes at the time, the author spoke with many Kurds (shopkeepers, laborers, traders) who expressed deep worry that such infighting could create an opening for outside powers (especially Baghdad) to assert control of the Kurdish area, an eventuality that almost proved true in 1996.[28] Some expressed regret that their own leadership was not paying greater heed to the interests of the Kurdish people as a whole. Officials of the KDP also expressed embarrassment about the events, seeking to minimize the importance of the fighting and stressing that such disagreements were temporary. Although the Kurdish population at large perceived the overarching need to unite in the face of the threat from Baghdad, KDP and PUK party elites were unable to put aside their differences.

Sporadic fighting endured until September 1998, when the two parties signed a cease-fire agreement in Washington. The agreement divided the Kurdish Autonomous Zone into two areas, with the KDP administration centered in Arbil and the PUK in Sulaymaniya. These zones boast their own separate prime ministers (Nechirvan Barzani for the KDP and Barham Salih for the PUK) and parallel administrations. Rather than institutionalizing their separation, however, the formal political division of Iraqi Kurdistan seems to have created a more stable political environment in which cross-cutting socioeconomic and political ties started to develop: neither has made any claim for the right to rule the adjacent unit; both have expressed a commitment to protect the rights of minorities within each zone;[29] there exists a good deal of travel and trade between the two areas; and cooperation on different issues has again become common. Both administrations have held municipal elections, and civil society is now flourishing like never before in the region's history.[30] As one observer of the Kurdish experiment in self-government commented, the emergence of separate administrations seems "in a curious way" to have been beneficial, making each administration more efficient and more honest than it would otherwise have been in their competition for public support.[31] Confirmation of this political dynamic was found in a PUK publication that stressed that "the PUK will work to promote a better model of governance" and that "this should become the mode of competition with rivals." The publication goes on to say that, "The continuation of the struggle will be based on the opportunity to choose the best and most suitable model to follow, which is the only path for success in public life."[32] In recognition of their improving relations, both the KDP and the PUK declared plans to hold KRG-wide parliamentary elections and return to a unified administration, in part as a way of demonstrating their commitment and suitability to eventual self-rule to the international community, although this has now been thrown into question as a result of the overthrow of the Ba'thist regime by the American forces.[33]

However, the emergence of viable political institutions also depends upon the ability to generate and maintain access to economic resources. Iraqi Kurdistan was not endowed with this kind of solid economic foundation. When the Iraqi government withdrew from the Kurdish Zone, it left a region devastated by genocide and war. In 1991, for example, it is estimated that 4,006 of the original 4,655 villages in the Kurdish Autonomous Zone had been destroyed, mostly during the 1987–1988 Anfal operations.[34] Moreover, immediately following its departure, the Iraqi government not only imposed an embargo on the KRG (as we have seen earlier), but also caused "incalculable financial losses" when the 25-dinar currency note was summarily canceled in May 1993.[35] In addition, the KRG was also subject to the same international sanctions regime that applied to the rest of Iraq wherein no trade was permitted with neighboring countries. Given that the infrastructure of the region (water treatment plants, roads, hospitals, and other facilities all nonfunctioning) was in ruins and hundreds of thousands of people were internally displaced, the economic future looked grim. It hardly seemed the basis on which to build an autonomous government. By fall 2000, however, the situation had turned around completely: visitors to Iraqi Kurdistan can now see modern supermarkets complete with scanners and uniformed cashiers, shelves stocked with items from canned food to imported vodka, modern electronics stores, internet cafes, and public parks full of people milling about.[36] Although many problems still exist, such as 900,000 internally displaced people, poverty-filled refugee camps, and an abundance of land mines, the region experienced an economic boom in the late 1990s and early 2000s. There were virtually no starving children in Iraqi Kurdistan, contrary to the situation in the rest of Iraq before the fall of Saddam. Moreover, both the PUK and the KDP have taken initiatives to develop the territories under their jurisdiction, building new schools, instituting compulsory primary school–level education, and opening up three universities, all of which now boast Internet facilities.[37] Of the region's 4,006 destroyed villages, 2,620 have been reconstructed.[38] The Kurds were even able to salvage a destroyed Iraqi oil well and, using machinery from abandoned factories, construct an oil refinery without any outside support or help.[39] Finally, the KRG has also opened a new central bank aimed at encouraging local business.[40] While one should not exaggerate the degree and extent of development of Iraqi Kurdistan since 1991, this experiment in autonomy has nonetheless done the region well. As David Hirst, a British journalist with extensive experience in the Middle East, argued in 2001, "it can't be said that prosperity has come to Iraqi Kurdistan . . . but it's obvious that these northern provinces, which until 1990 were the most backward, deprived and oppressed of President Saddam Hussein's domains, are now much better off than those where his writ still runs."[41]

The bulk of the resources available to the incipient Kurdish state for development purposes have come from the assistance provided to the KRG under Security Council Resolution 986 (more commonly known as "Oil for Food"). Under the scheme, 13 percent of Iraq's oil revenues were devoted to the Kurdish Zone, to be disbursed by the UN after Baghdad's approval concerning any and all projects, a share never before accessible to the Kurdish regions. Between the start of UNSCR 986 in 1997 until August 31, 2001, $5,767.8 million was allocated for the purchase of humanitarian goods in the KRG region of which $3,979.8 million has been approved for specific projects and items and disbursed;[42] indeed, Shafiq Qazzaz, the Kurdish regional government (KRG) minister for humanitarian affairs, commented, "it was 986 that saved us." Overnight, every inhabitant had a free, ten-item monthly food basket that would previously have cost a whole family's monthly income, or more. The WFP distributed it, with the willing collaboration of the KRG that, "officially," the UN did not recognize.[43] Between 1997 and 2002, projects funded by UNSCR 986 for housing, schools, roads, health centers, water projects, sewerage channels, and other endeavors were valued at $252,000,000.[44] The other source of income for Iraqi Kurdistan, until April 2003, has come from illegal (vis-à-vis the sanctions imposed on Iraq) trade and smuggling with Turkey and Iran. In PUK territory, for example, taxes are levied on smuggled goods (mainly consumer items and alcohol, which is illegal in Iran) and trade going over the Iranian border.[45] The largest and most profitable income from taxes on illegal trade, however, has gone to the KDP given that it controls the vast majority of KRG territory bordering Turkey. Indeed, as al-Khafagi notes, this lucrative illegal trade has become increasingly transnational, linking smuggling networks in Turkey, Syria, and Iran with those in Europe, Pakistan, and India—indeed, even with those in Iraq.[46] While no exact figures are available, additional revenue has also come from the "tourist trade," which revolves mainly around diaspora Kurds visiting or returning to the area, as well as some tourists from the south or even Iran, "who cross the border for a weekend's dancing, drinking and veil-free relaxation." For example, the KDP has collected US$50 cash from every man, woman, or child entering its area from outside Iraq. The fee is payable immediately upon entry, and by most accounts there is not much room for individual negotiation or payment in other currencies. The PUK also charges a much smaller fee in Iranian rials or Iraqi dinars to travelers entering its zone of control.[47]

The Future of Iraqi Kurdistan in the Post-Saddam Era

Iraqi Kurdistan remains an ambiguous political entity. On the one hand, there has been considerable political development over the last 12 years that includes parliamentary elections and the development of a competitive dynamic between the two Kurdish factions to improve governance within the territories that they administer. On the other hand, despite a marked improvement in economic indicators, the economic foundations of Iraqi Kurdistan remain uncertain. Although essential in the short term, the decision of the UN Security Council to continue the Oil for Food program in June 2003 is not a sustainable solution. Nor has its existence been an unmitigated success insofar as it has contributed to a culture of dependence, especially when the food provided was purchased from abroad rather than from local cultivators. The real key to the future viability of Kurdish autonomy, therefore, remains its access to revenue from the oil fields in Kirkuk. If Kurdish groups manage to retain control of areas around Kirkuk, where in May 2003 a Kurd was elected mayor, then the economic future of the Kurdish region (with or without Baghdad and/or UN Resolution 986) will be secure. Without control over, or a share of, the oil revenues of Kirkuk or Mosul, a quasi-independent Iraqi Kurdistan would face a much more precarious future.

This opens up the question of Iraqi Kurdistan's relations with the outside world. Iraqi Kurdish leaders, for example, have been very careful not to offend their regional neighbors with prominent displays of nascent statehood. During a recent visit to the KRG by a Turkish delegation, for example, the Kurdish administration sought to ease Turkish fears on the issue by removing its flag from the KRG Parliament building.[48] During the 2003 Iraq war, Turkey nonetheless threatened several times to send its troops into Iraqi Kurdistan in order to prevent the Kurds there from taking control of oil resources around Kirkuk and Mosul, resources that could give them the economic basis for a future independent state. This threat still looms large if Iraqi Kurds move to declare themselves independent from the new post-Saddam Iraq, although since May 2003 Turkey appears to have softened its position toward some form of autonomy for Iraqi Kurds. This seems to have occurred in recognition of the Kurds' stronger organization and position vis-à-vis other post-Saddam Iraqi groups, as well as their better relations with the United States (especially after the Turkish refusal to facilitate the American war effort). Iran and Syria do not wish to witness Kurdish independence from Iraq either. Foreign ministers from these countries as well as from Turkey periodically meet to discuss strategies for preventing any of their Kurdish minorities from achieving self-determination. None of Iraq's neighbors were pleased to see the Kurdish elections take place in 1992, viewing them as a move toward independence.[49] For years, Iran and Syria were happy to see their rival in Baghdad weakened by Kurdish dissent, but not to the point of allowing a Kurdish state to be established. Hence the policy of all has been to provide enough assistance to the Iraqi Kurds to keep them afloat, but not enough to see them succeed too much. Iran has also occasionally sent troops into the KRG area—in

July 1996 it sent roughly 2,000 Revolutionary Guards far into the region to attack bases of the Iranian Democratic Party of Kurdistan (KDPI). Iran has also successfully pressured the PUK on many occasions to keep the KDPI in check.

This ambivalence of Iraqi Kurdistan's neighbors is echoed by that of international actors. Despite the supportive activism of a variety of international nongovernmental actors, no nation-state has advocated Kurdish self-determination, independence, or statehood. Western policy currently places its primary concerns around the stability of the region (i.e. the sanctity of existing borders). Neither has the United Nations, guided by the policy decisions of the permanent members of the Security Council, played anything more than an ambiguous role in Iraqi Kurdistan. On the one hand, the Oil for Food program placed the United Nations in a kind of governing role in the area. The monthly food basket provided to residents of the KRG, as well as various aid projects under the auspices of the Food and Agricultural Organization (FAO) United Nations Development Programme (UNDP), and other UN organizations, buttressed the Kurdish de facto state. On the other hand, the United Nations has been scrupulously careful to support the territorial integrity of Iraq, waiting for permission from Baghdad before any project or food distribution was undertaken. It is also significant that the Kurds have never been granted observer status at the United Nations as have the Palestinians. With the overthrow of the Saddam regime in Iraq, this ambivalence toward the emergence of significant Kurdish autonomy in northern Iraq is likely to grow, overtaken by the desire to reverse the dynamic of the last decade and promote the reconstruction of an integrated Iraqi state.

Given the regional and international context cited earlier, Kurdish leaders in Iraq have become very adept at repeating the following mantra at every possible occasion: "Autonomy for Kurdistan within a democratic and federal Iraq."[50] It also seems that they are pragmatic enough to actually mean it, although their definition of autonomy may differ from that of Iraqi Sunnis and Shiites. Nonetheless, anyone familiar with the issue knows that although pragmatism may prevent them from declaring statehood for the next 100 years, virtually all Kurds feel they have such a right: "In spite of our right to our own state, we don't raise this slogan . . . We only seek federation within a democratic Iraq."[51] Indeed, Barham Salih, one of the two KRG prime ministers, argued that in contrast to the all-or-nothing violence of Abdullah Ocalan and his Kurdistan Workers' party's (PKK) that failed bid to win independence for the Kurds in Turkey, "we could be a model for all other areas of Kurdistan."[52]

It remains to be seen whether or not the new world order will have room for such aspirations, however. Well aware that they are currently a kind of ward of the United States, Britain, and the United Nations, Iraqi Kurds for the time being are content with the status quo, quietly establishing as many "facts on the ground" as possible during their fragile experiment in self-rule. Like many of the other cases examined in this volume, Iraqi Kurds responsible for the governing of their safe haven have in the meantime accomplished several goals. They have developed an institutional infrastructure that has served to protect Iraqi Kurds from a genocidal central government; they have begun to meet the social and welfare needs of the population under their jurisdiction; they have advanced the long-standing Kurdish aspiration to achieve independence and self-rule; and they have demonstrated to the international community (with a debatable degree of success) the Kurds' ability to manage their own affairs.

Particularly because they still lack unity, however, Iraqi Kurds need to maintain support from outside powers (particularly the United States) in order to safeguard the self-determination they have enjoyed since 1991. Additionally, they need to either establish a strong role in any future central government in Baghdad, or acquire strong institutional and material autonomy from a future Arab-dominated central government in Iraq. At the time of this writing, the KDP and PUK's strategy seems aimed at achieving all these objectives: continued American support, a federal democratic constitution for Iraq, and a strong Kurdish presence in Baghdad as well as the north.

Notes

1. David McDowall, *A Modern History of the Kurds* (London: I.B. Taurus, 1996), pp. 459–460.
2. Sabri Cigerli, *Les Kurdes et Leur Histoire* (Paris and Montreal: L'Harmattan, 1999), p. 20.
3. The two parties are the Kurdish Democratic Party (KDP) led by Barzani and the Patriotic Union of Kurdistan (PUK) led by Talabani. More leftist and urban than the predominantly tribal Barzani, the faction that would found the PUK had actually broken away from Barzani as far back as 1966. Jalal Talibani, who was from the Sorani-speaking Kurdish population rather than Barzani's Kurmanji-speaking area, became the leader of the PUK.
4. McDowall estimates that about 20% of Kurds in Iraq are still primarily "tribal." McDowall, *A Modern History*, p. 380.
5. For an extensive discussion of the role of tribal identity in Kurdish life, see Lale Yalcin-Heckmann, *Tribe and Kinship among the Kurds* (New York: P. Lang, 1991).
6. Ismet Chériff Vanly, *Le Kurdistan Irakien: Entité Nationale* (Neuchatel: Les Editions de la Baconnière, 1970), p. 153.
7. Robert Jackson, *Quasi-States: Sovereignty, International Relations, and the Third World* (Cambridge: Cambridge University Press, 1990).
8. This is a variation on Zartman's idea of a "hurting stalemate." See William Zartman, *Ripe for Resolution: Conflict and Intervention in Africa* (New York: Oxford University Press, 1985 (2nd edition, 1989)); and "Ripeness: The Hurting Stalemate and Beyond," in Paul C. Stern and Daniel Druckman, eds., *International Conflict Resolution After the Cold War* (Washington D.C.: National Academy Press, 2000), pp. 225–250.
9. McDowall, *A Modern History*, p. 319.
10. For a detailed examination of how Barzani viewed the events leading up to the 1975 defeat, see David A. Korn, "The Last Years of Mustafa Barzani," *Middle East Quarterly*, June 1994.
11. Kanan Makiya, "The Anfal: Uncovering an Iraqi Campaign to Exterminate the Kurds," *Harper's Magazine*, May 1992, p. 53. For more on the Anfal campaigns, see Dlawer Alaadin, *Death Clouds: Saddam Hussein's Chemical War against the Kurds* (1991); Gesellschaft fur Bedrohte Volker, *Germany and Genocide in Iraq: Persecution and Extermnination of Kurds and Assyrian Christians, 1968–1990* (1991); Samir al Khalil, *Republic of Fear: The Politics of Modern Iraq* (London: Hutchinson Radius, 1989); Human Rights Watch, *Bureacracy of Repression: The Iraqi Government in Its Own Words* (New York, February 1994).
12. McDowall, *A Modern History*, p. 362.
13. Nader Entessar, *Kurdish Ethnonationalism* (London: Lynne Rienner Publishers, 1992), p. 139.
14. Turkey did allow in one two-person UNHCR team during the month of September, many weeks after the chemical attacks had occurred. The team, after receiving some reports from Turkish medical authorities and quickly examining some of the refugees, stated that there was no evidence to substantiate the refugees' claims. Turkey's Foreign Ministry then announced that no additional teams would be allowed in the area to investigate the chemical weapons charge (*Tercuman*, September 15, 1988; also cited in

Entessar, *Kurdish Ethnonationalism*, p. 40). If evidence had been found, of course, Turkey would have been expected to join a sanctions regime against Iraq, from whom it received substantial amounts of oil and trade.

15. McDowall, *A Modern History*, p. 362.

16. Entessar, *Kurdish Ethnonationalism*, p. 146.

17. Peter Jennings, addressing General Brent Scowcroft I, stated: "The United States did want Saddam Hussein to go, they just didn't want the Iraqi people to take over. And what did you think of it at the time?" Scowcroft: "I, frankly, wished it hadn't happened. I envisioned a postwar government being a military government" ("The CIA's Secret War in Iraq—ABC News Report," February 7, 1998). The U.S. administration felt that a military government would be easier to deal with and do business with than a more popular government. Another Bush administration official stated: "It probably sounds callous, but we did the best thing not to get near [the Kurdish revolt]. They're nice people, and they're cute, but they're really just bandits. They're losers" (*Newsweek*, April 15, 1991, p. 27; cited in Entessar, *Kurdish Ethnonationalism*, p. 155).

18. Iran, to its credit, opened its borders to 1.5 million Kurdish refugees, spending up to 10 million dollars a day (with relatively little outside help) to care for them and exhorting Iranian citizens to welcome the refugees into their homes. Ibid., pp. 55–157.

19. For more regarding the geographical area left under Kurdish control, as well as particulars concerning the withdrawal, see Chirs Kutschera, *Le Défi Kurde* (Paris: Bayard Éditions, 1997), pp. 110–117.

20. Michael Gunter, "A *De Facto* State in Northern Iraq," in *Third World Quarterly*, Vol. 14, No. 2 (1993), p. 296.

21. McDowall, *A Modern History*, p. 79.

22. Personal interview with KRG Interior Minister Yu'nis Rushbayani, June 23, 1994, in Arbil, Iraqi Kurdistan.

23. Gunter, "*A De Facto* State," pp. 296–297. Gunter cites a report by Chris Hedges, "Kurds Dream of Freedom Slipping Away," in *The New York Times*, February 6, 1992, A1.

24. Michael Gunter, "The Iraqi Opposition and the Failure of U.S. Intelligence," *International Journal of Intelligence and Counterintelligence*, Vol. 12, No. 2 (1992), p. 299.

25. Ibid., p. 299.

26. Ibid., p. 300. For a detailed discussion of the electoral process, the results, and the structure of the resulting government, see Falaq al-Din Kakai, "The Kurdish Parliament," Fran Hazelton, ed., *Iraq Since the Gulf War: Prospects for Democracy* (London: Zed Books, 1994). Each cabinet position was assigned to one party or the other (or one of the Christian parties), with a deputy cabinet minister from the opposing party.

27. McDowall states that the elections, although a great achievement in a notoriously undemocratic region, "merely underlined the manifold and overlapping antagonisms between the two parties [the KDP and PUK]: personal between the two leaders, geographical between Bahdinan and Suran, linguistic between Kurmanji and Surani, and ideological between 'traditionist' and 'progressive' cultures," p. 385.

28. In August 1996 at the height of KDP–PUK hostilities, the KDP asked Saddam to intervene on its behalf, since the PUK was enjoying Iranian backing. This incredible invitation to the regime that used chemical weapons on Kurdish civilians embittered many Kurds against the KDP. Iraqi troops (30,000 Republican guards supported by tanks) spent about a week driving around the KRG area, helping the KDP push out the PUK from its strongholds and, of course, rounding up Saddam's opponents—including Arbil-based members of a CIA operation to oust Saddam. KDP leader Massoud Barzani may have even enjoyed seeing Saddam destroy a CIA operation that was badly organized in any case, after the CIA's betrayal of his father in 1975. His victory over the PUK was short-lived, however. After the Iraqis withdrew, the PUK returned from mountain hideouts and took back most

of its positions from the KDP, although it was unable to regain a presence in the city of Arbil. For more on this episode, see the postscript in McDowall, *A Modern History*; Gunter, "The Iraqi Opposition"; Michael Gunter, *The Kurdish Predicament in Iraq: A Political Analysis* (New York: Palgrave/MacMillan, 1999); or Chris Kutschera, "Invoicing the Future," *Current Affairs—The Middle East*, December 1996.

29. Prime Minister Barham Salih (PUK region) recently stated: "Here in Kurdistan we have a unique opportunity to demonstrate a model of tolerance and diversity. We cannot be true to our cause of Kurdish identity if we were to deny the Turkmen and Assyrians the rights we claim for ourselves. We pride ourselves in the strides that we have made in assuring, for example, educational and other cultural rights to the Turkmen and Assyrians living in this region. This is a work in progress, and the achievements so far are promising." Michael Rubin, "Interview with Barham Salih," *Middle East Intelligence Bulletin*, Vol. 3, No. 9 (September 2001).

30. BBC journalist Hiwa Osman comments that the Kurds seem to be making genuine efforts to establish some form of civil society. Words like democracy, civil liberties, and respect for human rights are heard in political, intellectual, and social circles. "Our people have for so long fought for freedom, we won't deprive them of it," was the KDP leader Mas'ud Barzani's reply when I asked him about his policy on openness. Internet access and satellite dishes are readily available without restriction. Hundreds of newspapers and magazines in Kurdish and other languages are published in the main cities. I asked the PUK leader Jalal Talabani about a weekly newspaper, Hawlati, published in his area, which openly criticizes his party. "We were not afraid of bullets. Why should we be afraid of words?" he said. Turkoman, Assyrian, and other minorities in the area also have their own political parties, newspapers, and schools. "We never had such freedoms in the history of Iraq," said a Turkoman leader in Arbil. "This is a golden age for the Iraqi Turkomans." "Iraqi Kurds—Waiting," BBC, August 11, 2001.

31. Cited in Charles Recknagel and Kamran Al-Karadaghi, "Kurdistan Developing Attributes of Statehood," August 10, 2001, *Kurdistan Observer*.

32. Kurdistan Newsline, "Talabani: Promotion of Good Models of Governance," July 10, 2001; www.kurdistanobserver.co.

33. Charles Recknagel, "Kurdish Parties Move to Normalize Relations," *Kurdistan Observer*, July 5, 2001. To publicize their success at self-rule, e.g., Kurdish leaders have been eager to have foreigners and journalists visit their Autonomous Zone.

34. Michael Rubin, "Interview with Nasreen Sideek, Minister of Reconstruction and Development, Kurdistan Regional Government," *Middle East Intelligence Bulletin,* Vol. 3, No. 7, (July 2001).

35. Alexander Sternberg, "Lifting Sanctions on Iraq: Center-South vs. Kurdistan," *Kurdistan Observer*, July 25, 2001.

36. Based on the author's own observations made during a recent visit to the area (September–October 2000).

37. Recknagel, "Kurdish Parties." Internet access is now helping to reduce Iraqi Kurdistan's isolation from the rest of the world. For more on this issue, see Michael Rubin, "Using the Internet to Overcome Isolation in Iraqi Kurdistan," in *Perspectives*, the newsletter of the Carnegie Council, available at www.kurdistanobserver.com (July articles).

38. Rubin, "Interview with Nasreen Sideek."

39. Charles Recknagel and Kamran Al-Karadaghi, "Kurdistan Developing Attributes of Statehood," Radio Free Europe/Radio Liberty in Prague interview with David Hirst, www.kurdistanobserver.com.

40. Reuters, "Iraqi Kurds Open New 'Central Bank' Building," August 21, 2001. Ever paranoid about Kurdish independence to the south, "Turkish officials voiced concern, saying the bank acted as a sort of central bank for the region and that could be a step toward an

independent Kurdish state in northern Iraq, a move Turkey fears could destabilize its own Kurdish areas."

41. "Kurds Reap Sanctions' Rewards," *The Washington Times*, August 15, 2001.
42. United Nations, "Report of the Secretary-General Pursuant to Paragraph 5 of Resolution 1360," September 28, 2001 p. 16.
43. Hirst, "Kurdistan."
44. Rubin, "Interview with Nasreen Sideek."
45. Recknagel, "Kurdish Parties."
46. Isam al-Khafaji, "Almost Unnoticed: Interventions and Rivalries in Iraqi Kurdistan," MERIP Press Information Note 44, MERIP Media, ctoensing@merip.org, January 25, 2001.
47. David Hirst, "Liberated and Safe, but Not Yet Free to Fly Their Flag," *Guardian Weekly*, August 16, 2001.
48. Ibid.
49. The *Toronto Star* carried the following short statement after the Kurds held their elections in 1992: Ankara (Reuter) "Iran, Syria and Turkey voiced disapproval yesterday of the self-declared Kurdish government in northern Iraq and vowed to prevent Iraq's disintegration" (November 15, 1992, A16).
50. For a specific treatment of what the Iraqi Kurdish definition of autonomy currently is, see Nouri Talabani, *The Kurdish View on the Constitutional Future of Iraq* (Kurdweb. human rights. de, 1999). This book contains a "Draft Constitution for the Iraqi Kurdistan Region." Some of the more striking articles of the constitution include Article 3: "1. All power rests with the people of the Iraqi Kurdistan Region, who will determine their future unilaterally. 2. The people exercise their power through their representatives or, in exceptional cases, through a plebiscite, according to the provisions of this Constitution or according to a decision of the Iraqi Kurdistan Region's Parliament" and Article 12: "No Federal legislation shall have any effect or validity in the Kurdistan Region without the approval of the Region's Parliament."
51. Massoud Barzani, quoted in Hirst, "Liberated and Safe."
52. Ibid.

Chapter Ten

State-Within-a-Failed-State: Somaliland and the Challenge of International Recognition

Matt Bryden

Introduction

The other chapters of this volume address the concept of a state-within-a-state. The subject of this chapter—the unrecognized Republic of Somaliland—brings a new twist to the genre: a state-within-a-failed-state. Since its implosion in 1991, the Somali Republic has been without a recognized and functional central government. Central governing institutions fell apart. Military and police forces disintegrated. Banks, ministries, and social services collapsed. Local government offices were abandoned or looted. As the twentieth century drew to a close, Somalia's advanced political and institutional entropy had come to epitomize the notion of state "failure."

The Somali Republic's ruin meant a new lease on life for the Republic of Somaliland. In January 1991, as the forces of the Somali National Movement (SNM) wrapped up their military campaign against Somali government forces in the northwestern regions, the regime of Mohamed Siyaad Barre crumbled and the situation in southern Somalia degenerated into inter-factional civil war. Within a matter of months, a conference of traditional and political leaders at the town of Bur'o announced the retrieval of Somaliland's sovereignty as an independent state.

More than 12 years later, Somaliland's claim to independence remains central to an understanding of the broader Somali crisis. First, Somaliland's success in establishing a de facto state has passed the point where it can realistically be addressed within the framework of a "national" reconciliation process intended to restore government to Mogadishu. The posture of Somaliland's leadership vis-à-vis eventual reunification with the South has become less compromising and public opinion less patient. Somaliland's political and administrative structures have matured, complicating the prospect of eventual integration with not-yet formed southern institutions. As the two territories drift further and further apart, their peaceful reunification is becoming an increasingly remote prospect.

Second, Somaliland's voluntary disengagement from the struggle for power in Somalia has complicated and perhaps postponed a solution in the south. Compared with the Somaliland authority, which controls close to a third of Somali territory, the claims to national leadership of the southern factions are lacking in credibility. But since Somaliland has removed itself from the southern political picture, numerous smaller factional groups in the south have succeeded in casting themselves as "national" actors. The fact that most southern factions lack the wherewithal either to impose their will on the battlefield or to administer significant blocks of territory has seriously complicated the prospects for settlement in southern Somalia, and especially in Mogadishu, where most aspirants to national leadership are clustered.

Third, Somaliland's secessionist agenda is in many respects an extreme manifestation of the desire for decentralization expressed by Somalis everywhere—a natural reaction to decades of abusive and corrupt centralized rule. Without a dramatic change in the nature of Somali governance institutions, not only will Somaliland and Somalia prove irreconcilable, but also peace and stability throughout the Somali territories will remain elusive.

The Somaliland issue has been exacerbated by international indifference. The inability or unwillingness of international actors to address Somaliland's demands while concentrating on building a government in Mogadishu has only heightened Somaliland's anxieties about being shoehorned into a one-sided and unworkable political union. In not one international peace initiative have Somaliland's main concerns—self-determination, war crimes, or confederation between two equal states—been on the agenda. On the contrary, knee-jerk insistence on the unity and territorial integrity of Somalia as a precondition to peace talks has effectively precluded serious participation by the Somaliland leadership. The purpose of this chapter is to elucidate Somaliland's claims to statehood, while assessing the prospects for its eventual reunification with southern Somalia.

Overview of Somaliland[1]

The Republic of Somaliland defines itself with respect to the territory, boundaries, and people of the former British Somaliland Protectorate, which was established in international law by a series of international treaties signed between 1888 and 1897. This territory represents a geographic area of 137,600 sq. km, of which about 850 km are coastline on the Gulf of Aden. Somaliland shares its western border with the Republic of Djibouti, its southern border with the Somali National Regional State of Ethiopia, and its eastern boundary with the self-declared Puntland State of Somalia.

Somaliland's climate is semi-arid and the territory contains no perennial rivers; average annual rainfall is 370 mm in most parts of the country, with a much lower precipitation in the dry coastal strip (*Guban*). These harsh environmental conditions have encouraged the economic and social predominance of transhumant nomadic pastoralism, giving Somaliland one of the highest proportions of pastoralists in the Horn of Africa. At cooler, more humid elevations, agropastoralism is also widely practised in various forms. In the second half of the twentieth century, subsistence pastoralism gave way to commercial, export-driven animal husbandry. Under normal circumstances, livestock exports probably represent Somaliland's single most important source of revenue, with a value of about US$175 million annually; the livestock trade is also the government principal source of income, accounting for $15 million of a total budget of about $25 million annually.[2] Remittances from the Somaliland diaspora account for a similar amount of foreign exchange earnings, but the available figures on this subject are far from complete.

There is no reliable demographic data on Somaliland and population estimates vary between 1.09 and 3 million inhabitants.[3] It is equally difficult to determine the distribution of the population between urban, rural, and nomadic groups. The Somaliland Ministry of Planning estimates that slightly more than half the population is nomadic and that the remainder live in rural or urban settlements, but there is currently no empirical way to test this assertion. The capital city is Hargeysa, with an estimated 500,000 inhabitants.

Somaliland's Case for Independence

Somaliland has gone to great lengths to persuade the international community that it is indeed an independent state. It has acquired all the abstract symbols of statehood—a flag, anthem, currency, and vehicle license plates—but it possesses the more tangible features of statehood as well: a defined territory, population, functional system of government, and relations, albeit limited, with other states. Perhaps more importantly, Somaliland has generally succeeded in maintaining a degree of peace and stability unknown in other parts of Somalia. This achievement, more than any other, has sustained a degree of international interest and engagement despite resistance to Somaliland's aspirations to independent statehood. The adoption of a democratic constitution, successful local elections in 2002, and credible presidential elections in 2003 have reinforced this trend, attracting foreign assistance and sympathy for Somaliland despite repeated international affirmations of the unity and territorial integrity of Somalia.

Somaliland's achievements, however, may not be sustainable in the absence of engagement and assistance from the international community. Restrictions on trade place the livelihoods of Somaliland's people under tremendous strain. The absence of banking and insurance services hampers both domestic and foreign investment. And the government's inability to prevent the steady deterioration of major economic infrastructure such as roads, ports, and airports that are vital to the territory's economic survival and to the administration's own revenue base.

Still, Somaliland is not so desperate for international assistance that it is prepared to compromise its claims to independence. Instead, the experience of the past 12 years has persuaded Somalilanders that they are capable of building and sustaining their embryonic state even—if necessary—under conditions of continued international isolation. And their determination to go alone reflects their confidence that the final verdict on Somaliland's claim to statehood will be handed down not by contemporary pundits, but by history itself.

Somaliland's Prior Existence as an Independent State

The existence of "Somaliland" as a geopolitical entity dates from 1897, when the British government concluded a series of treaties and protocols with other imperial powers—namely Italy, France, and Abyssinia—which defined the British sphere of influence in the Horn of Africa. The treaties, however, failed to precisely define the territorial limits of the British Somaliland Protectorate and several alterations were made before its borders were ultimately fixed in 1956.

The Protectorate's separate existence was interrupted twice between 1941 and 1948: first by the Italian conquest of Somaliland and its brief incorporation in the Italian East African Empire, then by the subsequent British reconquest and union of the Somali territories (except French Somaliland) under British military administration. Following the collapse of the British government's "Bevin Plan," which posited the unification of all Somali territories under a single flag, the Protectorate was restored to its separate, prewar status in November 1948.

On June 26, 1960 Somaliland was granted its independence by the British government, becoming a sovereign state with its own government and legislature. Over the next few days, a number of foreign governments—including the United States and Great Britain—formally recognized Somaliland as a new state. But when the United Nations Trust Territory of Somalia also obtained its freedom on July 1, the legislatures of the two newly independent states met in a joint session at Mogadishu and enthusiastically announced their unification as the National Assembly of the Somali Republic.[4] Somaliland was no more.

Somaliland's second declaration of independence, in May 1991, is therefore "predicated upon the territory's prior existence as a recognized, independent state."[5] In this respect, Somaliland's leaders argue that their demand for recognition is consistent with the charter of the African Union since it respects the integrity of international borders received at the moment of independence.

Absence of De Jure Union Between Somaliland and Somalia

Following the de facto unification of the two territories on July 1, 1960, the Somaliland government contends that the arrangement was never consummated de jure. Instead, two discrete Acts of Union were signed. On June 27, 1960, the Somaliland legislature passed the Union of Somaliland and Somalia Law. However, since the authorized representative of Southern Somalia never signed this treaty, it remained without force in the south.[6] Meanwhile, on July 1 the legislature of Somalia approved a significantly different document entitled Atto di Unione (Act of Union).

On January 31, 1961, the new National Assembly repealed the Unity of Somaliland and Somalia Law and introduced a new Act of Union, to come into force retroactively from July 1, 1960. The Somaliland government argues that the act of repealing could not have been effective in both parts of the Somali Republic, presumably on the grounds that the new National Assembly did not yet exercise its jurisdiction in the State of Somaliland.[7] In support of this view, Somaliland cites the acquittal, in March 1963, of a group of northern officers tried for treason before the Mogadishu Supreme Court. The British judge presiding over the case, according to the Somaliland government, dismissed the charges "on the grounds that there was no Act of Union between the North and South, the alleged offence having taken place in the North."[8] Northern rejection of the proposed unitary arrangements was manifest in the results of the referendum on the new Constitution in June 1961. Voter turnout in the former Somaliland was low owing to calls from political leaders for a boycott, and of the slightly more than 100,000 ballots cast there, over 50 percent voted against the unitary constitution. The poll was nevertheless carried by 1.6 million affirmative votes in the south.[9] In sum, the Somaliland government asserts that the de facto union between Somaliland and Somalia "fell short of legal requirements mandated by domestic and international law," leaving only "the recognition of other states to testify to the existence of Somalia as a unified state."[10]

Failure to Achieve Greater Somali Unity

The merger of North and South was widely perceived in both territories as a prelude to the unification under a single flag of all the Somali territories: Somaliland, Somalia, the French Territory of Afars and Issas (Djibouti), and the Northern Frontier District (NFD) of Kenya.[11] While this vision, espoused by the Somali Youth League, enjoyed wide currency among all Somalis, public interest in Somaliland was focused most immediately upon the retrieval of the Haud area, the rich traditional pastures that the British had surrendered to Ethiopian control in 1956.

The dream of a "Greater Somalia" was never to be realized. Britain delivered the first blow in 1963 by granting Kenya its independence, including the chiefly Somali-inhabited territory of the NFD. The second blow came in 1977, when the people of the French Territory of Afars and Issas voted in a referendum to reject unity with Somalia and to become instead the independent Republic of Djibouti. The *coup de grâce* was delivered in 1978, when the Somali army was served a crushing defeat by Ethiopian and Cuban forces in the Ogaden War, demolishing any hopes of ever placing the Somali-inhabited region of Ethiopia under Somali control.

Somaliland's marriage with the South in 1960 was contracted in the belief that other Somali territories would follow suit. With the unification of the Somali territories now beyond reach, the Somaliland government argues that the union was never consummated, and that an exclusively North–South interpretation of "Somali unity" is neither binding, nor desirable.

Legitimate Rebellion Against a Repressive Regime

In 1982, disaffection and disappointment in the North gave way to open rebellion under the banner of the SNM, a guerrilla force rooted mainly in the Isaaq clan. Although Barre's rule was becoming universally unpopular, discontent was felt most keenly among people of the former Somaliland, where economic neglect and deprivation (less than 7 percent of all development assistance was allocated to the region), stringent controls on trade, increasing centralization of administrative functions in Mogadishu, and the growing brutality of the Barre regime. As the wealthiest and most politically influential group in the north, the Isaaq were singled out for especially unpleasant treatment.

The Somali government responded to the insurgency in the North with disproportionate violence. The human rights organization, Africa Watch, documented the mounting repression:

> The government exploited the emergence of the SNM to justify indiscriminate violence against individuals and groups that criticized government policies and leadership, or merely because of clan affiliation. [. . .] Both the urban population and nomads living in the countryside have been subjected to summary killings, arbitrary arrest, detention in squalid conditions, torture, rape, crippling constraints on freedom of movement and expression, and a pattern of psychological intimidation. [. . .] Whenever the SNM launched an attack [. . .] that area was subject to harsh reprisals, including summary execution, the burning of villages, the destruction of reservoirs, the indiscriminate planting of landmines and the killing and confiscation of livestock, the lifeline of the nomads.[12]

Following the SNM offensive of May 1988 in which the guerrillas briefly took control of Hargeysa and Bur'o, government reprisals took the form of aerial bombardment and shelling of civilian targets. An estimated 50,000–60,000 people were killed before the final SNM victory in February 1991. Since 1997, a Committee for the Investigation of War Crimes, established by the Somaliland government, has been charged with compiling evidence about atrocities committed during the war years. The Committee has identified dozens of mass burial sites, compiled hundreds of hours of witness testimony, and identified over 200 individuals with alleged responsibility for the atrocities. Additional evidence of war crimes has been documented by various human rights monitors, including the U.S. Department of State, Amnesty International, and Africa Watch. The Somaliland government has qualified the atrocities committed by the Barre regime as "acts of genocide."[13] Although few others seem prepared to use such terminology, there is no dispute about the systematic, state-sponsored nature of the killing.

Somaliland continues to define itself with respect to the persecution of northerners under the Barre regime and thus with the generally accepted right to rebellion of a people subjected to the systematic violation of fundamental rights and freedoms. Since southern Somalia's post-Barre leaders have proven unwilling or unable to offer more robust guarantees for the protection of Northern citizens than those provided in 1960 (some have even refused to acknowledge the crimes committed in the North), Somaliland's rulers have argued that they had no alternative but to withdraw from the union and establish a state of their own.

Democratic Exercise of the Right to Self-Determination

On May 31, 2001, the Somaliland government organized a general referendum on a new constitution—one of its obligations under the interim arrangements that have governed Somaliland since the declaration of independence. Article 1 of the new constitution affirms the 1991 decision to withdraw from the 1960 union with Somalia. Many voters thus approached the referendum as a vote on the question of Somaliland's independence rather than a new constitution.[14]

The results of the plebiscite indicated that of 1.18 million ballots cast, 1.15 million (97.9 percent) approved the new constitution in a process described by international observers as having been conducted "openly, fairly, honestly and largely in accordance with internationally recognized election procedures," and that, despite allegations of irregularities, there appeared to be no "basis for questioning the final results of the referendum, or any reason to cast doubt on the integrity of its outcome."[15] Leaders in southern Somalia, however, denounced the referendum as "illegal" and described it as a "foreign-inspired conspiracy."[16]

The same observer report points out that an estimated two-thirds (66 percent) of those eligible actually turned out to vote. Even if all those who chose not to vote are assumed to have opposed the constitution (especially in the eastern Sanaag and Sool regions where many ballot stations were closed and turnout was low), then the total "yes" votes cast are equivalent to approximately 65 percent of eligible voters.[17] The Somaliland government thus advances the results of the referendum in support of its claim to the right of self-determination.

Perhaps more importantly, the introduction of the new constitution lent additional stability to Somaliland's political system. In May 2002, Somaliland's long-serving President Mohamed Haji Ibrahim Egal, died while undergoing surgery in South Africa. Within hours the vice president, Dahir Rayale Kahin, was sworn in by Parliament as Egal's successor, in accordance with Article 86 of the new constitution. The fact that

Rayale is a member of the Gadabursi clan, which is considerably smaller than the Isaaq and whose leaders sided with the Barre regime during the civil war of the 1980s, made the smooth transition all the more remarkable.

As interim president, Rayale's primary duty was to advance Somaliland's democratic transition. The constitution approved in May 2001 stipulates that Somaliland shall be governed by a democratic, multiparty political system. Accordingly, in December 2002, Somaliland held its first local elections in more than three decades. The elections took place throughout Somaliland territory except in the Sool region, which was declared to be under a state of emergency, and districts of eastern Sanaag region where only one political organization had registered and thus "ran" unopposed. Of the six political organizations to contest the local elections, the three to win the most votes went on to win accreditation as political parties, earning the right to stand for presidential and parliamentary elections in 2003. International and domestic observers, many of them informal, were favorably impressed with the conduct of the elections and generally deemed them free and fair. There was some consternation, however, at the turnout, which, at less than 500,000 voters, led some to question the reported turnout for the referendum the previous year.

A presidential poll was held in April 2003, producing the first popularly elected head of government in Somaliland for more than 34 years. The race was closely fought, with only 80 votes separating the winner—incumbent President Kahin—from the first runner-up. The narrow margin of victory appeared to ensure that the election's aftermath would be difficult—perhaps even turbulent. But there is little doubt that it was among the freest and most transparent democratic exercises ever to take place in the Horn of Africa.

Somaliland's steady progress toward democratization has advanced its case for independence in two ways: first, by engaging the interest and goodwill of concerned democratic states; and second, by demonstrating that the demands of Somaliland's leadership for the recognition of their government are a true expression of the will of their constituents.

International Perspectives

Somaliland's claims to independent statehood are unrecognized by the international community. No government has exchanged ambassadors with Somaliland, nor has the Somaliland government been admitted to any major intergovernmental organization. On the contrary, the United Nations, African Union (AU), Arab League, and Organization of Islamic Conference (OIC) have all extended membership to the "Transitional National Government" (TNG) in Mogadishu, implicitly endorsing its claims to jurisdiction over Somaliland.

Despite its lack of international juridical status, Somaliland has achieved a significant degree of de facto recognition. For example, very few member states of the above organizations have actually extended bilateral recognition to the TNG, and many maintain informal relations with Somaliland.[18] The Ethiopian government has established a "trade" office in Hargeysa and hosts a Somaliland liaison office in Addis Ababa. Somaliland government officials are permitted to enter and leave Ethiopia on a Somaliland passport. The two governments cooperate closely in security matters and have signed an agreement governing transit trade via the port of Berbera. A formal relationship exists between the Ethiopian Commercial Bank and the Central Bank of

Somaliland, and Ethiopian Airlines operates regular flights between Addis Ababa and Hargeysa.

South Africa has shown growing engagement in Somaliland, sending an unofficial team to observe the 2001 referendum and permitting a Somaliland Liaison Office to function in South Africa since June 2002. A visit by a high-level South African official to Hargeysa in early January 2003 pave the way for a reciprocal visit by Somaliland leaders later in the year. And a large South African mission, including representatives from the Electoral Institute of South Africa, the African National Congress, and the University of South Africa, observed Somaliland's presidential elections in April 2003.

Senegal took an unexpected interest in Somaliland in early 2003, inviting the president and a delegation of ministers on a visit to Dakar during the second week of January. Somaliland officials believe that Senegal is uniquely placed to understand Somaliland's case for international recognition since it has direct experience both of secessionist insurgency (in the southern region of Casamance) and of dissolution of a voluntary union between states (the 1982–1989 Senegambia Confederation). Senegal's advancement of Somaliland's case within the AU might therefore help to persuade other African governments that Somaliland's recognition poses no threat to their own unity and territorial integrity. It remains to be seen, however, how far Senegal is prepared to go in diplomatically promoting the Somaliland cause.

Many other governments acknowledge Somaliland's existence. Even Djibouti, which recognizes the transitional government in Mogadishu, has signed agreements with the Somaliland government—including one intended to improve understanding and cooperation between the two states. The EU member states, United States, and Canada continue to advocate a "building blocks" approach toward Somalia's eventual political reconstruction, which involves supporting the effort of de facto authorities like the Somaliland administration to maintain peace and stability. This has resulted in a number of governments, including the United Kingdom, Germany, Denmark, and the United States providing critical assistance to Somaliland's electoral process. Likewise, the level of reconstruction assistance to Somaliland, though very low, is greater than in any other part of Somalia.

Despite international awareness of Somaliland's accomplishments and growing sympathy for its cause, the government's efforts to obtain de jure recognition have made little headway. The next section of this chapter examines some of the reasons why Somaliland's appeals have fallen upon deaf ears.

International Law

Successive resolutions by the OAU, the Arab League, and the United Nations have reaffirmed the commitment of their members to the unity and territorial integrity of Somalia. The origins of this commitment lie in the 1963 OAU Charter, which makes no less than three separate references to the "sovereignty and territorial integrity" of member states. From this perspective, Somaliland's 1960 union with Somalia is characterized as irrevocable and its claims to independence illegal. Reports and resolutions issued by these intergovernmental organizations have been meticulous in either prohibiting the use of the term "Somaliland" or else situating it in quotation marks in order to ensure that no official reference to the territory could be misconstrued as a form of recognition.

Conversely, the historical application of the principle of territorial integrity of African states has not been absolute. Although no secessionist movement in Africa has been permitted to create an entirely new entity, the OAU has allowed (in varying degrees) several previously existing states or colonial territories to exercise the right to self-determination: among them the Gambia, Senegal, Eritrea, Western Sahara (the Sahrawi Republic), and Egypt.[19] The Constitutive Act of the African Union, which superseded the OAU Charter in 2001, continues to affirm the territorial integrity of states, but makes specific reference to "respect of borders existing on achievement of independence"—wording that could arguably be used to distinguish between states withdrawing from failed unions and other types of separatist movements.

The legal implications of Somaliland's de facto union with Somalia, like the principle of territorial integrity, are open to multifarious interpretations. No international body has ever officially reviewed Somaliland's case, and there are no signs that either the United Nations or the AU intends to do so. The Somaliland government has at times considered taking its case to the International Court of Justice, but has so far been hesitant to do so. This is in part because of uncertainty over the nature of the judicial ruling the government intends to seek, but also because the question of Somaliland's independence seems likely to be determined on political rather than legal grounds.

Prerogative

In the hierarchy of international politics, the Somali problem rates very low. Somali territory has lost much of its former strategic importance, and the notorious resistance of Somali crisis to externally led peacemaking endeavors has discouraged serious international engagement. The determination of Somaliland's international status has thus been devolved to those closest to the problem: the states of the region.

Somaliland's leaders consider this to be a less than ideal scenario. First, they believe that they will get a more sympathetic hearing from more distant powers than from either their African or Arab neighbors. A number of Western countries, the United States among them, have shown sympathy toward Somaliland, and are not necessarily as wedded to the principle of territorial integrity as the members of the AU and Arab League. The Somaliland government long believed that the United Nations would prove a more propitious forum in which to makes its case than regional intergovernmental organizations, asserting that "when claims of territorial integrity clash with self-determination, United Nations practice allows the latter to trump the former."[20] But the Somaliland government's faith in the United Nations looks increasingly misplaced: the world body has consistently played down Somaliland's demands, affirming in all of its decisions and statements its respect for the unity and territorial integrity of Somalia. The UN Department of Political Affairs actively promoted the establishment of the transitional Somali government in November 2000 and assisted in its efforts to claim Somalia's seat at the United Nations. Since 2001, Somaliland has therefore felt obliged to shift the focus of its efforts away from the United Nations and toward the AU instead.

The new emphasis is essentially pragmatic. Western powers continue to defer to the AU on the Somali question, partly because of lack of direct national interest and partly because of diplomatic convention: a French diplomatic visitor to Hargeysa in 2000 asked Somaliland government officials to consider what might have happened had African states rushed to recognize Croatia, Slovenia, or Bosnia before European states were ready to so. More concretely, Western governments must weigh any advantages in recognizing Somaliland against the potential damage to their relations with other

African states (and with each other) with whom they share more important economic or strategic interests.

On the other hand, persuading the AU to give Somaliland due consideration will clearly be an uphill battle. Notwithstanding the goodwill of Senegal, South Africa, and Ethiopia, Africa's commitment to resuscitating the Somali Republic whole and indivisible seems to be as firm as ever. The simultaneous membership of Somalia in both the AU and the Arab League works against Somaliland, since the League has lobbied in favor of Somali unity with diplomatic and financial resources not available to most African governments. And the membership of the Mogadishu-based TNG in both regional organizations since 2001 means that Somaliland's demands for recognition no longer receive the silent endorsement of an empty Somali chair, but are contested by aggressively hostile Somali "government" representatives (although this situation could change after August 2003 at the expiry of the TNG's three-year mandate if no credible successor entity has been established).

The AU has in turn devolved responsibility for handling the Somali crisis to the IGAD, whose governments are deeply divided in their interests and approaches.[21] Djibouti, which sponsored the 2000 Arta conference that the TNG, has become the TNG's principal ally in the international arena, providing diplomatic and limited military assistance in support of the TNG's claim to be the legitimate government of Somalia. The Djibouti government's unconditional patronage of the TNG is matched by its overt animosity toward Somaliland. Relations between the two governments thawed slightly in mid-2002, following the visit to Djibouti of Somaliland's President Kahin, but the diplomatic rapprochement has brought little in the way of tangible results and Djibouti continues to campaign openly against Somaliland's recognition.

Djibouti's ardent support for the TNG and its hostility to Somaliland are echoed by Egypt, the preeminent Arab power in the Horn of Africa region. Although neither a neighbor of Somalia nor a member of the IGAD, Egypt's abiding historical involvement in the Horn and its geopolitical rivalry with Ethiopia have helped to sustain its influence in Somali politics to the present day. Since the Arta conference, Egypt has been instrumental in securing Arab recognition of the TNG and persuading other Arab governments to provide financial, materiel, and military support to the Mogadishu-based "government." There is no reason to believe that Egypt will desist from active and uncompromising opposition to Somaliland's quest for international recognition.

Somaliland once pinned great hopes on Eritrea as a possible partner in the struggle for self-determination. But Eritrea's leadership has been anxious to reassure the AU that it does not intend to foment secession elsewhere in Africa and therefore reacted coolly to Somaliland's early approaches. Since the border war with Ethiopia, Eritrean foreign policy in the Horn has been motivated mainly by a desire to counter Ethiopian influence. This led in 2001 to the recognition of the TNG (which Ethiopia opposes) and an exchange of ambassadors. Unlike Djibouti, however, Eritrea holds no particular animus for Somaliland, leaving the door open to a more constructive relationship in future.

Ethiopia, the principal regional power, has maintained close relations with Somaliland since its inception in 1991—a relationship that built easily upon Ethiopian support for the SNM during the 1980s. During the second half of the 1990s, following the failure of numerous international initiatives to restore government to Somalia, the Ethiopian government advanced a "building blocks" approach to political reconstruction in Somalia that highlighted the achievements of Somaliland and administrations more recently declared in Puntland (1998) and Bay and Bakool regions (1999).

The strategy initially won international backing and Somaliland seemed likely to reap an important "peace dividend," but the Arta conference triggered an abrupt *volte-face* among donors and the "building block" approach was dropped in favor of the new central government declared in Mogadishu.

The Ethiopian leadership is deeply hostile to the TNG, whose formation served to destabilize Ethiopia's closest southern Somali allies, and which it perceives as a "stalking horse" for Arab and Islamic influence in the Horn.[22] The TNG's allegations that Ethiopia seeks to divide and destabilize Somalia in perpetuity, as well as its opportunistic relationship with Somali Islamist groups, served only to reinforce Ethiopia's suspicions. Ethiopia therefore moved to strengthen its ties with the leaders of Somaliland and Puntland, while supporting a coalition of southern factions opposed to the TNG.

Despite its close ties with Somaliland, Ethiopia has given no indication that it intends to recognize Somaliland, nor has it openly lobbied other states to do so. Instead, the Ethiopian government has repeatedly stated that the unity of Somalia is a matter for Somalis to decide and nudged Somaliland toward an "Eritrean" solution: that Somaliland seek the recognition of leaders in Mogadishu, just as the EPLF government in Eritrea was first recognized by its Ethiopian People's Revolutionary Democratic Front (EPRDF) allies in Addis Ababa. Realistically, however, the probability of a Mogadishu-based government recognizing Somaliland in the foreseeable future is virtually nil—an argument that will be addressed in greater depth later.

Ethiopian reluctance to move decisively in favor of Somaliland's recognition derives from a combination of factors. Ethiopian recognition of Somaliland would invite the enduring hostility of a rump "southern" Somali state (it might also create tensions within Ethiopia's own Somali population), which would probably seek to align itself with Ethiopia's strategic rivals, Egypt and Eritrea. Recognition of Somaliland could also damage Ethiopia's relationships with important African and Arab states without conferring comparable benefits. Ethiopia takes its role as host of the AU very seriously and thus is unwilling to be perceived as sponsoring the breakup of another member state. Ethiopia may also harbor doubts about Somaliland's durability and the depth of its commitment to maintaining good relations with Ethiopia.

Legitimacy

Hesitation within the international community concerning Somaliland's claims to independence is in part a function of uncertainty about the legitimacy of those claims. Somaliland's population is not unanimous in its endorsement of independence from Somalia. The difficulty in assessing the will of the majority is one of the obstacles to international acceptance of Somaliland's assertion of separate statehood.

The independence platform is associated primarily with the Isaaq clan, which represents a probable majority of Somaliland's population.[23] Opinion within other clans is more divided. The engagement of the western Gadabursi clan in the administration since the early 1990s has long helped Somaliland to claim an identity broader than the Isaaq clan. However, members of the Gadabursi in the diaspora, have been vocal in their support for Somali unity. The constitutional accession of a Gadabursi, Dahir Rayaale Kahiin, to the presidency upon the demise of President Mohamed Haji Ibrahim Egal in May 2002 has muddied the waters even further. Although Rayaale's brief presidency has persuaded many among the Gadabursi to be more supportive of the Somaliland cause, others see him as a situational leader with little real backing from his clan.

Among the eastern Harti clans (Warsengeli and Dhulbahante), resistance to the independence agenda has been more pervasive, and the Somaliland government has historically been less successful in exercising its authority in areas inhabited by these clans than in other parts of its territory. Since the late 1990s, numerous senior political and traditional leaders from the Warsengeli have pledged their support for Somaliland and have become increasingly engaged in the government apparatus. Among the Dhulbahante, however, public opinion remains deeply divided and the quality of representation in Somaliland from among the Dhulbahante is lower than that of other groups.

The establishment, in July 1998, of the Puntland State of Somalia, self-proclaimed subunit of a future federal Somalia, highlighted, and to a certain extent exacerbated, the divisions in eastern Somaliland. Representatives of the Warsengeli and Dhulbahante clans played a critical role in Puntland's founding conference, legitimating the Garowe administration's subsequent claims to parts of eastern Sanaag and Sool regions. The Puntland administration subsequently failed to substantiate its claims to those areas by establishing functional administration, and the areas remain under dispute between the two polities. A visit to Las 'Aanood, capital of Sool region, by Somaliland President Rayaale in December 2002, degenerated into a debacle when militia loyal to Puntland opened fire on him and his entourage, triggering clashes within the town. It therefore seems reasonable to assume a significant degree of ambivalence on the part of the Harti clan population and its leadership vis-à-vis Somaliland.

A second external challenge to Somaliland's legitimacy materialized in August 2000 with the formation of the TNG in Mogadishu. The TNG, which was formed at a Conference held in Arta, Djibouti claims sovereignty over the territory of the former Somali Republic, including Somaliland, although it actually controls only parts of Mogadishu and some areas of hinterland. The TNG's claims to national leadership have received a limited degree of recognition from the international community through the TNG's admission to the United Nations, OAU, the League of Arab States, and the OIC. But very few governments have extended bilateral recognition to the Mogadishu administration, presumably because of doubts about its legitimacy and its evident inadequacies as a national government. By mid-2002 it had become clear that the TNG existed in name only.

Somaliland's Constitutional referendum of May 2001 went some distance toward clarifying these issues by delivering a resounding vote (97 percent) in favor of independence. Although international observers gave the referendum a clean bill of health, they were not numerous enough to report authoritatively on the conduct of the poll through-out Somaliland's territory.[24] In particular, observer teams did not visit eastern Sanaag or Sool regions, where reports of the conduct of the poll differed significantly. Nevertheless, the referendum results appear to indicate with some certainty that a significant majority (at least two-thirds) of Somaliland's population favors independence from Somalia.

Regional Stability

One common objection to Somaliland's recognition is that it could lead to the "balkanization" of Somalia and set a precedent for other separatist movements around Africa. In view of the prevalence of ethnic grievance, armed rebellion, and weak states across the continent, the depth of the AU's aversion to secessionist movements should not be underestimated. This would appear to be the principal reason that the AU has been immovable in its commitment to the issue of the unity and territorial integrity of Somalia.

Fears about the breakup of Somalia are generally overstated. No other part of Somalia has shown any interest in secession: on the contrary, one of the few areas in which southern Somalis show unanimity is their determination to maintain the country's territorial integrity. Second, a successful bid for independence by Somaliland would inevitably refer to its internationally recognized boundaries and its prior existence as an independent state: a claim that no other part of Somalia can make. Few governments, however, and even fewer Somalis in the South, seem prepared to take that chance.

A more persuasive objection might be that two Somali states (three, if one includes Djibouti, which has been dominated by a single lineage of the Isse Somali subclan since independence in 1977) would be in constant competition with one another, providing a geopolitical playground for other regional rivals such as Egypt, Eritrea, Sudan, and Ethiopia. Somalia and Somaliland might then be mired in proxy conflict for years to come.

Practical Aspects of Nonrecognition

Somaliland's late president, Mohamed Haji Ibrahim Egal, used to liken Somaliland to a boxer with both hands tied behind his back: on the one hand, international partners urge Somaliland to consolidate peace and stability, establish systems of good governance, and persevere in social and economic development. On the other hand, they seemed indifferent to restrictions on Somaliland's ability to trade (since the Saudi livestock ban), its total lack of access to bilateral and multilateral aid, and the multiple other ways in which the territory is politically and economically excluded from the world community. Egal spent his final years alternately bemused and exasperated by these contradictory and seemingly impossible demands on his leadership.

Somaliland's chief demand is for diplomatic recognition. During the 1990s, in the absence of a recognized Somali government, Somaliland pursued political recognition as an end in itself. Following the formation of the TNG in 2000, however, the issue of political recognition acquired a more urgent meaning as well: the opportunity to be heard in the international arena. The TNG's limited recognition offered its leadership access to foreign governments, international media unequalled by other Somali political actors, including the Somaliland government. International perceptions of Somaliland began to shift from "breakaway region" of a failed state, toward clan-based rebellion against legitimate state authority. Only the failure of the TNG to win international credibility prevented this contradiction from triggering a new crisis. The experience appears to have spurred the Somaliland government to redouble its efforts toward obtaining international recognition.

Foreign Aid

After political recognition, access to international assistance ranks first in the Somaliland government's order of priorities. At present, Somaliland has no access to loans or grants from multilateral financial institutions like the World Bank or the IMF. Bilateral donors give no direct assistance either: their funds are typically channeled through NGOs or the United Nations.

Between 1999 and 2002, the Somaliland government pursued "special interim international status" analogous to that of the Palestinian Authority, pending full international recognition. This proposal was intended, inter alia, to provide the Somaliland government with access to Bretton Woods institutions, multilateral donor resources such as the European Development Fund, and the bilateral aid resources of well-disposed governments. The proposal failed to attract international attention and seems to have been abandoned by President Rayaale, who asserts that Somaliland will be satisfied with nothing less than independent statehood.

The Somaliland government's desire for foreign aid is easily explained. The administration's meagre annual budget leaves few resources available to catalyze economic development, soften the impact of repatriation and reintegration of returning refugees, accelerate the pace of demobilization and reintegration of ex-combatants, or hold elections. In the year 2000, about 80 percent of the government's $25-million-dollar budget went to general administration and security. The reimposition of the Saudi livestock ban in late 2000 cut government revenues by about half, meaning that nearly the entire budget must now be allocated to general administration and security expenditure.

On the other hand, overdependence on foreign aid was one of the central elements in the collapse of the last Somali government. Given the fragility of Somaliland's political and financial institutions, ineffectual parliamentary oversight of the budget, and the prevalence of corruption within the local and central administrations, large-scale external assistance could potentially nudge Somaliland toward the dependency trap, sapping the government's legitimacy and undermining the fragile political consensus.

Livestock Trade

Freedom to trade poses a more immediate problem for Somaliland than access to aid. In 1998 and again in 2000, Saudi Arabia imposed a ban on the import of livestock from the Horn of Africa, citing an outbreak of Rift Valley Fever, a potentially dangerous hemorrhagic disease. As of February 2003, the September 2000 ban was still in effect, slashing livestock exports by more than 60 percent over normal years, and representing an estimated $100 million or more per year in lost revenues for Somaliland.[25] Given the overwhelming importance of the livestock trade to Somaliland's economy, the ban has prompted international aid agencies to warn of impending economic and humanitarian crisis if it is not lifted.

Part of the problem involves the Somaliland government's inability to certify the health of its own livestock. Somaliland's certificates are not internationally accepted, nor is it party to any international protocols governing export veterinary standards. In 2002, the government sought to circumvent this problem by contracting a private Swiss company to monitor and certify export veterinary services, but there is no guarantee that an agent's services will satisfy the Saudi government, whose imposition of the ban may be in part politically motivated (a way to punish Somaliland for its repudiation of Somali unity) and in part driven by Saudi commercial interests seeking to replace Somali livestock with chilled meat from Australia and New Zealand. Somaliland's suspicions in this regard have been heightened by the fact that an FAO technical assessment declaring Somaliland clear of the disease has not persuaded the Saudis to lift the ban.

It is difficult to assess the importance of recognition to such issues: certainly it is not a substitute for professional expertise or integrity in the livestock and veterinary sectors. But it is clear that, lacking international status, Somaliland possesses little diplomatic leverage to engage its trading partners more forcefully or to resist unfair trading practices.

Financial Services

In the absence of international banks, Somaliland is also deprived of financial services. The gap left by international banking institutions has been partly filled by the *xawaalaad* enterprises: money transfer agents. Dahabshiil is the largest Somaliland-based *xawaalaad*, with offices in 33 countries and over 1,100 employees worldwide. Other major Somali *xawaala* agents include Barwaaqo, Mustaqbal, and Damal, and there are dozens of smaller agents. Precise figures of their volume of business are hard to obtain, but most estimates place remittances to Somaliland in the range of $150–200 million annually—an amount approximately equivalent to the territory's livestock export revenues in a normal year.

Following the September 11 attacks on New York and Washington, allegations that the *xawaalad* company Al-Barakat provided financial services to the *al-Qa'ida* network fueled speculation that the remittance flow might dry up. Barakaat's chairman, Ahmed Nur Jim'aale has denied the allegations, but his company is virtually defunct. Its local partners across Somalia have divested from the parent company and changed their names. Other *xawaalad* businesses, led by Dahabshiil, have moved rapidly to claim Barakat's market share, and the remittance flow does not appear to have slowed significantly, in defiance of aid agency predictions of imminent disaster.

On the other hand, tighter international control and monitoring of financial transfers may yet drive other Somali *xawaalaad* out of business. With livestock revenues in Somaliland hit hard by the Saudi livestock ban, a contraction in the flow of remittances could tip the economy into decline and perhaps still trigger a humanitarian crisis.

Travel

Most Somalilanders who need to travel continue to use the old Somali passport, which can be readily purchased in most major markets, or have obtained foreign passports. During the late 1990s, Ethiopian procedures for issuance of travel documents were unofficially relaxed, allowing many Somaliland residents to obtain Ethiopian passports. But few countries continue to accept the old Somali passport as a valid travel document. Immediate neighbors such as Ethiopia, Kenya, Djibouti, and the United Arab Emirates still selectively honor the passport, but it is of little or no use for travel outside the region. This problem principally affects members of the urban elite and the business community, whose livelihoods may depend upon their ability to travel. In the aftermath of the terrorist attacks in the United States in September 2001, international concerns about terrorism and identity theft have restricted travel opportunities for Somalis even further.

Somaliland attempted to circumvent this problem by producing its own passport in 1999, but this initiative has met with only limited success. A number of African and European countries have permitted the use of the Somaliland passport by government representatives on official business, but do not officially recognize it as a travel document, and it remains invalid for travel elsewhere in the world. Somaliland has therefore limited issue of the new passport to select government officials and members of official delegations, thus avoiding the potential embarrassment of its widespread refusal by foreign immigration authorities.

Somaliland's attempts to introduce a new travel document have been replicated elsewhere. Soon after its inception, the TNG in Mogadishu also designed and printed a first consignment of new Somali passports. This would have potentially provided the TNG with an important political advantage over its rivals, including Somaliland, but the TNG's lack of international credibility prevented the issue of the new passport. As the TNG's prospects continue to decline, the issue of a new Somali passport appears to be an increasingly remote prospect, and a growing number of countries seem likely to allow limited use of the Somaliland travel document.

Security

The designation of Somalia as one of the possible targets in the U.S.-led campaign against terrorism has highlighted a number of international security concerns. The attention of the United States is generally focused on other parts of Somali territory— namely Mogadishu, Bosaaso, and Kismayo, but Somaliland is also of interest for a number of reasons. First, some of the same groups that interest the United States elsewhere in Somalia (chiefly *al-Itihaad al-Islam*, but also *Takfir wal Hijra*, *Tabliiq*, and *al-Islah*) are active in Somaliland or transit its territory en route to Somalia and Ethiopia. Second, Somaliland's proximity to southern Somalia makes it an attractive location for certain types of intelligence-gathering activities. And third, Somaliland's police, security, and immigration authorities promise greater scope for cooperation in counterterror activities than elsewhere in Somalia.

Somaliland does not participate in Interpol, nor does it subscribe to arrangements for the extradition of criminal suspects to or from other countries. A limited degree of intelligence sharing takes place between Somaliland and Ethiopia on issues pertaining to their common security. Likewise, Somaliland's security services are unaware of intelligence from other countries on foreign individuals and groups operating on or from Somaliland territory.

Though tolerated for over decade, this lacuna in the international system is likely to become more sensitive as terrorists and militant Islamist organizations come under greater international scrutiny. Over the past decade, Somaliland and Somalia have experienced the proliferation of Islamic groups with a wide range of social and political agenda, some of whom are extremists with connections to foreign militant organizations.

Al-Ittixaad Al-Islam, one of the most radical groups, is present in all parts of Somalia and has been listed by the U.S. State Department as a terrorist organization with links to Usama Bin Laden and the *al-Qa'ida* network. *Al-Itixaad's* profile as a radical, violent organization is in no doubt: its forces have participated in military operations within Somalia and in Ethiopia's Somali region, and have been linked for bomb attacks on hotels and assassination attempts in Ethiopia. *Al-Itixaad's* presence in Somaliland has been more low key than it has elsewhere on Somali territory: training camps active in the early 1990s have since been closed and government security forces monitor the organization closely.

Other groups of concern to the Somaliland authorities include *Takfir wal Hijra*, a radical offshoot of Egypt's *Ikhwaan Muslimiin* (Muslim Brotherhood), and the Pakistani-based missionary organization, *Tabliiq*, which is widely perceived as being apolitical and moderate. Somaliland government officials, however, have expressed concerns that *Tabliiq* inadvertently provides cover for the movements of members of more radical groups. Somaliland's capacity to monitor the movement and activities of members of such groups, as well as those of more mundane criminal organizations, is severely limited.

Refugees and Returnees

The peace and security prevailing in Somaliland have encouraged the return to the territory of hundreds of thousands of refugees from camps in Ethiopia, and thousands of others from elsewhere in the diaspora. In 2001, over 50,000 refugees were repatriated from Ethiopia by the UNHCR, leaving only 66,932 remaining of an original camp population of more than half a million. The UNHCR aimed to repatriate another 35,000 by the end of 2002.

In addition to the returnees, Somaliland plays host to tens of thousands of refugees from southern Somalia, mainly from the regions of Bay and Bakool, who fled the conflict in their home regions in the mid-1990s, as well as hundreds (possibly thousands) of Ethiopian migrants.

During the 1990s, security issues involving Somalis were less of a preoccupation for Western governments than immigration. The total number of Somalis who have settled in foreign countries since the onset of the civil war is unknown, but in North America and Europe Somali refugees who have arrived since 1991 number in the hundreds of thousands. Although a majority have been granted asylum, the reluctance of Western governments to consider Somalis as bona fide refugees has been growing.

The relative peace and stability that have prevailed in Somaliland in recent years has led a growing number of governments to reject asylum requests from claimants of Somaliland origin. Since 1995, a number of Western governments, notably the Netherlands, Canada, Norway, Denmark, Sweden, and the United Kingdom have sought to encourage the repatriation of Somali asylum seekers, voluntarily where possible, forcibly where required.

This has proved problematic for a number of reasons. Although refugee-screening procedures in many countries differentiate between conditions in Somaliland and Somalia (as even between different regions of Somalia, such as Puntland), ordinary courts have often been hesitant to accept the distinction and to order deportation of individuals to a country seized by civil war and without a recognized central government.

Some governments have successfully deported limited numbers of denied asylum seekers to Somaliland and Somalia without the permission of local authorities, others have suffered the seizure of their charter aircraft, the detention of aircrews, and the imposition of hefty fines. Most governments seeking the return of Somalis to Somaliland, whether voluntary or involuntary, now prefer to seek the consent of the Somaliland government.

Since 1991 Somaliland has reintegrated close to half a million returnees and a greater number of internally displaced with negligible foreign assistance, and the government has been reluctant to add to this burden with rejected asylum seekers and returnees from Western countries. Nevertheless, Somaliland has by-and-large acceded to foreign requests in order to strengthen relationships with Western governments and to earn international acceptance. Certain governments, notably Denmark and Sweden, have accompanied their return programs with complementary aid packages, providing an incentive for the Somaliland authorities to accept their proposals.

This generally constructive attitude toward return programs appeared to shift in early 2002 when, arguing that "present economic and social conditions in Somaliland are not favourable to the reintegration of returnees," the Somaliland government announced that it would no longer accept the compulsory return of denied asylum seekers.[26] The memorandum's assertion that Somaliland lacks the "conventional diplomatic and legal instruments that provide protection for deportees"[27] and its reference to a UN Human Rights report calling on European governments not to return asylum seekers to Somalia in the absence of a recognized government would seem to indicate that Somaliland's government has decided to forego its obligations as an international citizen until it is recognized as one.

Prospects for Recognition or Reunification

Somaliland's prospects for international recognition ebb and flow according to the fortunes of the Somali peace process at any given moment, and seemed to hit an all time low following the establishment of the TNG in Djibouti, which received a limited, but nevertheless significant degree of international recognition. The inescapable failure of the TNG and the subsequent difficulties of the IGAD-led peace initiative in Eldoret, Kenya have given Somaliland a new lease on life. But to what end? Is Somaliland truly headed for independent statehood, or is it destined to be reabsorbed into a united Somali Republic?

This question is among the most emotive and hotly disputed issues in contemporary Somali politics. Attempts to answer it are typically polemical, reflecting a strong prejudice one way or the other. It is not the purpose of this chapter to engage directly in this debate, but rather to offer some practical considerations that are too easily overlooked.

Independence

Legality aside, the most common arguments against Somaliland's recognition pertain to its viability as a polity. In other words, even if Somaliland received international recognition, it is far too poor and underdeveloped to succeed. It is an argument that Somaliland's leaders cannot—and should not—dismiss. Potential oil and mineral wealth notwithstanding, Somaliland is among the most resource-scarce territories on the continent, possibly in the world, and there is good reason for the international community to discourage the emergence of yet another basket-case government, dependent in perpetuity on foreign aid.

Somaliland's strongest rebuttal to this argument is that it has achieved so much against such formidable odds.[28] It is hard to conceive of many (if not most) other states on the continent maintaining stability and security for over a decade were they to be simultaneously deprived of aid and their largest export markets. The fact that Somaliland has managed to do so would appear to suggest a more robust political economy than some would believe. No doubt, the receipt of remittances from the Somaliland diaspora, has played an important part in keeping the homeland afloat. But other diasporas have also played vitally important roles in other countries in political distress or chronic poverty, without the validity of the state itself necessarily being called into question. An impartial, comparative study of the political economy of Somaliland would probably help to put this issue in perspective. Even without such a study, it is probably fair to state that Somaliland's odds of survival are no worse than Eritrea's and much better than Djibouti's. And as experience elsewhere has shown, political leadership and economic management appear to be more important determinants of a state's success or failure than its intrinsic wealth. Whether or not an independent Somaliland's leaders would prove equal to the task is entirely a matter of conjecture.

Another potential problem involves the existence of a substantial minority, mainly among the non-Isaaq clans, who remain attached to the notion of a united Somalia. This does not necessarily invalidate the Somaliland platform: many other modern states (the former Yugoslav republics, East Timor, Eritrea etc.) have encountered similar problems upon independence. But Somaliland's leadership has not done enough to persuade its domestic opposition that it is committed to a national identity for Somaliland that transcends Isaaq clan hegemony. In many ways, the Isaaq political elite has continued to subordinate minority clans in much the same way that the southern leadership subordinated the Isaaq after independence. Non-Isaaq politicians are often token representatives of their clans, expected to pacify their constituents through patronage rather than building real bridges across clan and regional differences. Unless Somaliland's leaders work harder to construct an identity beyond Isaaq liberation ideology and to offer genuine political equity to all groups and individuals, it is likely to face chronic discontent and instability in parts of the territory.[29]

A more disturbing possibility is that the recognition of Somaliland might produce two mutually antagonistic Somali states, each attempting to subvert the other and possibly bringing other regional actors into their conflict. While the leadership of each state might resist such a scenario, there exist (and no doubt will continue to exist) extremists and opportunists on both sides who would reject peaceful coexistence. Neither Somaliland nor Somalia can afford the costs of such a conflict, but neither has full control over its relationship with the other.

Voluntary Association

Assuming that Somaliland does not simply implode, either before or after international recognition, cooler heads in the Somali and international community perceive an opportunity for a form of voluntary association. This is typically described as a type of confederal or federal association, in which Somaliland is one of two or more partners.

In theory, this is probably the most promising scenario for an "all-Somali" settlement. After all, if the Tamil Tigers are prepared to contemplate autonomy in Sri Lanka rather than outright secession, and if the perpetrators and survivors of the Rwandan genocide can continue to live together, then why not Somalis?

In practice, however, a negotiated reunification of the Somali territories is rapidly receding as a possibility, and there is reason to believe that it may have already passed the point of no return.

Just getting the parties to the negotiating table will be no mean feat since a dialogue entails significant risks for both sides. For Somaliland's leaders, any dialogue must include among its possible outcomes the continuation of its independent status and the eventuality of recognition by the South. Any formula for dialogue that does not offer this option is tantamount to political suicide and hence a nonstarter. From a southern perspective, this means that one of the possible outcomes of dialogue would be a scheme to break up the Somali Republic requiring the complicity of southern leaders—also tantamount to political suicide and thus totally unacceptable.

Hopeful observers believe that a compromise can be struck through federation. In reality, Somaliland and Somalia will find it difficult to agree on a formula. Somaliland's point of reference is the 1960 unification process, in which northerners received about one-third of the seats in the executive and the legislative. In any future merger, Somaliland's leaders would demand considerably more. Southern notions of a federation typically envision a Somalia comprising four or five regions or provinces, of which Somaliland would be one. This arrangement would leave Somaliland with an even smaller share of power than it had in 1960, and would therefore be unacceptable to Somaliland, even as a basis for negotiation.

A formula for asymmetrical sovereignty could conceivably bridge the gap: for example, a southern federation of three or four provinces might collectively confederate with Somaliland. But there are groups in southern Somalia who will resist such an arrangement, believing that it awards undue power and influence to Somaliland and its Isaaq majority. Puntland for example, has consistently sought to portray itself as an entity on par with Somaliland and should be expected to fight a North–South federation tooth and nail. And there are many in the South who object to any kind of federal structure at all, hoping instead for a return to some kind of decentralized, unitary arrangement in which entities like Somaliland would cease to exist.

A skilled mediator with commanding diplomatic leverage might nevertheless be able to arm-twist both sides to the table. But timing will also be critical if talks are to have any chance of success: a window of opportunity must exist in which both sides have leadership with sufficient vision, courage, and popular support to be able to come together and compromise. Such a window is unlikely to open any time soon: Somaliland's leadership will confront a radically altered and fragile political landscape following presidential and parliamentary elections in mid-2003—the first such exercise in over three decades. The new government will have its hands full adapting to the unfamiliar demands of multi-party politics and will be disinclined to take on additional risks—especially the kind that could invigorate a post-election opposition and potentially destabilize the territory.

In the South, no such window of opportunity will exist until a functional and representative authority comes into being. But that moment may yet be several years away, and when it does arrive the new government is unlikely to enter into a dialogue of equals with Somaliland, and certainly not one that might lead to Somaliland's recognition by a rump Somalia. Even were Somalia's leaders prepared to engage in such an exchange, it would be so unpopular and divisive an issue that it could jeopardize the stability of a southern government. Somalia's first government in well over a decade will have its hands full with domestic challenges, without taking on such an explosive political risk. More likely, a southern government would feel obliged to claim jurisdiction over Somaliland, polarizing relations between the two entities even further and possibly "opening a new and potentially bitter phase in the civil war."[30]

A conflict over Somaliland is not a prospect to be shrugged off lightly. Somaliland's armed forces are better trained and equipped than the SNM was when it launched its guerrilla campaign in the early 1980s, and the forces they would face in any conflict will be far less formidable an adversary than the old Somali National Army. In addition, the defense of Somaliland's hard-won freedom from southern domination provides a compelling rallying cry, especially among the Isaaq, whose diaspora is much wealthier and better able to contribute to the war effort than in the 1980s. Most probably, such a scenario would evolve into a bitter conflict within and between the clans of Somaliland with no decisive military victory for either side—yet another festering sore in Africa's Horn.

Notes

1. Much of the information in this section is drawn from Somaliland Centre for Peace and Development, *A Self-Portrait of Somaliland: Rebuilding from the Ruins* (Hargeysa: WSP, 2000).
2. The imposition of a ban on Somali livestock by the Kingdom of Saudi Arabia, Somaliland's largest export market, has dramatically reduced both export earnings and government revenues since 1999.
3. In 2000 the official figure from the Somaliland Ministry of National Planning and Co-ordination was 3 million, whereas the UN estimate was 1.09 million.
4. Somaliland received 33 of 123 seats. The new cabinet reflected a similar balance of northern and southern interests.
5. *GOS Position on the IGAD Peace Process for Somalia*, Ministry of Foreign Affairs Memorandum, Hargeysa, April 10, 2002. For a more detailed presentation of Somaliland's arguments for recognition see *The Case for Somaliland's International Recognition as an Independent State*, Ministry of Foreign Affairs Briefing Paper, Hargeysa, August 2002.
6. Anthony J. Carroll and B. Rajagopal, "The Case for the Independent Statehood of Somaliland," *American University Journal of International Law and Politics*, Vol. 8 (1993), p. 653.
7. Carroll and Rajagopal, "The Case for the Independent Statehood," endorse this view.
8. Government of Somaliland. *Somaliland: Demand for International Recognition*. Hargeysa: Ministry of Information, 2001, p. 5
9. Saadia Touval, *Somali Nationalism* (Cambridge: Harvard University Press, 1963), p. 121. Touval cites Agence France Presse figures reporting 54,284 votes out of 103,811 votes cast, or 53%. However, Drysdale states that over 60% opposed the Constitution *Whatever Happened to Somalia* (London: Haan, 1994), p. 133. It is interesting to note that the total number of ballots cast in southern Somalia exceeded the total estimated population of the South (including women and children, who could not vote) by over half a million, suggesting serious irregularities.
10. Carroll and Rajagopal, "The Case for the Independent Statehood."
11. For a contemporary account of the controversy attached to the Greater Somali issue, see John Drysdale, *The Somali Dispute* (London: Pall Mall Press, 1964).
12. Africa Watch, *A Government at War With Its Own People* (New York: Africa Watch, 1990), pp. 8–9.
13. *The Case for Somaliland's International Recognition as an Independent State*, Ministry of Foreign Affairs Briefing Paper, Hargeysa, August 2002.
14. Final Report of the Initiatives and Referendum Institute's (IRI) Election Monitoring Team, *Somaliland National Referendum—May 31 2001* (Washington, D.C.: Citizen Lawmaker Press, July 27, 2001), p. 2.
15. Ibid., p. 55.
16. United Nations Integrated Regional Information Network (IRIN), *A Question of Recognition (Part I)*, Nairobi, July 10, 2001, p. 1.
17. The Initiatives and Referendum Institute estimates 66%. IRI, *Somaliland National Referendum*, p. 58.
18. Egypt, Libya, Eritrea, and Djibouti have signalled their recognition of the TNG by appointing ambassadors.
19. The destiny of the Sahrawi Republic remains unresolved: although the OAU and the UN have accepted in principle the right to self-determination of the territory's inhabitants, Morocco's opposition has prevented resolution of the issue.
20. Government of Somaliland, *Somaliland*, p. 50.
21. The Intergovernmental Authority on Development (IGAD) comprises Djibouti, Eritrea, Ethiopia, Kenya, Somalia, Sudan, and Uganda.

22. International Crisis Group Africa Report No. 45, *Somalia: Combating Terrorism in a Failed State*, Nairobi/Brussels, May 23, 2002, p. 7.

23. According to British colonial administration figures, the Isaaq constituted 66% of the population of the Protectorate in 1959. See Touval, *Somali Nationalism*.

24. The IRI ten-person team observed 57 polling stations (out of a total of 600) in five out of six regions of Somaliland. The South African observer team of similar size coordinated its efforts with the IRI team but did not publish a report.

25. This estimate is based on figures presented by the Academy for Peace and Development in *Regulating the Livestock Economy of Somaliland* (Hargeysa: WSP-International), unpublished draft.

26. Memorandum, *Return of Denied Asylum Seekers to Somaliland*, Ministry of Foreign Affairs, Hargeysa, April 10, 2002, p. 1.

27. Ibid., p. 2.

28. For an in-depth discussion of this issue see M. Bryden, *The Importance of Being Somaliland: An Emerging Paradigm of Governance for the Somali Territories*, paper presented to the First Post-War Reconstruction Strategies Conference, IPRT, Hargesya, May 2000.

29. It is perhaps worth speculating that the challenge of integration in Somaliland is considerably less daunting than the potential challenge of reintegration of Somaliland and Somalia.

30. International Crisis Group Africa Briefing, *Salvaging Somalia's Chance for Peace*, Nairobi/Brussels, December 9, 2002, p. 7.

Conclusions and Policy Options
Paul Kingston and Ian S. Spears

This volume has presented a wide array of case studies of states-within-states—some as predatory and others as potential models of emerging states. Each has been born out of a unique set of historical circumstances although most have in common their emergence in situations of armed conflict. However, regardless of whether they are potential avenues of political or socioeconomic development or simply new forms of threats to already precarious states in the Third World, states-within-states are a significant new phenomenon in comparative and global politics that cannot be ignored by either scholars or practitioners. After reviewing and summarizing some of the definitional features of states-within-states, this conclusion will turn to a series of contingent policy options aimed at those in the international community struggling to come to grips with these challenges to conventional processes and means of diplomacy and development.

We have defined states-within-states as political entities that have some or many of the attributes normally associated with statehood but which nonetheless lack formal recognition from the international community. While the strength and durability of these entities varies considerably across our cases, many of them have some capacity in the areas of fiscal extraction and coercion. A few have gone further, developing a deep-rooted sense of identity and legitimacy in contradistinction to the juridical state. In some cases such as Somaliland and Eritrea this sense of self was quite powerful and, as is often the case in the formation of a *national* identity, was in part a consequence of their respective wars with centralized governments. Most states-within-states, however, also have a weak capacity when it comes to the development of representative institutions (a tendency that is perhaps rationalized by a proclaimed solidarity between the leaders and the citizenry) with others demonstrating predatory characteristics and no interest in giving citizens a political voice.

The emergence of states-within-states is directly linked to the phenomenon of state weakness or state failure. This is the case both for Africa and the Middle East with its relatively new states and for Latin America with its relatively older states, some of which predate the emergence of those in Europe. With limited presence in their societies and unable to prevent the penetration of alternative transnational forces, be they geostrategic or financial, weak states have found themselves increasingly challenged by autonomous political movements below. However, the fact of state failure does not mean that the state is finished as a prevailing norm unit of the international system. On the contrary, what this volume has shown is that states remain its principal building blocks.

Moreover, from the various case studies in this volume, it is also not clear that states-within-states are simply states in the making. Rather, their trajectories are unclear.

At one level, they are blocked from achieving juridical statehood by the prevailing international norms and practice surrounding sovereignty—in short by the structure of the present international system. On another, their political leadership is not necessarily interested in formal or separate statehood nor with the responsibilities that go with that status. Instead, we see a variety of alternative political inclinations, ranging from the long-term objective of reforming or overthrowing the existing regime, to the medium-term objective of providing for the welfare needs of their own people, to short-term and more predatory purpose of accumulating capital. It was a conclusion of some contributors to this volume, for example, that predatory inclinations have become an increasing tendency among many substate elites who have positioned themselves to take advantage of opportunities created by the reduction in the regulation of national and global economic activity that characterize globalization. Indeed, this decision of certain substate elites to depart from their "shadowed" and parasitic relationship with the juridical state and to "go it alone" may be one of the most distinct features of the post–Cold War era in the developing world.

In their quest for autonomy, however, states-within-states have not become isolated political entities but have developed numerous, alternative, and complex connections to a variety of transnational actors and networks, be they embedded in the global economy, in networks of regional actors, in diaspora populations, or even in the international humanitarian bureaucracy itself. The combination of these connections has proved to be essential for the survival of states-within-states entities although, as we shall see, they may also provide an important means by which the international community can exert leverage over them.

It is in this light that we would like to return to the questions posed at the beginning of this volume. Born as many of them are in situations of humanitarian disaster and conflict, what are the challenges of using states-within-states as channels for humanitarian and development assistance? Moreover, what are the consequences in terms of the future practice surrounding the norm of sovereignty? Many contemporary scholars see more hazard than promise in tinkering with the existing state system. William Zartman, for example, has argued that a more cautious approach that seeks "to reaffirm the validity of the existing unit and make it work" is more likely to yield positive results in the long term.[1] Others have argued that conditions in regions such as Africa have deteriorated to such an extent—epitomized by the emergence of numerous states-within-states—that more creative solutions beyond the "steel grid" of the current state system need to be considered if progress is to be made. Jeffrey Herbst has gone even further by arguing that the international community's "dogmatic devotion to the current boundaries" should be discarded in favor of new forms of sovereignty. For Herbst, "The inevitable disruption caused by state creation will also have to be balanced against the profound harm that existing states . . . do to their populations every day."[2]

While the contributors to this volume did not arrive at a definitive resolution of this issue, a number of them make clear that policy makers should exercise skepticism and caution when approaching the issue of states-within-states. As Kenn Crossley argues in his discussion of the SPLM/A in Sudan, despite rhetorical pretenses of a functioning and viable bureaucracy and infrastructure, there is often less of substance on the ground than their proponents claim. Moreover, elites may be more interested in advancing their own political interests through predatory behavior than the welfare of their populace. On the other hand, while we concur that states remain the principal building blocks of the international system, there also exists a serious problem of state collapse that requires a substantive response from the international community. The selective support and, perhaps recognition, of states-within-states offers a potential solution. Indeed, the international community should be careful not to recreate the errors of the past by relegitimizing states that have already proven to be unviable. Nor should we ignore the fact that some minority groups will often see formal statehood as the only sufficient hedge against oppressive government in the future. This means that the international community needs to be skeptical about offering unquestioned recognition of both existing formal states *and* the substates within them. But it also may mean rethinking whether issues of sovereignty should prevent the international community from considering other approaches to the international state system. Indeed, if there was a degree of unanimity among our participants it was that a formal and exclusive form of sovereignty does not reflect the reality of situations on the ground in many regions and that the international community needs to develop more flexible and diverse approaches to the question of political order and development. Consequently, instead of embracing a single approach to reforming the state system, there is a need for a more fluid system of norms that allows different types of units to exist simultaneously.

It is in this light that we would like to propose a number of general policy options, each of which depends upon the viability of the state in question:

1. In situations of humanitarian disaster precipitated by the state-within-state, for example, (such as Liberia's "Taylorland" or RUF-controlled regions of Sierra Leone), the international community should publicly acknowledge the sovereignty of the existing state and support the recognized government in the neutralization of the coercive capacity of the state-within-a-state.
2. Alternatively, in situations of humanitarian disaster, precipitated by the existing state, it may be necessary for the international community to step in and provide protection—in a sense creating a state-within-a-state (e.g. as occurred in Northern Iraq).
3. In cases of indeterminate conflict between the state and the substate, the international community must find mechanisms that help diffuse tension between them. This could involve the closing off of financial linkages to both sides and the promotion of a negotiated coexistence (efforts to reduce UNITA's ability to export diamonds during the mid-1990s, e.g. was an effort to push it into a negotiated solution). The objective here is to provide space and incentives for an agreeable settlement rather than a specifically two-state solution.
4. Finally in rare cases where the state-within-a-state is viable and exists in an irreconcilable relationship with the formal state, or when it exists in situations of profound state collapse, the international community may have no choice but to consider some sort of recognition of states-within-states. However, in the short term, formal recognition should be kept in reserve as a means of exercising leverage to ensure good and accountable governance.

In all these situations, it is imperative that the international community not only meet its own obligations by continuing to provide humanitarian assistance but also that it encourage and promote the public mindedness of all actors, both state and substate.

The authors are under no illusions about the logistical and political implications of these issues or the very difficult dilemmas or trade-offs that would have to be addressed in implementing policy decisions. The imperative of aid delivery, for example, may entail the unintended and perhaps undesirable recognition of a "government" of one such state-within-a-state. Moreover, aside from dilemmas associated with the recognition of a substate entity, the delivery of aid may force international organizations to make decisions over whether to deal with—and thereby to offer tacit or de facto recognition of—one of multiple rebel groups as the authority within a region over another. A second problem is that humanitarian organizations may not be able to offer assistance on their own terms. Because substate units often exercise exclusive control over a territory and are often the only means of access to an affected population, they may set conditions beneficial to them that run contrary to the norms of international humanitarian assistance. In short, they may serve as gatekeepers to the provision of aid and other goods. Moreover, the aid provided by international organizations may work to strengthen substate entities in ways undesired and unintended by the international community. Finally, states-within-states may demand the reorganization of international bureaucracies to reflect and respond to the reality of the situation on the ground. In some locations, the NGOs and other international organizations may be forced to set up multiple country programs to address the fact that separate authorities control different regions of a country.

Finally, there is the issue of how to manage predatory behavior of some states-within-states or their leaders. While the prospect of relations with warlords in Sierra Leone or Liberia can be particularly unpalatable, ignoring hitherto unrecognized governments and local actors undoubtedly does little but encourage them to continue their involvement in objectionable activity. Careful decisions need to be made as to whether such individuals are incorrigible and can be sidelined, or whether they can be engaged and steered toward more legitimate activities that take into account the well-being of those ostensibly under their authority. In any event, it is unwise to neglect more benevolent indigenous subunits whose leaderships actively solicit the support of their inhabitants in return for the provision of key services. As Herbst has argued, a refusal to deal with them may only force them to engage in illicit activities in order to survive.[3] Indeed, channeling them into more conventional behavior may go a long way to making them constructive partners in meeting local development needs and in the larger project of rebuilding the state.

Addressing the challenges faced by states-within-states will undoubtedly require considerable flexibility on the part of the international community. But at a time when many scholars and practitioners are advocating decentralized approaches to development and conflict resolution, states-within-states also offer potential avenues through which these objectives can be achieved. Overlooking their existence may jeopardize an opportunity to encourage governments that better meet and reflect the needs of the local population.

Notes

1. See I. William Zartman, *Collapsed States: The Disintegration and Restoration of Legitimate Authority* (Boulder: Lynne Rienner, 1995).
2. Jeffrey Herbst, *States and Power in Africa* (Princeton: Princeton University Press, 2000), p. 266.
3. Ibid., pp. 268–269.

Notes on Contributors

Ana Maria Bejarano completed her Ph.D. in Political Science from Colombia University and is an Assistant Professor of Political Science at the University of Toronto at Mississauga. Her publications and research interests focus on the politics of electoral democracy and democratic transitions in Colombia and Latin America.

Matt Bryden works for the International Crisis Group and is based in Addis Ababa, Ethiopia.

Kenn Crossley works for the United Nations World Food Programme, Resource Mobilization for the Southern Africa Crisis Response.

Paul Kingston is Associate Professor of Political Science and International Development Studies at the University of Toronto at Scarborough. His published works include *Britain and the Politics of Modernization in the Middle East, 1945–58* (Cambridge: Cambridge University Press, 1996) and he is currently working on a book on postwar reconstruction and the politics of civil society in Lebanon.

Lauchlan T. Munro is Director of Policy and Planning for the International Development Research Centre in Ottawa. From 1989 to 2003, he worked for UNICEF in Uganda, Zimbabwe, DR Congo, and at headquarters in New York.

Scott Pegg teaches in the Department of Political Science at Indiana University-Purdue University Indianapolis (IUPUI). He is the author of *International Society and the De Facto State* (Aldershot, UK: Ashgate, 1998) and has published journal articles in *The Washington Quarterly, Security Dialogue*, and *Third World Quarterly*.

Eduardo Pizarro is Associate Professor at the National University in Bogotá, Colombia and Visiting Fellow at the University of Toronto. His publications include *Las Farc 1949–1966: De la autodefensa a la combinacion de todas las formas de lucha* (Bogota: IEPRI—Tercer Mundo Editores, 1991) and *Insurgencia sin revolucion: La guerrilla columbiana en perspectiva comparada* (Bogota: IEPRI—Tercer Mundo Editores, 1996).

William Reno is Associate Professor of Political Science at Northwestern University. His extensive publications on the history and political economy of West Africa include *Corruption and State Politics in Sierra Leone* (Cambridge: Cambridge University Press, 1995) and *Warlord States and African States* (Boulder: Lynne Reinner, 1998).

David Romano completed his Ph.D. in Political Science from the University of Toronto on Kurdish nationalist movements in Turkey and Iraq. He has lectured at McGill University and presently holds a postdoctoral fellowship from the Canadian Department of National Defense with which he will spend nine months in Iraq conducting further research. He has spent over one-and-a-half years in Ankara and the Kurdish regions of Turkey, Iran, Syria, and Iraq.

Ian S. Spears is Assistant Professor of Political Science at the University of Guelph. He has published extensively on the issue of power sharing as a mechanism for conflict resolution in Africa and has published articles in *The Review of African Political Economy*, *International Journal*, and *The Journal of Democracy*.

John Young is Research Associate, Institute of Governance Studies, Simon Fraser University. He has worked in the Horn of Africa for ten years and, with respect to Sudan, has worked as a journalist, peace advisor to the Canadian International Development Agency (CIDA), advisor to IGAD Special Envoy for Peace, Ambassador Daniel Mboya, and in the field of security analysis. His publications include *Peasant Revolution in Ethiopia: The Tigray People's Liberation Front, 1975–1991* (Cambridge: Cambridge University Press, 1997).

Marie-Joelle Zahar is Assistant Professor of Political Science at the Université de Montréal. She has contributed several chapters to edited collections on conflict resolution and peace implementation in addition to articles in *International Peacekeeping* and *The International Journal*. She is currently director of a United States Institute of Peace collaborative research project on foreign assistance to postconflict reconstruction and has served as consultant to the UN Office for the Coordination of Humanitarian Affairs.

Index